This volume brings together a selection of Brian Bond's most interesting contributions to books and journals on British Military History in the 20th century. They are arranged around three large subjects: the First World War, the inter-war decades, and the Second World War with concluding reflections on the author's 'farewell to arms' at the end of a distinguished career in the Department of War Studies at King's College London. Brief new introductions have been written to provide background information and contexts for each essay.

Sir Basil Liddell Hart's name appropriately forms part of the title since he was the author's original inspiration and mentor. His early career and influential publications on the First World War are critically discussed, as is his later 'partnership' with the reforming War Minister, Leslie Hore-Belisha. Professor Bond also acknowledges his tremendous debt to his research supervisor and 'founder' of War Studies, Sir Michael Howard. Other essays provide fascinating examples of the author's main interests, including the Western Front and civil-military relations; the significance of post-1918 war memoirs; the nadir of the Army's fortunes between the World Wars and its performance in France and Belgium in 1939–40. This section is complemented by earlier studies of Field Marshals Gort and Ironside.

In recent years, Professor Bond has been a leading critic of the 'Lions led by Donkeys' school who have misrepresented and denigrated Britain's achievement in the First World War. His target, the concluding essay in this volume, are the historical shortcomings of the stage and film versions of *Oh! What a Lovely War* – hence the inclusion of Joan Littlewood's name in the title.

Brian Bond spent most of his teaching career at King's College, London where he played a role in developing the Department of War Studies from its early days in the 1960s. He was awarded a personal Chair in Military History and was also appointed a Fellow of the College (FKC). He was President of the Commission for Military History (BCMH) from 1986 to 2006, and was a Visiting Fellow at Brasenose College and, later at All Souls College, Oxford. He delivered the Lees Knowles lectures at Cambridge in 2000, published two years later as *The Unquiet Western Front*. His other numerous publications range, in time, from *The Victorian Army and the Staff College* (1972) to *Britain's Two World Wars against Germany* (2014). Other noteworthy books include *British Military Policy between the Two World Wars* (1980) and *Survivors of a Kind. Memoirs of the Western Front* (2008).

He has been extremely fortunate to be able to combine an academic career in London while living most of his life, with his wife Madeleine, in a beautiful village in the Thames valley.

From Liddell Hart to Joan Littlewood

Studies in British Military History

Brian Bond

 Helion & Company Limited

Helion & Company Limited
26 Willow Road
Solihull
West Midlands
B91 1UE
England
Tel. 0121 705 3393
Fax 0121 711 4075
Email: info@helion.co.uk
Website: www.helion.co.uk
Twitter: @helionbooks
Visit our blog http://blog.helion.co.uk/

Published by Helion & Company 2015

Designed and typeset by Bookcraft Ltd, Stroud, Gloucestershire
Cover designed by Paul Hewitt, Battlefield Design (www.battlefield-design.co.uk)
Printed by Lightning Source Limited, Milton Keynes, Buckinghamshire

Text © Brian Bond 2015
Maps © as individually credited

ISBN 978-1-910777-57-2

British Library Cataloguing-in-Publication Data.
A catalogue record for this book is available from the British Library.

For details of other military history titles published by Helion & Company
Limited contact the above address, or visit our website: http://www.helion.co.uk.

We always welcome receiving book proposals from prospective authors.

Contents

Foreword

I am grateful to Gary Sheffield for suggesting that it would be worthwhile to publish a selection of my public lectures and contributions to various volumes and journals. Brian Holden Reid's *Studies in British Military Thought* (1998) provided a model for inserting brief introductions to each essay to explain its origins and put the subject into historical context. Hugh Cecil, Simon Doughty and Frances Parkes helped me to obtain copyright clearance from some of my original publishers whose addresses had sometimes changed in the interval. Emily McLeish skilfully typed my introductory notes and the new opening and closing essays. Above all, my thanks are due to Duncan Rogers for encouraging the project and his remarkable efficiency in transforming my miscellaneous scripts into a handsome volume.

It is a relief, and a pleasure, to record that my wife Madeleine and I have not been flooded while preparing this book.

Medmenham, Bucks, June 2015

Acknowledgements

I am grateful to the following publishers for graciously giving me permission to reprint copyright material:

New York University Press for 'The Somme in British History' in G. Jensen and A. Wiest (eds), *War in the Age of Technology* (2001)

Oxford University Press for 'The Army between the Two World Wars' in D. Chandler and I. Beckett (eds), *The Oxford Illustrated History of the British Army* (1994) and for 'Alanbrooke and the Mediterranean Strategy, 1942–1944' in L. Freedman, P. Hayes and R. O'Neill (eds), *War, Strategy and International Politics* (1992)

Manchester University Press for 'Leslie Hore-Belisha at the War Office, 1937–1940' in I. Beckett and J. Gooch (eds), *Politicians and Defence* (1981)

Pimlico for 'Britain's Field Force in France and Belgium 1939–1940' in P. Addison and A. Calder (eds), *Time to Kill. The Soldier's Experience of War in the West, 1939–1945* (1997)

Weidenfeld and Nicolson for 'Gort' and 'Ironside' in J. Keegan (ed), *Churchill's Generals* (1991)

I.B. Tauris for 'Oh! What a Lovely War. History and Popular Myths in Late Twentieth Century Britain' in Wm. Roger Louis (ed), *Yet More Adventures with Britannia* (2005)

I have done my best to establish that I possess the copyright to republish the following essays but apologise for any misunderstandings or mistakes:

'A Victory Worse than a Defeat?' Liddell Hart Lecture, King's College London, 1997

'Liddell Hart and the First World War' in *Look to Your Front. Studies in the First World War* (Spellmount Ltd, 1999)

'Soldiers and Statesmen. British Civil–Military Relations in 1917' in *Military Affairs* Vol XXXII, Fall 1968

'The Anti-War Writers and their Critics' in H. Cecil and P. Liddle (eds), *Facing Armageddon* (Leo Cooper, 1996)

'Arras, May 1940: A Case-Study in the Counter-Stroke' in *Old Battles and New Defences* (Brassey's Defence Publishers, 1986)

'General Sir William Slim and the Fourteenth Army in Burma' in B. Bond and K. Tachikawa (eds), *British and Japanese Military Leadership in the Far Eastern War 1941–1945* (Frank Cass, 2004)

Introduction: A Wasted Life? Military History in My Time

A few years ago, after I had given a lecture at Oxford, a female undergraduate asked me bluntly: 'Why have you wasted your life studying war?' I replied that if you were at all interested in history, war was the most dramatic and absorbing aspect, but I doubt if this was persuasive. On reflection, I thought that the question was anachronistic. In the 1940s and 1950s this would have been a common reaction based on puzzlement or downright hostility.

In retrospect I believe such negative attitudes sprang from three inter-related sources. In the post Second World War era many people felt that they had had enough of war: it was horrific and evil, and studying it would only serve to lend it credibility, even respectability. Secondly, war was seen as a technical subject best left to retired officers and a handful of defence journalists. Thirdly, war was not deemed a suitable academic subject with scarcely a foothold in universities and, indeed, openly derided by some scholars in other historical fields; justified to some extent by the narrow prevailing notion of what was meant by 'military history'. As a corollary of this third point, it followed that there was no point in considering military history as a possible profession because there were no job prospects. This depressing outlook was evident in my own early experience. My senior history master, at a good grammar school, had been wounded in the First World War and embittered by his experience. He skipped over the wars as though they were irrelevant interruptions to the flow of interesting non-military developments. At Oxford my college tutor held similarly negative views based on his Second World War experience and became markedly unenthusiastic when I opted for the military history special subject (taught by Norman Gibbs at All Souls College) in my final year. While doing research and looking for an academic job between 1959 and 1962, no positions in military history were advertised and only a handful in modern history. Sandhurst was the only exception and I was offered a teaching post there, only to be thwarted – for good or ill – by the withdrawal of MOD funding. The only possibility, and of course an entirely respectable one, was to win a junior post in modern history, play down one's hopes of specialising in military history, and hope to introduce it in the course of time.

The event that transformed my own career prospects, and remarkably quickly, the entire subject area of military history and 'war studies', was the successful struggle of a young history lecturer, Michael Howard, to establish an independent department at King's College, London.

In his autobiography *Captain Professor*,[1] Sir Michael has revealed what a tough struggle he had to overcome opposition from the History Department and, later, to outmanoeuvre opponents of further development of the subject in the university. He was awarded a chair in 1963 but remained essentially a 'one man band' until 1965, when the Department of War Studies was founded, admitting only graduates and with a one year MA in War Studies as its core course. I was very fortunate to join the Department as a lecturer in 1966, joining Professor Howard and Wolf Mendl, who specialised in contemporary international relations.

As with most trailblazers, there was a large element of luck in the early development of Michael Howard's emergence as 'the father of War Studies' as he has memorably described in his memoirs.[2] He realised that the history of war 'was more than the operational history of armed forces. It was the study of entire societies. Only by studying their cultures could one come to understand what it was that they fought about and why they fought in the way that they did.'[3] Conflicts in turn had a reciprocal impact on the belligerent states' social structure. Howard does not claim to have invented the concept of 'War and Society' but he certainly provided the initial impetus. With much more emphasis on the social dimension, Arthur Marwick would soon afterwards popularise the study of 'War and Society' at the Open University.[4]

This is not the place for a full discussion of Michael Howard's profound and continuing impact on the study of war. As Brian Holden Reid has written: 'It is difficult to think of a single scholar who has had more influence on thinking about military issues, contemporary strategy or the practice of military history than Sir Michael Howard. He more than any other scholar, has conferred on the study of war a degree of academic respectability that has offered protection against later outbreaks of renewed hostility.' Under his inspiration, 'war studies' has offered to military history a fresh impetus and permitted it to develop new dimensions.[5] Before these pioneering achievements in the 1960s and 1970s 'the number of scholars interested in war and conflict (mostly retired military men) could be numbered on the fingers of one hand; it is now... an overcrowded field'.[6]

Of course the proliferation of war studies in Britain, the United States and many other countries does not in itself answer the student's question as to whether or not I had 'wasted my career' though what has been written above does show that the 'pariah' subject of the 1950s had become not merely respectable but also enormously popular within two decades.

It is not for me to assess how successful or influential I was as a teacher; it is surely a profession particularly prone to melancholy reflection about these matters once the marking of essays, the discussions and the classrooms have been left behind. A kind or flattering remark from a former student is the best one can hope for. I can only say that, despite the inevitable disappointments and low points, I always enjoyed teaching the subject I had specialised in and never felt that I had chosen the wrong career.

As suggested above, from the outset Michael Howard had stressed that all the courses in the Department would be based on a broad, disinterested study of armed conflict over the past two hundred years. It was emphatically not intended to equip students with technical or tactical knowledge designed to enhance their career prospects in the armed services. I can report that only a handful of MA candidates, mostly airmen for whom technical qualifications were so important, challenged our philosophy or felt that they had signed up under a misapprehension.

I enjoyed the challenge of teaching at three different levels; undergraduate, MA candidates and MPhil/PhD research students. The Department did not admit undergraduates until the early 1990s, but I myself and some other colleagues always offered a military history survey course (war since the mid 18th century), and a special subject for the University Board of History. As regards the BA courses, always stimulating because they were small groups of students who had opted for these topics and were mostly based at other London colleges, I briefly continued Michael Howard's 'special' on the Franco–Prussian War before changing to 'Gallipoli' around 1970 and later to 'British Military Policy and Strategy from Munich to the Fall of France'. All special subjects involved the study of a large selection of original documents, usually including some in a foreign language, to which a separate examination paper was devoted. Initially some students resented this precise attention to documents, but as I had found at Oxford, it was a sure and satisfactory method to ensure a real command of a limited period which could then be applied to other topics.

The one year Masters Degree in War Studies was our staple course during nearly all my time at King's, that is until the huge influx of undergraduates in the early 1990s. In my first year (1966–7) we had only 11 MA candidates, from nearly as many countries, but competition for entry, from all over the free world, was intense so the annual intake soon rose to what I considered the maximum of 30, where all could get to know each other and meet in one large seminar room for each of the core elements. When this number was exceeded, more attention inevitably focused on the MA special subjects, my own included 'The Face of Battle' and 'The First World War' (always popular because it permitted an optional visit to the Somme battlefield).[7] I especially enjoyed the special subjects, not only because of my own input, but also for the strong sense of group identity that often developed within the class. Mature students, mostly, though not all, MA candidates, were particularly beneficial because they had seen something of the wider world, had sometimes taken a break from their careers and brought to the class an enhanced self-discipline, punctuality and keenness to learn. These annually changing small-group classes were high points that I particularly missed when obliged to retire at 65.

On leaving for Oxford in 1968, Michael Howard bequeathed to me eight or ten of his MPhil/PhD candidates, which was a large commitment for a young-ish lecturer developing his own courses and writing projects. Inevitably they were a mixed bunch, some (like John Gooch and David French) were brilliant and needed little guidance, while others were more pedestrian or lacking in the necessary commitment to the lonely business of archival research. Throughout my time at King's the situation regarding PhD candidates remained essentially the same: always ten or so active candidates on a variety of topics which stretched my boundaries; many reliable, hard-working and a pleasure to supervise; and a few with the opposite traits. Inevitably quite a few fell by the wayside, for financial or other reasons, but I am proud of the fact that of the 50 plus who presented their theses, not one failed.[8]

The last, but by no means least important, of Michael Howard's institutional creations in the University of London was the Research Seminar in Military History at the Institute of Historical Research at Senate House. It had originally been given an anodyne title, 'Military Organisation and the Great Powers', and Michael Howard admitted much later that in 1957 it would have been impossible to gain approval for its eventual and more accurate name.[9]

I first attended this seminar as a graduate student of Howard's in 1959. It was a small but already distinguished group, containing some established historians such as M. R. D. Foot, Kenneth Bourne and Peter Paret. It convened weekly in a tiny room off the main first floor corridor so that even allowing for the occasional guest speaker, one's turn to read a paper came round alarmingly often. Returning to the seminar as a lecturer in War Studies in 1966, I soon took over as principal chairman and convenor and remained in this quite demanding but enjoyable role until 2006, when I retired on reaching the age of seventy. I can fairly state, leaving aside any personal influence, that this seminar attained an international reputation witnessed by the facts that distinguished scholars from various countries would usually be pleased to offer a paper on brief visits to London; and that several members who had obtained their doctorates would attend regularly (the meetings being now fortnightly) or drop in whenever their other duties permitted. In my very long stint as chairman I recall only one speaker failing to turn up and two going to King's College first by mistake. As most attenders already held a PhD or were aspirants to that distinction the debates could be probing and at times sharp. But the atmosphere was nearly always congenial and supportive of the speaker, if only because most had submitted themselves to the ordeal or would do so in due course. The pursuit of historical truth based on the best available evidence was the dominant concern. Just occasionally I would come away into the maelstrom of the evening rush hour wondering why I had wasted my time on a boring or impenetrable paper, but mostly I would stride to the tube at Euston Square with uplifted spirits, feeling that this was an academic plateau which more than compensated for the darker valleys in the donnish life.

Michael Howard would be the first to admit that he was not the only military historian teaching in British universities in the 1950s and 1960s: there were a large number of mostly ex-Second World War officers including Harry Hinsley, Noble Frankland, Norman Gibbs, M. R. D. Foot, Piers Mackesy and John Erickson. But most of them (with Gibbs an exception at Oxford) did not lecture mainly, if at all, in military history and none headed a department in the subject.

Not only did Michael Howard succeed in founding an independent department at an inauspicious time, but subsequently outstanding graduates from this 'stable' would establish other centres of excellence in the wide field of War Studies both in Britain and overseas. At the risk of causing offence by omission I can at once think of, in rough seniority, in achieving PhDs and significant publications, John Gooch, Ian Beckett, David French, Brian Holden Reid, Philip Towle, Jim Beach, Gary Sheffield, Mathew Hughes and Robert Foley. Many others have 'spread the gospel' in related institutions such as Sandhurst, the Imperial War Museum, the Royal United Services Institute and the Ministry of Defence. War Studies, with a firm foundation in military history, now flourishes not only at King's and Queen Mary College, London, but also at Kent (Canterbury), Birmingham, Wolverhampton, Liverpool, Edinburgh, Leeds, Oxford, Northampton and Exeter.

Reading the above *apologia*, the doubting Oxford student might still remark, "Well, he would say that, wouldn't he", to which I can only reply that I was fortunate to be in at the foundation, and to have played a small part in the development of a new academic field of study which has achieved world-wide recognition and tremendous popularity.

References

1. Michael Howard, *Captain Professor* (Continuum, 2006) pp. 144–47.
2. Ibid, pp. 123–52.
3. Ibid, p. 145.
4. See, for example, Arthur Marwick, *Britain in the Century of Total War* (Pelican Books, 1970). See also the series on *War and Society* edited by Geoffrey Best (Fortana paperbacks) in the 1970s and 1980s.
5. Brian Holden Reid, 'Michael Howard and the Evolution of Modern War Studies' *Journal of Military History* vol 73, no 3, July 2009, pp. 869–70.
6. Ibid, p. 875.
7. In most years a brazen student would tell me that he or she wished to visit the Somme but was not interested in the course. The request was refused.
8. I cannot precisely count the total beyond 50. On occasions when I had several more PhD candidates than my equally hard-working colleague Michael Dockrill, he would take over some of mine. This applied particularly to candidates in air power topics, which was one of his special interests.
9. Holden Reid, op cit, pp. 875–6n.

Part I
The First World War

1

'A Victory worse than a Defeat? British Interpretations of the First World War'
Liddell Hart Lecture at King's College London, 17 November 1997

This essay originated as the Liddell Hart Lecture delivered to a packed audience in the Great Hall at King's College London on 17 November 1997. It was a bold attempt to tackle head-on the main controversies surrounding Britain's role in the First World War and, in particular, how these had evolved right up to the present. The lecture was very well received, partly no doubt due to the hilarious entries from the index of Lloyd George's *War Memoirs*, and I proudly noted, on returning home, that it had been, academically, my 'finest hour'. In terms of professional military historians, I believe that many of the controversies I discussed have gained full acceptance, but as regards the media and its influence on the general public there has been, at best, only a gradual thawing in the ice-field. Many of the ideas and opinions I advanced in 1997 have been more fully discussed in my later work, notably *The Unquiet Western Front* (2002), based on the Lees Knowles lectures at Cambridge in 2000, and *Britain's Two World Wars Against Germany: Myth, Memory and the Distortions of Hindsight* (C.U.P., 2014). Inevitably there are echoes, but not, I hope, too much repetition of views, examples and supporting evidence in later pages of the present volume.

A few years ago, in a Radio 4 discussion about the public schools, a female novelist remarked 'and that is why we lost the First World War'. Since no one challenged this revisionist view, I wrote to the chairman suggesting that the victory celebrations had been held in London and Paris rather than Berlin or Vienna. 'My dear professor', Robert Robinson replied, 'you may well be right', but it seemed I had voiced a politically incorrect opinion. Many people do indeed apparently believe that the war had been lost, especially those influenced by the film *Oh! What A Lovely War*. Its poignant culminating scene shows the whole landscape filled with white British crosses. If everyone had been killed, how could one speak of victory? More recently the theme of a whole generation of 'lions' needlessly sacrificed by 'donkeys' has been reinforced by that authoritative source – Blackadder!

Let us briefly examine three additional negative assumptions. First, that the war was not about great political issues. As that influential but unreliable writer, Paul Fussell, put it: 'In the Great War eight million people were destroyed because two persons, the Archduke Francis Ferdinand and his Consort, had been shot.'[1] Suffice it to say that at the time the British and Dominions governments believed that a German victory would endanger vital national interests and, despite all the revisionism about war aims and war guilt, this still seems convincing. Propaganda certainly exaggerated enemy atrocities but could not account for the sustained British and imperial war effort. The vast majority believed, in Trevor Wilson's phrase, that it was a 'necessary war'.

Secondly, there is the seductive argument that Britain could and should have remained neutral, but even with hindsight this is not persuasive. A very unwarlike Liberal government agonised over its decision in August 1914, but eventually felt compelled to intervene for reasons both of honour and national interest. Governments also have to calculate the risks of non-intervention: what if Britain had stood aside and France had been overrun?

Thirdly, there is a charge that is harder to counter; that victory was indistinguishable from defeat. Siegfried Sassoon voiced this opinion during the war and Churchill afterwards in *The World Crisis*. But these were emotional reactions to the very high costs of staving off defeat: they could not be taken literally and acted upon in the light of the draconian terms imposed on Russia in the Treaty of Brest-Litovsk. Even historians are apt to neglect the iron law of chronology: victory in the early months of 1918 seemed far off and even unlikely. Then, after 1919 it appeared disappointing, first on the home front ('homes for heroes'), and later in international affairs ('the war to end all wars'). But this was due to unrealistic hopes encouraged by deceitful slogans, and by unpredictable events after the war. These disappointments were not the fault of those who had won the war, and indeed the achievements of Britain and her allies were substantial: Belgium liberated, Alsace-Lorraine recovered by France, the German drive for European dominance checked and her fleet destroyed. Moreover the revolutions and prolonged political and social turmoil experienced by the losers starkly exposes the muddled thinking of those who claim to perceive no difference between victory and defeat.

In the immediate post-war years, military historians like J.F. Maurice and Spenser Wilkinson were well aware that the British and imperial forces had achieved an outstanding series of victories from 8 August 1918 onwards, all the more remarkable since the allies had been on the brink of defeat in March and April. More recently, however, the tendency has been to dwell on the earlier years characterised by attrition and heavy casualties for minimal territorial gains. So obsessive has been the focus on 1 July 1916 that a generation of schoolchildren could be forgiven for thinking that the war had ended there and then in a catastrophic defeat.

On the contrary, in 1918 the Allies – with British and imperial forces playing the leading role – clearly defeated the German armies on the Western Front. Between 18 July and 11 November the British forces took 188,700 prisoners and 2,840 guns, far more in each category than the French, Americans and Belgians. Following the brilliant operations in late September to break through the Hindenburg Line, the five British Armies skilfully outmanoeuvred the stubborn defenders from a series of river and canal lines on which Ludendorff had hoped to stabilize the front during the winter. In the final days of hostilities the Fourth Army crossed the Sambre canal and the stage was set for a great battle on the Germans' last defensible river line of the Meuse, but the armistice was signed before this could take place.[2]

Conditions did not permit a breakthrough and the advance to victory was steady rather than dramatic – about 60 miles at an average rate of less than a mile per day. The Germans fought stubbornly against superior artillery assisted by dominant Allied air forces. Despite a few cases of large-scale surrenders there was no general disintegration. Nevertheless, the imminence of complete defeat was demonstrated by Ludendorff's resignation and the acceptance of armistice terms which precluded any hope of renewing the struggle.

Few military historians would dispute these facts or the inference that the defeat of the German armies on the Western Front was crucial in accounting for the collapse of the Central Powers. In the past decade or so new approaches and original research have moved on to more specific issues related to 'the learning curve' which, it is widely accepted, rose steadily and impressively from mid-1916. Thus attention focuses on such topics as technical and tactical innovation and the levels at which they were implemented; the performance of individual commanders and units, especially the divisions. Even staff officers, the butt of so much uninformed criticism, are now viewed more favourably. While the old debate about the relative merits of tanks and artillery rumbles on, there is now growing appreciation of improvements across the board in doctrine, training and all-arms co-operation. As Trevor Wilson eloquently expressed this a decade ago:

> What was particularly noteworthy in the operations of these last 100 days was the co-ordination between the various elements. Infantry, artillery, machine-guns, tanks, aircraft, and wireless telegraphy all functioned as parts of a single unit. As a result of meticulous planning, each component was integrated with, and provided maximum support for, every other component. Here, more than

anywhere else, was the great technical achievement of these climactic battles. It was not that the British had developed a war-winning weapon. What they had produced was a 'weapons system': the melding of the various elements in the military arm into a mutually supporting whole.[3]

Why then have these remarkable achievements by what was essentially an amateur and, from 1916, a largely conscript Army been obscured in the public consciousness by the notions of unrelieved horror, disillusionment and futility? The outpouring of a flood of 'disenchanted' and even bitter war literature in the late 1920s and early 1930s was certainly influential in some quarters, but several critics, including myself, have challenged the definition, depth and extent of 'anti-war' sentiments regarding the First World War. Firstly, bitter individual memoirs, mainly by sensitive intellectuals, did not represent what the vast majority of ordinary soldiers or their relatives felt about the war, or what they read. Secondly, the influence of the best-known 'war poets' at that time was by no means as important as is now assumed. Wilfred Owen's published verse had achieved only very modest sales by 1930 and, on this criterion, even the readership of poets like Sassoon and Rosenberg was minute – in comparison with the consolatory poets such as John Oxenham, the Rev G. A. Studdert Kennedy ('Woodbine Willy') and Robert Service. During the war, for example, Oxenham's verses sold in hundreds of thousands and his 'Hymn for the men at the Front' sold seven million. It is not difficult to understand why these versifiers were vastly more popular than poets of a much higher literary calibre. As Martin Stephen sums up:

> In their different ways, Oxenham and Woodbine Willie told those who read them that this was a war for decency and peace, and that suffering and salvation had ever been allied in the form of a young man nailed to a cross. Service told them that to fight was both the decent and manly thing to do, and brought a sense of humour to telling the tale.[4]

Thirdly, and even more damaging to the literary myth, scholars such as Hugh Cecil and Rosa Maria Bracco have shown that the bulk of middlebrow fiction cannot be construed in any way as 'anti-war'. 'It is often forgotten', Cecil writes, 'that this early wave of patriotic war books enjoyed far more acclaim than any of the later "disenchanted" British war novels, such as Richard Aldington's *Death of a Hero* (1929)... Book for book, the British public over a 30 year period... seem to have preferred the patriotic to the disenchanted type of war book'.

Cecil goes on to make the case that these best-selling novels by V.M. Yeates, Richard Blaker and others now largely forgotten, were welcomed by ex-combatants because they 'told the truth about the war' and are consequently still valuable for contemporary students of the conflict.[5]

Rosa Maria Bracco's argument is epitomised in her title *Merchants of Hope*.[6] Middlebrow writers of fiction did not attempt to camouflage the horror of war but their main aim was to soften the impact of the break it represented by reasserting links with the past. Their tone was essentially conservative and reassuring, for example in stressing the absolute value of war-time comradeship, the history of the regiment, past great battles, home comforts and the English countryside.

Above all, as I've argued in my contribution to *Facing Armageddon* (1996), the very term 'anti-war' is far too general and vague to provide any precise indication of individual writers' beliefs about the Great War, and hence much less, their influence on the public. Nearly everybody is 'anti-war' in principle in detesting the prospect of large-scale killing, destruction, suffering and social disruption. Those who survived the war of 1914–18, whether combatants or civilians, had many legitimate grounds for bitter reflections: the dreadful conditions and uniquely heavy casualties; the rash promises, deceitful propaganda and political incompetence; and, most serious of all for combatants, the feelings of betrayal by those at home: the shirkers, strikers, profiteers and 'civilian militarists'.

Moreover, it is now more widely understood that even writers generally agreed to be 'anti-war' such as Owen and Sassoon (both awarded the Military Cross) were ambivalent alike in their military careers and their reactions: they were efficient and even bellicose officers leading soldiers who were killers as well as victims; enjoying some aspects of the war while savagely denouncing others. As Robert Wohl neatly puts it:

> Ambivalence toward the war is the main characteristic of the best and most honest of the war literature. The same men who cried out at the inhumanity of the war often confessed that they had loved it with a passion and wondered if they would ever be able to free themselves from the front's magic spell.[7]

Most significantly, of the millions who fought, only a handful would subsequently write that the war had been futile and not worth pursuing to victory. Even C. E. Montague's famous title *Disenchantment* was misleading because what he chiefly criticised was the decline in idealism from the heady days of 1914 which, perhaps, only a minority of his fellow volunteers had fully shared.

I now propose to examine briefly the ambiguities of three well-known components of the 'anti-war' myth: a personal rebellion, an autobiography and a play. In June 1917 Siegfried Sassoon invited court-martial by denouncing the war as unjust in a letter to the press, resigning his commission and throwing his medal ribbons into the Mersey. His anger was inspired as much by the atmosphere in England and the perceived duplicity of politicians as by the conditions at the front. Indeed Sassoon could be classed as a 'war lover' and warrior who was never happy when away from the front, but this side of his character is absent from his poetry. Later, in *Siegfried's Journey* he came close to admitting that his brave moral gesture had been an error:

> I must add that in the light of subsequent events it is difficult to believe that a Peace negotiated in 1917 would have been permanent. I share the general opinion that nothing on earth would have prevented a recurrence of Teutonic aggressiveness.[8]

Robert Graves was another dubious recruit to the anti-war brigade. He was indignant to be classed with anti-war writers on the publication of *Goodbye to All That* in 1929, and for the remainder of his long life remained very proud of his war service with the Royal Welch Fusiliers.

> In any case Graves' title was accurate: he was saying goodbye to *all* that; including the stuffy conventions of pre-war society; war-time hysteria and immorality on the home front; and personal problems at the time of writing, including a marital crisis and being grilled by the police on suspicion of attempted murder.[9]

Lastly – the play. R. C. Sherriff's *Journey's End* has long occupied such a key position in the myth of anti-war literature that it comes as quite a shock to discover (notably from R. M. Bracco) that this was entirely at odds with the dramatist's intention, not only when the play made its amazingly popular debut in 1929, but for the whole of his life. The origins of this ambivalence lay in the complete contrast in outlooks between Sherriff and his first producer, Maurice Browne. Sherriff's career had been transformed for the better when he was commissioned into the 9th Battalion of the East Surrey Regiment and saw active service in France. Like Graves he remained extremely proud of his regiment and the comradeship he had found there.

By contrast Browne was a pacifist and a conscientious objector who had remained in America throughout the war. Sherriff would later write that his characters were 'simple, unquestioning men who fought the war because it seemed the only right and proper thing to do… (it was a play) in which not a word was spoken against the war… and no word of condemnation was uttered'. When the first reviews appeared in 1929, Sherriff had protested that he had not tried to point any kind of moral; he had merely wished to perpetuate the memory of some of the men he had known. One perceptive critic noted that while the play answered the question 'What was our war like?' it did not address the issue 'What did the war mean?'. Dr Bracco charts the various answers given to the latter question. Among recent misinterpretations of Sherriff's own beliefs and intentions, she cites the blatant example of a Methuen's Study-Aid book for young students which describes the play's theme as 'basically depressing… a message-carrying play designed with a definite purpose in mind: to make people ponder the stupidity and horrors of war'.[10]

These examples illustrate the tendency to misread or misrepresent complex personal experiences and texts in the light of later and quite different political and cultural assumptions. Phrases such as 'the horror of the trenches' are then repeated endlessly without much knowledge either of history or even of the supposed anti-war texts. In any case harrowing personal accounts of dreadful conditions and heavy casualties do not add up to a national revulsion against Britain's role in the war. They were controverted by many former combatants who stressed their positive experience in the war and especially the unique value of comradeship. These writers included Douglas Jerrold, Charles Carrington, Guy Chapman, Graham Greenwell, Sidney Rogerson and many more. In 1929, T. E. Lawrence warned his friends against blaming all their current problems on the war. The war, he noted, seemed more horrible in retrospect... than when they were in it. He dismissed *All Quiet On The Western Front* as 'post-war nostalgia shoved into the war period'.[11]

I have so far tried to suggest that disenchantment with the First World War was mainly literary in character, ambivalent or confused in the selection of targets and, above all, limited in its impact on the general public. Despite the boom in war books and severe criticisms directed against military leadership in the First World War, it is surely significant that a new generation proved willing to make a similar sacrifice in the late 1930s to stop German aggression a second time, and that long before the full horrors of Nazi extermination policies had been publicized.

In a curious way, coming to terms with the justification of Britain's role in the First World War has been made more difficult by participation in the Second. The Kaiser was obviously not such an evil force as Hitler, and German atrocities in the First World War, greatly exaggerated by propaganda, were dwarfed by Nazi barbarism in the Second. Consequently, A. J. P. Taylor's judgement that the Second World War was, ultimately, 'a good war' has been widely accepted, whereas it is hard to apply any term of moral approbation to the First. Nevertheless, both wars were fought mainly for reasons of British national self-interest, and only towards the end did the Second World War acquire the mantle of a moral crusade.

So far I have concentrated on literary rather than historical interpretations of the war, but it was clearly the historians' responsibility to bring home to the public the magnitude of the war effort and the British forces' leading role in the final, victorious phase of the war. This task was necessarily left largely to non-professional historians, since at that time very few academics were interested in the subject and only one, C. R. M. F. Cruttwell of Oxford, tackled the First World War as a whole, publishing in 1934 a lively and quite critical study which is still worth reading.

It is safe to assume that the multi-volume official history had little influence on the public. Its volumes on the Western Front appeared irregularly and out of sequence over many years; they were mind-numbingly detailed; and expressly intended for a professional military readership.

One official historian who did evince concern to reach a wider public was Cyril Falls, whose survey of *War Books* in 1930 was robustly critical of the 'disenchanted' school. Unfortunately, for the historiographical debate, his admirable volume *The First World War*, which praised Haig and stressed that the German Army had been soundly beaten in 1918, was not published until 1960.

The two military critics and historians who dominated the inter-war scene were Major-General J.F.C. Fuller and Captain B.H. Liddell Hart. As a convalescent subaltern in 1916 Liddell Hart had written a fulsome eulogy of the British high command and staff, but by the 1930s his views had swung full circle and he became sharply critical, especially of Haig and Robertson. His (and Fuller's) plausible defence of their critical stance was that more could be learnt from defeats than victories, coupled with anxiety that the Army hierarchy had learnt nothing and would repeat the bloodbaths of the Somme and Passchendaele in a future war. Fuller became particularly sarcastic and intemperate, for example remarking of one despised general who had been awarded the GCB that the initials must stand for 'Great Cretin Brotherhood'. As critics of the inter-war Army many of their shots were probably on target, but as influential historians of the First World War their approach was too polemical.

But the work which surely did most damage to the generals and their part in winning the war was Lloyd George's *Memoirs*, published in six volumes between 1933 and 1936. The former Prime Minister, assisted by Liddell Hart, clearly delighted in demolishing the reputation of Field Marshal Earl Haig, by then safely dead. Haig's entry has five columns in the index, including this sample:

> His reputation founded on cavalry exploits.
> Insists on premature use of tanks.
> His refusal to face unpleasant facts.
> His limited vision.
> Viciously resists Lloyd George's attempts to get Unity of Command.
> His stubborn mind transfixed on the Somme.
> Prefers to gamble with men's lives rather that to admit an error.
> Completely ignorant of the state of ground at Passchendaele.
> Painstaking but unimaginative.
> Narrowness of his outlook.
> Incapable of changing his plans.
> His liking for great offensives.
> Unequal to his task.
> Did not inspire his men.
> His ingenuity at shifting the blame to other shoulders than his own.
> Only took part in two battles during the war.

So, it is clear, the Prime Minister was not wholly satisfied with his Commander-in-Chief! But note also two further entries:

> Lloyd George had no personal quarrel with…
> (and) No conspicuous officer better qualified for highest command than.

One should also not miss the index entries under 'Military Mind' which include:

> Military Mind, narrowness of.
> Stubborness of, not peculiar to America.
> Does not seem to understand arithmetic.
> Represented by Sir Henry Wilson's fantastic memorandum.
> Obsessed with North-West Frontier of India.
> Impossibility of trusting.
> Regards thinking as a form of mutiny.

In reacting to the often dreadful conditions on the Western Front some historians found consolation or escapism in strategic 'might have beens'. This contrast to the Western Front has given a special appeal to the tragic failure at the Dardanelles, epitomised by John North's elegaic *Gallipoli: the Fading Vision* (1936).

Even more attractive as a romantic alternative to the Flanders bloodbath was the Palestine campaign where the spotlight obsessively focused from the early 1920s on T. E. Lawrence's peripheral exploits rather than Allenby's vastly larger armies. Here the terrain gave scope for rapid and far-reaching mobile operations, culminating in spectacular victories – the recovery of Jerusalem with its echo of the Crusades – and the advance to Damascus.

Finally, as regards the inter-war period, an all-too-brief reference to the influence of films. In the late 1920s, surprisingly, it was still possible to produce a series of patriotic – indeed jingoistic – films, including the battle of Jutland, and even the Somme. Then in 1930, Lewis Milestone's celebrated film of E. M. Remarque's *All Quiet on the Western Front* made a tremendous impact in Britain, as in New York, Paris and Berlin, where it was eventually banned by the Nazis. On the enormous popularity of Remarque's book and the resultant film, Modris Eksteins has written persuasively that both were manifestations not of the 'real war' but of attitudes in the late 1920s. Many veterans, for example, denounced Remarque's works and their runaway success 'as evidence of the malaise that had engulfed the postwar world, and as a symptom of the spirit that had betrayed a generation and its hopes'.[12]

Disappointment with the fruits of victory and the terrible prospect that another war might be looming diverted attention – already flagging – from how the First World War had been won to why it had broken out and how a Second might be avoided. In the quest to promote peace and international co-operation the public was deemed to require a new iconography of war: one which emphasized its suffering, destruction and futility.

I now come to my main contention or thesis; namely that much of what the public today believes to be the objective truth about the First World War really derives from the radical anti-war and anti-authority movement of the 1960s.

A portent of the new wave of ultra-critical interpretations of the First World War was Leon Wolff's *In Flanders Fields*, published in Britain in 1959. Wolff's searing description of conditions at Passchendaele introduced the horrors of the Western Front to a new generation, including myself, satiated with a decade of accounts of how Monty had beaten the Desert Fox and knocked him for six out of Africa. Wolff's anger and indignation suffused the book: the futile offensive should have been stopped but it had dragged on into November, mainly due to Haig's obstinacy. The 'butchers' were fair game but, by contrast, 'the curs' (politicians) got off relatively lightly. Wolff tried to be fair and even-handed but his conclusion was devastating: the war had 'meant nothing, solved nothing and proved nothing', and in the process had killed eight and a half million men.[13]

The new spirit of iconoclasm and ridicule was encapsulated in the title and contents of Alan Clark's *The Donkeys* (1961). Here was revived a potent myth of a generation of soldier lions sacrificed by incompetent officer donkeys who were too stupid to appreciate that the war could have been won more economically in the East. Haig, not yet Commander-in-Chief but already cast as Donkey-in-Chief, was excoriated as a 'combination of ambition, obstinacy and megalomania'. Academic reviewers were not impressed either by Mr Clark's scholarship or his judgement. Michael Howard found the book entertaining but worthless as history. It was a 'petulant caricature of a tragedy' and, as a memorial to the dead of 1915, 'a pretty deplorable piece of work.[14] Nevertheless, it sold well and remains popular, due perhaps in part to the celebrity of its author.

On a completely different scale was the BBC's epic 26 part series *The Great War*, first shown in the summer of 1964 and immediately repeated during the following winter. As Alex Danchev has pointed out, the series made a tremendous impact on the public with an average of eight million viewers for each episode. The distinguished team of script writers were given an unusual amount of influence in relation to the visual material, even in the final production. Chief among them was John Terraine, already the author of *Douglas Haig: the Educated Soldier* and emerging as a doughty defender of the primacy of the Western Front and champion of the British performance there. Despite much friction and disagreement among the script writers, Terraine's 'positive' interpretation featured prominently in many of the episodes.

Ironically, the medium proved to be much more powerful than the message. Audience Research Reports revealed that the visual images of the ravaged battlescapes, the broken bodies and the faces of the haggard survivors had made a vastly greater impact than the text. Viewers were struck by the horrors of war and the appalling waste of young men. Thus the series mainly served to confirm the myths which Terraine and some of his colleagues had hoped to demolish or modify; above all the 'horror of trench warfare' and the utter futility of the First World War.[15]

Lastly, I will discuss briefly the play and, even more influential, the film of *Oh! What a Lovely War*, produced in 1963 and 1969 respectively. I am indebted again here to Alex Danchev for bringing out the inspirational role of Raymond Fletcher, who acted as more than 'historical adviser' to Joan Littlewood's Theatre Workshop production of the play. Fletcher, later a Labour MP, was a journalist, a fan of Liddell Hart and a fierce opponent of Terraine and any author who 'white-washed' Haig and the generals. Fletcher revealingly described his three hour harangue to the Theatre Workshop group as 'one part me, one part Liddell Hart, the rest Lenin!'. He injected a powerful, two-pronged impetus to the play: as an entertaining vehicle in the class war it championed the working class or ordinary soldiers against the upper class officers who callously sacrificed them; and also served as a contemporary warning – drawn from the supposed miscalculation of 1914 – against the risks of nuclear war.

The historical limitations of the play are evident in its structure: Act 1 dramatises 'innocent' hope of victory and optimism; Act 2 stages recognition of defeat, despair and pessimism. The play leans heavily on three recent popular historical texts; namely Barbara Tuchman's *August 1914* (1962), Alan Clark's *The Donkeys* and Leon Wolff's *In Flanders Fields*. These books focus respectively upon the years 1914, 1915 and 1917. There is some effort in the play to cover events in 1916, but on 1918 it has almost nothing to say. Thus the awkward, embarrassing issue of eventual victory was avoided and the message came over loud and clear: 'the War as a whole was visited upon a compliant lower class by an upper class which claimed a superiority it could not justify'. This sort of clap-trap reminds one of Wully Robertson's derisive snort 'I've 'eard different!',-which is particularly relevant in this context since he had risen from private to field marshal. As the theatre and film critic Derek Paget disarmingly admits, reliance on these sources and the emphasis on contemporary concerns made the play 'a poorish source for knowledge about the Great War, (but) such an excellent source of knowledge about the early 1960s'.[16]

Richard Attenborough's film adaptation has largely eclipsed the play in the public memory. It caused a sensation worldwide when first screened in 1969, and has been described as 'the perfect TV extravaganza', not least because of its all-star cast. The setting on Brighton Pier was frivolously satirical, and the dialogue displayed little concern with historical accuracy or fairness. Though obviously 'anti-war', it was more specifically anti-authority and especially anti-officer. The First World War was a disaster because the officer-donkeys 'combined homicidal imbecility with vainglorious ambition'. A composite 'Haig figure' representing all the red-tabs shouldered most of the blame; there were 'butchers' aplenty but 'The Cur' (Lloyd George) was conspicuously absent. As Danchev concluded, 'it was the greatest exercise in debunking for 40 years'.[17]

This all-too-brief discussion suggests that a new wave of campaign histories and military biographies, an outstanding TV series and a radical, debunking play, later turned into a film, introduced the post-1945 generation to the Great War. But, inevitably, it was history given a very powerful 'spin' by contemporary concerns, including a new phase of the class war, a challenge to traditions and hence resentment of authority – particularly in uniform – and fear of war both conventional (as in Vietnam) and nuclear.

Through their texts and references these works revived interest in the anti-war writers of the 1930s and thereby prompted a further surge of popular, non-scholarly publications. I need mention only the obsession with the first day of the battle of the Somme which, for example, features prominently even in Sebastian Faulks' novel *Birdsong* and John Laffin's *Butchers and Bunglers*, a late emotional throw-back to earlier polemical tirades.

With a few honourable and encouraging exceptions, such as the balanced *Timewatch* reassessment of Field Marshal Haig in July 1996, television programmes have generally taken the easy option of reinforcing received views and recycling myths which might be summarised as Oh! What a Ghastly and Futile War. This was, alas, true of the seven part series *1914-1918* produced by the BBC Education Department at the end of 1996. While admirable in its evocation of atmosphere and with stunning photography, it deserved Correlli Barnett's stinging critique (in *The Spectator*) entitled 'Oh What a Whingeing War'.[18] It dwelt heavily on the dreadful conditions, suffering and casualties, but largely evaded the hard political questions about the great power issues at stake and why a 'peace without victory' proved unobtainable. Most directly relevant to this lecture, it failed to explain how the blundering Allied military leadership of the middle war years had won a remarkable victory in 1918. These defects and omissions may perhaps be put right next year in commemorating the 80th anniversary of the remarkable transformation of Allied fortunes from the nadir of March 1918 to the victorious conclusion of the war in the autumn. Let us hope that a balanced and well-informed television series is, even now, in the making.

During the long period when the politically correct views of the First World War prevailed, ie, of military incompetence and futility, 'Colonel' John Terraine, supported by a few trusty NCOs, remained doggedly in his forward command post. He insisted, in book after book, that: (1) conditions in the 20th century's first great industrialised war ruled out brilliant generalship in the main theatre or any quick route to victory, (2) from 1916 Britain bore the main burden of the war on the crucial front against a very powerful enemy, and wore him down through attrition warfare and (3) the war had to be won, and was won on the Western Front by the Allies, with Haig and his armies playing the leading role.

Now, Terraine's sector has been relieved and soldiers (scholars) from Britain, the Commonwealth and the United States are carrying the war (debate) forward into fresh ground only lightly scarred by the barrages (polemics) of Terraine, Laffin, Alan Clark, Denis Winter et al. Since the publication of the pioneering study *Fire-Power* by Shelford Bidwell and Dominick Graham in 1982, a brigade of scholars, including Tim Travers, David French, Peter Simkins and John Bourne have exploited the full range of sources now available to throw new light on such issues as civil-military relations, biographies of lesser-known generals, controversial campaigns and the higher conduct of the war. There are also encouraging group projects in progress examining the performance of all the divisions on the Western Front and the levels at which innovations were implemented. The Australasian team of Robin Prior and Trevor Wilson have demonstrated how successful combined operations for limited advances ('bite and hold' tactics) were introduced in 1916, but only fitfully applied in 1917. Gary Sheffield has shown that officer-other rank relations were generally very good, *pace* the *Monocled Mutineer*. Paddy Griffiths has gone furthest in arguing that in doctrine, training and tactics the British forces had achieved parity at least with the Germans in the final year of the war. Paul Harris has contended that Haig and GHQ welcomed the tank but were realistically aware of its limitations. Even if some claims for the British Army's receptivity to new ideas and weapons are disputed as excessive, a broad consensus is clear: historians are now exploring and charting the improvements which were so-successfully implemented in the final months of the war.

Military historians such as Ian Beckett,[19] Correlli Barnett and myself have expressed frustration at the persistence of myths and obsolete judgements on key aspects of the First World War. I have written on several occasions in the last decade that the time must surely be coming when the First World War can be treated objectively as history (like the Napoleonic wars or even World War Two) rather than viewed – often from a narrow selection of literary sources – as a national trauma whose myths can be used to inculcate the futility of all wars.

As I have suggested today, within the ranks of military historians that time has already come, but on the popular front we still struggle against the appeal of the ubiquitous 'war poets' on the one flank and their television ally *Blackadder*, on the other. I place on record, with no satisfaction, that *Blackadder* has been cited as a historical source in an undergraduate essay.

Still, I believe it is possible to end on a positive note and I trust you will excuse the military metaphors. Military historians have now sorted out their command problems, their Intelligence is sound and they are perfecting their operational skills – not least in the Centre for Military Archives here! They have summoned their reserves and built up their stocks of tanks, guns and ammunition. They must attempt one more 'big push' to obtain the decisive breakthrough. Their offensive will not be motivated by a triumphalist or militaristic spirit, but will seek simply to re-establish what was common knowledge to the generation which fought the war;[20] namely that for Britain, the First World War was a necessary war. Though unexpectedly costly, and in some respects disappointing in its aftermath, the conflict was worth pursuing to victory – a victory which was undoubtedly preferable to defeat.

References

1. Martin Stephen, *The Price of Pity* (1996), p. 230.
2. John Terraine, *To Win a War. 1918 the Year of Victory* (1978), p. 258.
3. Trevor Wilson, *The Myriad Faces of War* (1986), p. 586.
4. M. Stephen, op cit, pp. 138–147.
5. Hugh Cecil, 'British War Novelists' in Hugh Cecil and Peter H. Liddle (eds) *Facing Armageddon: the First World War Experienced* (1996), pp. 801–16.
6. Rosa Maria Bracco, *Merchants of Hope. British Middlebrow Writers and the First World War, 1919–1939* (1993), pp. 12, 198.
7. Robert Wohl, *The Generation of 1914* (1980), p. 219.
8. Ibid pp. 98–100. Siegfried Sassoon, *Siegfried's Journey, 1916–1920* (paperback edition, 1982), p. 57.
9. Brian Bond, 'British "Anti-War" Writers and their Critics' in Cecil and Liddle (eds), *Facing Armageddon*, p. 821.
10. Bracco, op cit pp.149, 152–-3, 178, 185–6.
11. Wohl, p. 120.
12. Modris Eksteins, *Rites of Spring. The Great War and the Birth of the Modern Age* (1989) p. 298. Bond, *The Pursuit of Victory*, p.126.
13. Brian Bond, 'Passchendaele: Verdicts, Past and Present' in Peter H. Liddle (ed) *Passchendaele in Perspective* (1997), p. 481.
14. Michael Howard's review of *The Donkeys* in *The Listener*, 3 August 1961.
15. Alex Danchev, 'Bunking and Debunking: the Controversies of the 1960s' in Brian Bond (ed), *The First World War and British Military History* (1991), pp. 263–288. I have drawn heavily on this brilliant essay in the discussion of *Oh! What a Lovely War.*
16. Derek Paget, 'Remembrance Play: Oh! What a Lovely War and History' in Tony Howard and John Stokes (eds), *Acts of War: The Representation of Military Conflict on the British Stage and Television since 1945* (1996), pp. 86–90. While correcting some

historical errors, the author commits one himself; namely that Alan Clark had been Liddell Hart's pupil at university! I am indebted to Dr Steve Badsey for drawing my attention to Derek Paget's chapter.

17. Danchev, p. 285.
18. Correlli Barnet, 'Oh What a Whingeing War!' in *The Spectator*, 18 January 1997.
19. Ian Beckett, 'The Military Historian and the Popular Image of the Western Front, 1914–1918' in *The Historian*, Spring 1997, and his bibliographical essay in *Facing Armageddon*, op cit pp. 891–5.
20. 'The task of the historian is often to recapture for a new generation the meaning of events that were perfectly well understood at the time they occurred.' Lawrence Freedman reviewing a history of the Cold War in *The Evening Standard*, 22 September 1997.

2

Liddell Hart and the First World War

This essay first appeared in *'Look to Your Front'. Studies in the First World War* (Spellmount, 1999). It was a pioneering venture by members of the British Commission for Military History, of which I was then President. A year earlier, Alex Danchev had published his authorised biography *Alchemist of War*, which was extremely well written and full of interest but tailed off badly after 1945. I had known Liddell Hart very well in the last 11 years of his life and had the inestimable advantage of living in the same village where, I should make clear, he was the newcomer, arriving only in December 1958. I felt qualified to write his biography but was only permitted to publish a study of his military thoughts, and that under strict conditions. This, I felt in retrospect, was a back-handed compliment because his ideas were much more interesting than his private life. Now that his career, his huge list of publications and wide-ranging influence can be seen in perspective, the time is surely right for a more comprehensive and definitive study than either Danchev or I could achieve. I hope that in due course this will be undertaken by my friend and former colleague, Brian Holden Reid.

When the First World War began Basil Hart had just completed his first year at Cambridge reading history. In his initial reactions he was typical of thousands of middle class ex-public school boys: patriotic, idealistic and anxious to prove himself in combat before the war's anticipated early conclusion. On his own admission a spoilt 'mother's boy' who had outgrown his strength, Basil at first enjoyed the rigours of officer training in England and was fortunate to arrive on the Somme, still 'all quiet', in the autumn of 1915.'It reminds one most of a great picnic,' he wrote cheerfully to his parents in September. In mid-October he was struck low by a sudden fever and had difficulty in persuading the doctors not to send him home. His second tour of duty later that winter introduced him to the mud and nerve-shattering noise of the Ypres salient. After a brief spell in the front line, which he privately transformed into heroic mode, he was concussed by a shell exploding above the entrance to his shallow dug-out. This time he raised no objection to an immediate return to England.

Like so many of his contemporaries who survived combat, the war made a profound impression on Basil's conception of his own character (which he was already analysing in 'notes for history'), and his attitude to armed conflict. Yet, when he came to write his memoirs in the 1960s, he devoted only a few pages to the critical experiences in 1915 and 1916 which had fundamentally shaped his outlook and his career.[1] Moreover his surprisingly brief account of his experiences in the front line, and particularly of the reasons for his rapid evacuation to the rear on all three occasions, is cool, detached and – in modern parlance – economical with the truth. What was the precise nature of Basil's wounds and disabilities? Was the damage he suffered more psychological than physical? What were the immediate and more lasting effects of experiences seemingly bordering on the traumatic? These questions pre-occupied and baffled Liddell Hart's only son, Adrian, in his later years, and have recently been subjected to close and imaginative scrutiny by his biographer, Alex Danchev.[2]

Danchev rightly allots the most thorough discussion to Liddell Hart's third and final experience of front-line combat – on the Somme near Fricourt between mid-June and 18 July 1916. Liddell Hart was fortunate indeed to be in reserve for the first attack when his battalion, 9th KOYLI suffered very heavy casualties, but he went up later that day, 1 July, and 50 years later was still disputing Lance Spicer's right to temporary command of the company rather than himself. His physical and mental ordeal occurred – or culminated – between 16 and 18 July at the northern end of the devastated charnel-house of Mametz Wood. It was in the darkness of the wood that Liddell Hart suffered flesh wounds in a heavy bombardment and was then badly gassed with phosgene, though unaware of this until later. The effects of gassing were quite sufficient to explain Liddell Hart's subsequent collapse and evacuation to England but, scrutinizing his contemporary accounts and later hints – notably in correspondence with General Ironside – Danchev speculates boldly and persuasively that he also experienced a devastating psychological revelation which affected his whole outlook on war and, more specifically, on command. To summarize a complex matter: Liddell Hart had a nightmare vision of being left alone on the battlefield and in Mametz Wood he apparently yielded to the fear of being afraid. He discovered that he was not physically brave or, in Danchev's phrases, he 'lacked intestinal fortitude. In and out of Mametz Wood the liver had been searched, painfully, and found wanting'.[3]

This self-discovery that he lacked physical and mental robustness of the story-book variety is not a matter for censure, particularly for those of us who have not endured a comparable trial, but it was a catastrophic blow for the immature but ambitious subaltern who dreamt of becoming a great commander. Liddell Hart found consolation in becoming a famous writer instead and a demanding critic of commanders ancient and modern (in Yigal Allon's perfect phrase 'The Captain who teaches Generals'), but he was too self-critical and introspective not to be naggingly aware that he had failed to 'hack it' in his brief opportunity on the Somme. Danchev speculates, in my view persuasively, that Liddell Hart was henceforth handicapped in dealing with a profession which prizes physical courage above all other virtues. He was obliged to dispute this priority in his writings and to award the palm to moral courage. I would also invoke in this context his lifelong tendency to lay stress on the role of the individual genius as against the mass; on the crucial importance of surprise and psychological unsettling of the enemy; and on the ideal of winning battles without bloodshed. He was reluctant to admit that even when his ideals were most nearly realised, for example in France in May 1940, a great deal of hard fighting and bloodshed was still unavoidable.

During the war, however, Liddell Hart's obligatory withdrawal from combat did not entail a sudden evaporation of patriotic idealism and uncritical reverence for the British high command. Quite the contrary, as is now well-known, though the booklet remained unpublished (until 2010), while convalescing in the autumn of 1916 he wrote a eulogy entitled *Impressions of the Great British Offensive on the Somme* by 'A Company Commander who saw three and a half weeks of it'. As I commented when writing on Liddell Hart's military thought in 1977, 'there could hardly be a more comprehensive catalogue of the assumptions about British generalship in the First World War which he would denounce with increasing severity for the remainder of his career'.[4]

A few phrases must suffice to convey the tone of this youthful effusion: he praised 'the amazing perfection of our organisation which in its generalship and staff work were super German'. The Somme area was well chosen for the offensive and the strategy was masterly. Sir Douglas Haig was 'the greatest general Britain had ever owned'. 'Whilst not all our staff are brilliant, it is safe to say that 90 percent of our general staff officers are really brilliant men, with quite a large number amongst them who have a genius for war... We have produced fully a hundred first-rate generals'. While he acknowledged that war, as waged on the Western Front, is 'horrible and ghastly beyond all imagination of the civilian', he was still able to conclude that 'with all its faults and horrors, it is above all a man's life, in the fullest and deepest sense of the term'.[5]

How can we account for the complete sea-change in his views of British strategy and tactics, and above all of British generalship, which occurred in the 1920s, hardened in his intensive writing on the war in the early 1930s and never significantly changed thereafter?

It could be argued that in his own brief experience, particularly on 1 July 1916, he had seen enough tactical ineptitude with its horrific cost in lives, to justify an obsession with improving the quality of professional officers and the theoretical and practical development of tactics. These concerns he shared with a whole generation of surviving junior officers including Bernard Law Montgomery, though going beyond most of them in his emphasis on tanks as a war winning weapon which would also be more economical with soldiers' lives.

We must surely, however, take into account a number of other factors relating to Liddell Hart's post-war career and the influence of individuals in explaining his transformation from near-idolater of the generals to harsh and unremitting critic. The following seems to me a significant, but not necessarily exhaustive, list.

Soon after the war Liddell Hart came under the powerful influence of the Army's most original, irreverent and iconoclastic thinker, J. F. C. Fuller, already a colonel and his senior by 12 years.[6] Fuller had little patience with senior officers less intelligent than himself (ie, nearly everybody), and few were spared from his scathing sarcasm. Liddell Hart, though possibly less arrogant, was also unimpressed by the intellectual shortcomings of senior officers whom he met, penning for example, a belittling description of General Horne's inability to understand a simple sand-table exercise.

He was also very reluctant to abandon a touching but naive belief in the moral integrity and gentlemanly code of behaviour of senior officers. Thus he was one of those who declared himself shocked by the posthumous publication of Field Marshal Sir Henry Wilson's edited diaries in 1927 – despite the fact that Wilson had long been known as a notorious gossip, a 'political soldier' and an arch-intriguer.

A quite different consideration is that Liddell Hart shared the conviction common to virtually all military writers and historians of that era that operations should be studied primarily for the 'lessons' that they yielded. He readily took a further step in arguing that it was more rewarding to concentrate on failures and shortcomings since they would produce more valuable lessons. His role as a professional military journalist from 1925 onwards surely reinforced this tendency; indeed he would protest to critics that he had to avoid at all costs appearing to be an apologist or propagandist for the Army or the War Office.

One can only speculate about the precise effects of his enforced departure from the Army on health grounds in 1924, but it clearly freed his egotism and natural critical bent from the severe restraints prevalent within the Service. As Danchev brings out well in his biography, Liddell Hart reluctantly abandoned his dream of becoming a 'Great Captain' and substituted that of 'Great Writer'. By 1930, still aged only 35, he had achieved an international reputation as a military theorist, critic and historian. As Fuller told him, he now had the power to shake the Amy Council to its roots.[7]

Finally, by 1925, in his little book *Paris* subtitled 'The Future of War' he already displayed the main elements of his methodology or 'keys' to historical development. In his approach, the First World War was depicted as the negation of classical strategy, and the fatal aberration from Britain's traditional strategy in particular. In short, Britain's leaders in 1914 had wilfully abandoned her traditional – and economical

– maritime strategy in favour of a total commitment to Continental war waged by mass conscript armies. One may suggest that it was Liddell Hart's Whig or Liberal sympathies which were appalled as much as his military sensitivity.[8] He saw it as part of his duty as a military critic to warn against the dangers of repeating such a catastrophic mistake; the corollary being that Britain would fight a Second World War with a group of generals who had learnt as little from the First as had Frederick the Great's mule from its campaigns.

Let us turn now to Liddell Hart's sources. The British Cabinet and War Office Papers remained closed throughout his working life, but he enjoyed some unofficial access to them via Brigadier-General Sir James Edmonds and other official historians. He did not read German and even his command of French is uncertain. He therefore depended mainly on published books and journals, especially *The Army Quarterly* (established in 1920) with its summaries of foreign accounts of the war; supplemented by innumerable interviews with participants or witnesses – a source which he exploited brilliantly throughout his life.

Although the thrust of this article is deliberately critical, it needs to be stressed that given his limited sources and busy working life as a journalist, Liddell Hart's early attempts to provide a structure and an outline for the war as a whole were very successful. His bibliography was impressive; he provided a fair narrative coverage of fronts other than the Western; and above all he developed an attractive style with a plethora of images and metaphors; and with his confident personal judgements well to the fore. But he conspicuously lacked some notable scholarly attributes: such as an interest in past events for their own sake or a willingness to make substantial alterations in the light of later evidence. Indeed, given his stance as the widely-recognised authority whose personal philosophy was bound up with his historical judgements, he found it increasingly difficult to admit to shortcomings in matters of fact or perspective. In his later decades he was committed to a somewhat dogmatic and, on some sensitive issues, even ruthless defence of positions adopted by the early 1930s.

The main works under discussion are *Reputations* (1928), *The Real War* (1930) and *A History of the World War* (1934). The war was depicted, in the latter two volumes, chronologically and geographically in a series of episodic scenes and sketches rather than by an attempt at a sustained narrative of the war as a whole. In this respect he compares unfavourably with C.R.M.F. Cruttwell (an Oxford don and ex-combatant) whose substantial single volume treatment, *A History of the Great War*, was first published in 1934.[9] Surprisingly, even major campaigns such as the Somme and Passchendaele receive progressively shorter treatment, with striking images and phrases substituting for analysis. Above all, the fundamental error of Britain's primary commitment to the Western Front, the unwisdom of the strategy of attrition waged there and the inadequacy of the high command (ie Generals Haig and Robertson as Commander-in-Chief and Chief of the Imperial General Staff respectively) are taken as established facts.

If a personal reminiscence may be inserted here, I was flattered, in the 1960s, by Liddell Hart's meticulous 'vetting' of my early forays into the history of the First

World War, but also embarrassed by the pressure he placed on me to alter even moderately sympathetic or favourable statements about Haig or Robertson. In some cases I decided to risk his angry reaction by sending off articles or contributions to volumes without first showing them to him. As I now approach the age he was then, I have more understanding of the natural tendency to identify ever more defensively with positions one has taken in print; but even so I must say that Liddell Hart carried this tendency to unusual extremes, perhaps reflecting more deep-seated feelings of insecurity about his career and reputation.

In a perceptive critical essay,[10] Hew Strachan has noted the unintentional irony of Liddell Hart's title *The Real War*, published in 1930 during the spate of trench memoirs which really did try to recapture the conditions and experiences of ordinary soldiers. Here, as in his other works, Liddell Hart resolutely (and puzzlingly) set his face against dealing with such emotive personal aspects. Rather he aimed to view the war, loftily, 'as an episode in human history', and to argue that 'the decisive impressions were received and made in the cabinets and the military headquarters'. As Strachan aptly comments, by omitting any glimpse of operations at the tactical level or any depiction of hardship and suffering, Liddell Hart was effectively helping to perpetuate a false image of the war, resting on the wartime claims of politicians and generals. Lord Beaverbrook's volumes might be cited as the supreme example in this genre; namely of the 'battles' waged in Whitehall and at Westminister by politicians to whom the nostalgic line of the war-time song might be applied: 'There was a Front, but damned if we knew where.' In contrast to the Generals, however, the politicians who were ultimately responsible for Britain's strategy largely escaped Liddell Hart's censure.

By this time (1930), Liddell Hart's main interest in the war and its 'lessons' was clear. He had moved beyond his war-time and early post-war concern with tactics, and had never been much concerned with the broader considerations underlying operations such as munitions, logistics, manpower and morale on the home front. No, his overriding concern was with British strategy (essentially Army or land-based) and the terrible error which he traced back to Sir Henry Wilson (as Director of Military Operations between 1910 and 1914), of committing the small British Expeditionary Force to a mass continental war of attrition. Wilson's original error had been compounded – from December 1915 – by an obstinate and unimaginative Commander-Chief, Sir Douglas Haig, abetted by an excessively loyal and single-minded CIGS Sir William Robertson. Liddell Hart's sympathies seem to have lain increasingly (in the post-war 'battle of the memoirs') with David Lloyd George, in the compilation of whose multi-volume account he played an influential role.

Hew Strachan has accurately described *The Real War* as 'a sustained strategical critique',[11] but even as such it is flawed by its emphasis on the (long) period of British failures almost to the exclusion of the final phase of outstanding success in the summer and autumn of 1918. As mentioned earlier, this approach was defended on the grounds that more is to be learned from the study of failures, but one cannot avoid the suspicion that he found *British* failures more congenial, and was reluctant to confront the awkward facts that the British Army (and the newly constituted Air Force) had improved markedly in 1918, and that Haig and his general headquarters had contributed significantly to the eventual victory.

One explanation for Liddell Hart's concentration on the years of British failure, in the senses that little ground was gained and enormous casualties incurred, might be that he had left the Western Front in July 1916 before the debut of the tank and before the 'learning curve' in such aspects as the roles of artillery, airpower and combined all-arms tactics had become apparent. But against this, he had ample post-war evidence that such positive improvements had occurred, and indeed made his reputation largely by concentrating on one dramatic facet of British operational innovation – the tank.

A more persuasive insight is Hew Strachan's suggestion that a more sophisticated gambit was adopted.[12] By largely ignoring the successful culminating battles of 1918, Liddell Hart was able to imply a natural progression from the British commanders' incompetence on the Western Front to their conservatism and failure to learn lessons in the 1920s and 1930s. In short, the British Army and its leaders were not up to Continental standards and never would be. Britain had been drawn into a Continental struggle based on material and manpower attrition rather than on psychological effect and the optimum exploitation of new technology. The obvious inference or 'lesson' that such a costly strategic error must not be repeated exercised considerable appeal in the 1930s. David Low's cartoon caricature of the Army's leaders as 'Colonel Blimps' reinforced this message. Liddell Hart's alternative national policy was clearly outlined in *The British Way in Warfare* (1932), where he urged a return to the primacy of a maritime strategy whose main features were economic blockade and reliance on superior naval power to mount amphibious operations in an 'indirect approach' to the enemy's vulnerable coast.[13]

It would be pedantic and 'academic', in the popular sense of 'pointless', to place so much emphasis on the omissions and limitations in Liddell Hart's coverage of the First World War were it not for the pretentions – and enduring influence – of the theories based upon such faulty foundations. Liddell Hart's relative lack of interest in the Eastern Fronts, or other peripheral aspects from a British viewpoint, may be excusable, but it is very strange indeed that he should make such high claims for the decisive effects of the blockade of Germany (in comparison with attrition on the Western Front) without subjecting the whole operation to careful scrutiny.[14]

Again, given his youthful eulogy of British generals and staff officers, it is surprising that as a mature writer he should display so little sympathy for commanders confronted with the unexpected conditions of siege warfare on a vast scale, maintained by the near-total mobilisation of industry and manpower. In these conditions the learning process was likely to be slow and costly, but Liddell Hart contended that the principles of military leadership were eternal and could be derived from a study of the 'Great Captains' such as Scipio Africanus (a 'greater than Napoleon' in Liddell Hart's league table), Maurice de Saxe or Napoleon himself. Sherman was a more recent and more relevant model, but there was much more scope for strategic mobility and an indirect approach in the western theatre of the American Civil War. Also

Sherman's deliberate policy of undermining Confederate morale by destroying crops, buildings and communications was at odds with Liddell Hart's essentially humane and moderate philosophy.

Were there, then, any generals or commanders in the First World War who found favour with Liddell Hart? General Sir John Monash appealed to him as an 'outsider' whose background contrasted sharply with the standard British commander. He was Australian, Jewish and a civil engineer. Far from being a handicap, his lack of a Staff College education and failure to jump the usual hurdles of the regular officer's career, was believed to bring a fresh and original 'business mentality' to the problems of the Western Front. Danchev also interestingly develops the point that Monash's alleged lack of physical courage in the Gallipoli campaign provided Liddell Hart with a plausible example of a successful commander who lacked the traditional physical leadership qualities but made up for them 'by an uncanny mastery of what was reported and by a masterly organisation of his intelligence'. Above all he displayed moral courage.[15]

Two senior British commanders retained Liddell Hart's admiration: Sir Edmund Allenby because he had achieved victory by a brilliant example of strategic mobility in Palestine; and Sir Ian Hamilton because he had failed gallantly in the campaign (Gallipoli) which might have transformed the whole course of the war. But the commander, or at any rate leader, who most closely approached Liddell Hart's ideal was T. E. Lawrence.[16] His personal qualities and achievements were as remote from those of Haig and other Western Front commanders as could be imagined. Here was a completely un-military intellectual and scholar who had proved himself a brilliant leader through strength of character and intelligence; had achieved strategically significant victories through boldness, cunning and mobility rather than in attrition by protracted battles; and had aspired to literary fame by writing his war memoirs, *The Seven Pillars of Wisdom*, on an epic scale. Liddell Hart was too intelligent and too well-informed to suggest that Lawrence would have succeeded in a high command on the Western Front (and Lawrence himself stressed that his methods were peculiarly suited to Arabia/Palestine and not of universal validity). Nevertheless, through Liddell Hart's (and others') idealisation of T. E. Lawrence and his romantic operations the notion was firmly implanted that his was the 'real war' or war as it should have been conducted had intelligence and genius been allowed wider play than the sordid, unimaginative slogging match on the Western Front.

One further puzzle or paradox needs to be discussed. As mentioned earlier, Liddell Hart, with one outstanding exception, displayed little interest in the materiel or 'sinews of war' such as guns, munitions and the enormous quantity of stores which had to be transported and replenished in order that the armies could survive, let alone advance. The great exception was, of course, the tank whose utility in the recent war and revolutionary potential Liddell Hart began to extol, under the influence of J. F. C. Fuller, from the early 1920s. The paradox, only to be suggested here, is that in his military career and in civil life alike, Liddell Hart was notoriously un-mechanical and impractical. He also, surprisingly, neglected the tactical application of airpower. Such limitations do not necessarily of course invalidate theories based upon observation, reading and reflection, but they should cause us to examine more critically the relationship between the available technology and means of waging war and the theories built upon them. Liddell Hart was by no means unique in his hope that mechanization would restore mobility and decisiveness while at the same time greatly reducing casualties, but did he perhaps come to see tanks almost as chess pieces or symbols which would again make possible a conflict between small, high-quality forces in which there would be the opportunity for the superior mind to triumph over matter?

Liddell Hart did not write much specifically on the First World War after 1939 except for the long-gestating first volume of his history of the Royal Tank Corps *The Tanks* (1959). However, in the same year he published an important revisionist article 'The Basic Truths of Passchendaele', which served to re-awaken slumbering controversies before the volcanic eruption of these issues in the 1960s.[17] Here was Liddell Hart at his best in puncturing, or at least challenging myths and errors. He argued convincingly that Haig had not been pressured by the French into launching his ill-fated offensive, nor had he felt obliged to continue it into the autumn to prevent a general French collapse. These were excuses put forward by Haig's supporters after the war. Charteris's reputation was again questioned for providing over-optimistic reports on German casualties which Haig had accepted. More generally, the article raised the complicated issue of comparative casualty statistics on which the chief culprit was said to be the senior British official historian, Sir James Edmonds, who had deliberately 'cooked the books' to suggest that attrition had in fact worked in the Allies' favour.[18]

Although he never revisited the First World War to produce a significant publication, Liddell Hart continued to publicize and inculcate his views in various ways. Though some might detect a veiled and calculating motive, it must also be stressed that he was an extremely generous host and a brilliant teacher manqué who delighted in encouraging young scholars and writers to pursue the numerous controversies in military history which had enthralled him for so many years.[19] He thus opened for many of us the dazzling prospect of making our own contributions to living issues whose protagonists we might meet (as I, for example, on one occasion was left alone to entertain 'Boney' Fuller), or at least study their private correspondence in his vast and haphazardly organized archives.

In my own experience, as mentioned earlier, I do not think he found it easy to follow Clausewitz's advice that the wise teacher should be content to guide and stimulate his students' intellectual development but be careful not to lead them by the hand for the rest of their lives.[20] All teachers experience this dilemma in some degree with promising pupils, and Basil was not good at letting go, particularly where the acolyte reached opinions contrary to his own on issues which he regarded as critical and on which his judgement represented 'The Truth'. Nevertheless, while it would be invidious to name names, I can assert with confidence that several of my contemporaries derived tremendous benefits from Liddell Hart's enthusiasm, encouragement and practical help without forfeiting their integrity and independence of mind. This reflection applies even to the highly emotive issues discussed here; namely British strategy and generalship in the First World War.

On the wider 'front' of popular opinion it must be acknowledged that Liddell Hart's unremitting efforts to propagate his interpretation of the First World War have been remarkably successful. In the 1960s his controlling hand and distinctive authorial 'voice' seemed to be omnipresent. Thus he was the consultant or adviser for the BBC's celebrated *'Great War'* series, Joan Littlewood's play *'Oh! What a Lovely War'*, the screening of *'Lawrence of Arabia'* and the play *'Ross'*. His was the chief inspiration behind Purnell's best-selling part-work series on the First World War.

Moreover, in this radical, revisionist decade it was almost obligatory to obtain Liddell Hart's approval and imprimatur for publications on the First World War. Thus he vetted the drafts of Alan Clark's *The Donkeys* and A. J. P. Taylor's irreverent *History*, which depicted British Western Front generals as donkeys and the war itself as meaningless; praised Leon Wolff's poignant dirge about the Passchendaele campaign (*In Flanders Fields*), and passed an anathema on John Terraine for his heretical presumption in daring to write sympathetically about Haig. Clinching evidence is provided by Raymond Fletcher, a self-confessed fan of Liddell Hart and a significant contributor to the script of *'Oh! What a Lovely War'*, who revealingly described the play's message as 'one part me, one part Liddell Hart, the rest Lenin!'.[21] Interestingly, in the 1960s Liddell Hart's personal contacts were mostly with Labour politicians concerned with defence issues such as Dennis Healey, George Brown, Reginald Paget and Richard Crossman.

Liddell Hart died in January 1970. Nearly 30 years on (now 45) he is beginning to take his place as an historical figure as distinct from a ubiquitous brooding presence. We can begin to place him as a late Victorian autodidact with a polemical approach to history, grandiose ambitions and excessive confidence in his own judgement. If his various overlapping accounts of the First World War were generally seen to be outdated and of mainly historiographical interest like, say, the war histories of Conan Doyle or John Buchan, there would be no problem. But, due to his immense readability, his Olympian tone and his politically appealing message for a generation which assumes the First World War to be the epitome of vain slaughter and pointlessness, his histories are still reprinted, widely translated and read uncritically. This is anomalous because in the last 20 years or so, since the opening of the Cabinet and War Office Papers, a new generation of scholars such as David French, Peter Simkins, Robin Prior, Trevor Wilson, David Woodward and Ian Beckett (the list could easily be doubled), have truly begun to delineate the 'real war' and, though by no means reaching consensus on the great issues, have moved the debates forward onto ground where archival evidence, historical perspective and reasoned argument are in the ascendancy.[22]

Unfortunately, with some honourable exceptions, many popular authors and producers of television documentaries seem to be more than ever obsessed with the Somme, Passchendaele, Haig's generalship and the historical significance of the 'War Poets', or to be more precise, two of them. To hold Liddell Hart primarily responsible for late twentieth century interpretations of the meaning and relevance of the First World War would be as unreasonable as his indictment of Clausewitz as posthumously responsible for the actual nature of the war itself. Nevertheless, whether we approve or not, it is in large part Liddell Hart's remarkable achievement and legacy that so much of the British discussion of the First World War still takes place in the arena and under the guidelines which he established more than 60 years ago.

References

I am grateful to Professor Hew Strachan and Dr Brian Holden Reid for their comments on this essay in draft.

1. B. H. Liddell Hart, *Memoirs* Vol I (Cassell, 1965), pp. 11–-28.
2. Alex Danchev, *Alchemist of War. The Life of Basil Liddell Hart* (Weidenfeld & Nicolson, 1998).
3. Danchev, pp. 47–67.
4. Brian Bond, *Liddell Hart: a Study of his Military Thought* (Cassell, 1977), pp.15–21. Liddell Hart's *Impressions of the Battle of the Somme* constitutes the core of Brian Bond (ed), *Liddell Hart's Western Front* (Tom Donovan Editions, 2010).
5. Bond, p. 18.
6. See Brian Holden Reid, 'Fuller and Liddell Hart: a Comparison' in his *Studies in British Military Thought* (Lincoln: University of Nebraska Press, 1998), pp. 168–82.
7. Fuller quoted in Dianchev, p. 73.
8. For a discussion of Liddell Hart's political inclinations, see Brian Holden Reid op cit, pp. 187–93.
9. Hew Strachan, 'The "Real War": Liddell Hart, Cruttwell and Falls' in Brian Bond (ed), *The First World War and British Military History* (Oxford: The Clarendon Press, 1991), pp. 41–67.
10. Ibid, pp. 46–47.
11. Ibid, p. 47.
12. Ibid.
13. For criticisms of 'The British Way in Warfare' see Bond, *Liddell Hart*, pp. 65–85.
14. In *The Real War*, for example, there are only passing references to the naval blockade of Germany on pp. 94, 227 and 336.
15. Danchev, pp. 66–67. B. H. Liddell Hart *Through the Fog of War* (Faber & Faber, 1938), pp. 149–51.
16. Allenby was allotted an essay in *Reputations* (1928) and all three (Allenby, Hamilton and Lawrence) were discussed in *Through the Fog of War* (1938).
17. Liddell Hart, 'The Basic Truths of Passchendaele' in *RUSI Journal* (November, 1959) and my brief comments in Peter H. Liddle (ed), *Passchendaele in Perspective* (Leo Cooper, 1997), p. 481.
18. M. J. Williams, 'Thirty Per Cent: a Study in Casualty Statistics', *RUSI Journal*, (February 1964), pp. 51–55.
19. See the list in Danchev, p. 251.
20. Michael Howard and Peter Paret (eds), *Carl von Clausewitz On War* (Princeton University Press, 1976), p. 141.
21. See Alex Danchev, '"Bunking" and Debunking' in Brian Bond (ed), *The First World War and British Military History*, p. 282.
22. See Brian Bond, 'A Victory Worse than a Defeat?' Liddell Hart Lecture at King's College London, 17 November 1997. Reprinted in this volume.

3

The Somme in British History

This paper was prepared for a conference to mark the official opening of a new kind of military museum, The Historial, at Péronne in July 1992. A great number of books about the Somme campaign have been published since but in general they tend to reinforce my central theme that these operations are now emphasised, at least in British historiography, more than those around Ypres which are often misleadingly referred to simply as 'Passchendaele'. Just a few significant titles need to be cited to show that the Somme is constantly under scrutiny by historians.

In 2005 Robin Prior and Trevor Wilson published an unrelenting critique analysing the campaign battle by battle which was simply titled *The Somme* (Yale UP). The year before however Gary Sheffield had published a more moderate and sympathetic account, also called *The Somme* (Cassell paperback). In 2009 William Philpott's excellent study put the campaign into a much wider context as is evident from his title *Bloody Victory. The Sacrifice on the Somme and the Making of the 20th Century* (Little Brown). Both Philpott and Sheffield stress that the overall result of the campaign was to deal a fatal blow to German chances of victory on the Western Front. For an interesting exploration of 'the other side of the hill', Jack Sheldon's *The German Army on the Somme 1914–1916* (Pen and Sword, 2005) is highly recommended. The steady trickle of books about the Somme will doubtless become a torrent in 2016.

What's in a name? For most Frenchmen the Somme is simply the name of a river like the Thames or the Severn, but for the British 'the Somme' has become a potent myth – grim, dark, sombre – epitomising the 'horror' and 'futility' of the First World War. Ironically, although the 'battles of the Somme' were mentioned from 1916 onwards, none of the British offensives in that year took place on or across the river. Indeed the official designations were more accurate, stretching from the initial Battle of Albert (1–13 July) through Flers-Courcelette (15–22 September) to the final muddy phases of the Ancre and the Ancre heights in October and November. The Somme could just as well be associated with the Anglo-French retreat in March 1918 or the victorious Allied advance a few months later. But who, except a handful of misguided military historians, would dream of linking the words 'Somme' and 'Allied victory'? The Somme must, for the media, evoke notions of incompetent generalship, horrendous losses and failure. There is a further enormous distortion between myth and historical reality: the campaign lasted from 1 July to 18 November (141 days), yet only the first day with its unprecedented British casualties (before or since) of 57,740 officers and men is popularly remembered. Indeed, as Ian Beckett has remarked 'there can be few historical episodes where the gap between professional and public comprehension is greater.'[1]

It is doubtful if this obsession with the Somme campaign in general and 1 July in particular as the symbol of unnecessary losses and incompetent generalship has been consistent and continuous since the end of the First World War. Indeed it seems more appropriate that that doubtful distinction should have been bestowed on Flanders, and especially Ypres, where the British effort on the Western Front was concentrated from October 1914 and culminated in the Third Ypres offensive of 1917 which was more costly in casualties, fought in more hellish conditions and harder to justify politically than the Somme. This offensive produced the perfect name for pacifists, satirists and critics of the Western Front – Passchendaele (Passion Dale): a terrible valley in which thousands of British soldiers met their sacrificial deaths.

My contention is that historians' attitudes to the Somme have never achieved a consensus since 1918 either as regards the campaign's significance in British strategy and tactics or its contribution to the outcome of the war. Much of what is now assumed, by all but a handful of specialists, to be the objective 'truth' established during or soon after the war, probably dates only from the rediscovery of the Western Front in the radical 1960s. Although the controversialists of the 1960s did not of course invent the catastrophe of the first day, 1 July, they gave it lurid prominence in books articles, radio and television programmes. 'By implication they seem to ask, in effect, why on the 133rd day of the Battle of Verdun, the British Command did not tell the French (and Russians) that one day of this sort of thing was quite enough.'[2] Without in any way wishing to excuse military miscalculations or ignore the resultant heavy casualties, it may be suggested that this ritual invocation of 'the first day of the Somme' tells us more about the assumptions and attitudes of the 1960s and later generations than about the actual history of the war and its impact on the British public at the time.[3]

Even if the course and outcome of the battle had been more obviously successful, the Somme would still occupy a central and controversial place in British interpretations of the war due to its timing and the exaggerated expectations placed on it. Though it did not mark the debut of the Kitchener volunteer armies nor, as modern myth implies, was it fought solely by them, it was nevertheless by far the biggest British offensive to date, assisted by far the greatest concentration of artillery (more than 1,500 guns firing 1.7 million shells in the preliminary bombardment). No less than 97 of the 143 infantry battalions consisted of New Army volunteers, some of whom annoyed the Territorials and regulars by their supreme confidence in their ability to finish off the war.[4] On the home front over-optimistic press reporting, magnified by propaganda, created a dangerous delusion that this was the 'Big Push' which was bound to succeed. In particular, overwhelming attention was given to the supposedly irresistible power of the preliminary bombardment which, it was assumed, would so shatter and demoralise the enemy that victory would be gained with minimal casualties. It would literally be a walk-over. The reporters, magazine illustrators and the mass of the public alike were willing the attack to succeed and could not conceive of failure.[5]

The public's notion of war was founded on pre-industrial romantic and patriotic imagery (exemplified by Caton Woodville's illustrations), and in 1916 these illusions were still being nourished by the handful of war reporters in France sanctioned by the High Command. Some reporters were irked by the strict censorship but others, such as W. Beach Thomas, were to become notorious because of the deceitful picture they continued to convey. Popular notions of war as a glorified game were encapsulated by the famous incident of Captain Nevill of the 8th East Surreys leading his men by kicking a football into No Man's Land. Most popular papers stressed the heroic courage of the British attackers but Beach Thomas went to nauseous lengths: 'The very attitudes of the dead, fallen eagerly forward, have a look of exuberant hope. You would say that they died with the light of victory in their eyes.'[6] This and much more in similar vein would later provoke a furious reaction when the truth about conditions, casualties and the very limited progress eventually filtered through.

It would be a great mistake, however, to assume that the horrendous losses on the first day were immediately known at GHQ, much less at home. Press censorship, willingly abetted by patriotic editors, muffled and delayed the impact of the heavy losses, but these could not be long concealed from towns like Accrington whose localised 'Pals' battalion suffered particularly severely. Taking this as an example, the first terrible indication of the tragedy occurred about 10 days after the battle when a train full of wounded soldiers arrived in Accrington causing anguished rumours of a massacre. This was substantiated when the local newspaper published half a page of photographs of the killed and wounded. Even two weeks after the attack the War Office still refused to release the full statistics of losses to the Mayor of Accrington, but it eventually emerged that on 1 July in just 20 minutes the Accrington Pals had suffered 585 casualties out of about 700 men: 235 were killed and of these it is grimly significant that 135 have no known grave.[7] Given the pre-battle euphoria and the subsequent official evasiveness about the scale of casualties, it is easy to comprehend how an extreme reaction of bitterness and disillusionment might set in. Who for example, except professional military historians, now remember that on 1 July the southernmost sector of the British offensive was successful?

Neither the early books about the battle nor the celebrated film *The Battle of the Somme*, first shown to mass audiences in Britain in August 1916, conveyed a realistic sense of the conditions or any idea of the casualties. The film, shot by G. Malins and J. B. McDowell, contains some genuine combat footage, notably the explosion of the enormous mine under the Hawthorn Redoubt, but much of it was recreated or filmed behind the lines. Its emphasis on the artillery preparations and bombardment, plus the absence of sound, conveyed little impression of the realities of battle. The film's captions and the accompanying publicity were reassuring, exciting and patriotic.[8]

After the war Haig and his supporters were quick to establish a defence of British strategy in the Somme campaign. The campaign had been forced on an unwilling Haig by Joffre to take pressure off the French at Verdun, in which it had succeeded. Haig's persisting belief in a breakthrough with 'decisive' results was played down in favour of the need to wear down the enemy. In this, so the argument ran, it had been the real turning point in the war: the Germans suffered irreplaceable losses and were steadily forced to give ground, culminating in the retreat to the Hindenburg Line in the early months of 1917.

This is not the place for an extended discussion of this controversial topic; especially as one of the key issues – comparative casualty statistics – can never satisfactorily be resolved.[9] Suffice it to say that a positive interpretation of the purpose, course and outcome of the campaign was established early on and has continued to have reputable supporters, even if for the general public it has now become an article of faith that the operation was a complete and unmitigated failure.

A brief sampling of the British press after 1918 shows that surprisingly little attention was paid to the battle on the anniversaries of 1 July.[10] In 1925, for example, *The Times* recorded (on p. 16) that it was the anniversary of the opening of the battle: it included 98 *in memoriam* notices of individuals and nine collective (regimental) notices. On that day the *Daily Express* contained no references to the battle. Five years later *The Times* published 67 individual notices and seven collective entries; the *Daily Express* nothing. By 1935 *The Times*'s individual entries had declined to 38 (three not for Somme casualties) while collective entries remained on seven; the *Daily Express* again ignored the anniversary.

On 1 July 1966, however, the modern preoccupation with the Somme is evident. In addition to individual (14) and collective (seven) entries, *The Times* included a long editorial prefaced by Siegfried Sassoon's poem 'When the Barrage Lifted'. There had, it stated, been many previous bloody British battles 'But the Somme has become a national symbol for the waste of human life'. Some 410,000 British casualties had been suffered for a strip of land 30 miles long by, at most, seven miles deep, of no strategic or tactical value. Both armies (British and German) had been pretty well destroyed, but whereas the German losses had been irreplaceable, Kitchener's Army to some extent was. The post-Somme conscript army could meet the Germans on level terms. 'Yet, when all the defence arguments have been heard, the fact remains that "the flower of Britain's generous manhood" was lost at the Somme.'

Significantly on 1 July 1966 the *Daily Express* published a long article by Henry Williamson about the first day of the battle, and on 2 July there was an account of six Somme VC winners revisiting the battlefield. Recollections by survivors, such as the distinguished economic historian R. H. Tawney, became almost obligatory on succeeding anniversaries, and now that these 'old soldiers' have all 'faded away' journalists make the annual pilgrimage to contrast the present tranquillity of the Picardy landscape with the scarcely imaginable noise and desecration of that sunny morning in 1916 ('Could so vast a slaughter – in all history none was ever greater – so enormous a destruction, have been accomplished in so arcadian a landscape, so small a compass?' wrote Nigel Buxton in 1986).

It is a shock to retrace our steps from these post 1960s commemorations of ruination and losses to a second film of *The Somme* directed by M. A. Wetherell, produced by Gordon Craig and scripted by Geoffrey Barkas in 1927.[11] This 80 minute silent film is positive, even celebratory and patriotic, in the tone of its captions. It describes the main episodes (1 and 14 July, 15 September and the final successful offensive) in detail, not ignoring the depiction of casualties and dreadful conditions, but stressing that the enemy (characteristically called 'Jerry') was outfought. The battle as a whole is termed 'a glorious tragedy' but only near the end are 'appalling losses' mentioned. The winning of four VCs (only one an officer) is re-enacted, a few battalions are named, and prominence is given to the contributions of Scots, Anzacs, Canadians and South Africans. 'Our victorious forces' had been deprived of a crowning achievement only by torrential rain. As a Tommy puts it: 'Jerry's 'opped it' ie pulled back to avoid a worse disaster but thereby abandoning 900 square miles. Consequently, 'the sacrifice had not been in vain'. Further research might reveal how audiences received the film. One reviewer criticized it as 'unreal' for taking 'a romantic boy adventure book angle', but elsewhere, along with the director's other war films, it was said to have earned a great deal of prestige for the British film industry.

It is hard to imagine such an unapologetic, patriotic film being made a few years later after the remarkable impact – particularly on the middle classes – of the spate of memoirs, novels, poetry and plays about the Western Front which appeared between 1928 and 1932. There is no need to list them here or discuss them at length.[12] By no means all of them were concerned with the Somme, there is no consensus about what they were recalling in bitterness or saying goodbye to, and a minority could not be construed as 'anti-war' in a polemical or any other sense (e.g. Charles Edmonds' *A Subaltern's War*). Nevertheless, for all the differences in form, tone and attitude a broad message was conveyed to the readers: of idealism turning to disenchantment; the incompetence of the higher command and staff and the futility of the fighting; the obscenity and terrors of the modern battlefield. Their popularity is undeniable. R. C. Sherriff's play *Journey's End* was reprinted 13 times in 1929, and several of the memoirs and novels were immediate best-sellers. Correlli Barnett has argued that this outpouring of 'anti-war' literature was unrepresentative of the officers and other ranks alike, and Douglas Jerrold pointed out in a celebrated pamphlet that by focusing on the anguish of individuals these works ignored both the collective activity of armed forces and the wider purposes for which they fought.[13]

Nicholas Hiley has formulated the most original interpretation of the 'war books boom' as a deliberate re-working of war time experience to meet the perceived public need of the late 1920s.[14] This need was to prevent the recurrence of war by demonstrating that democratic opinion was naturally pacific. The message made a profound impact, at least among the intelligentsia, but had the unfortunate effect of obscuring for a time the unpalatable truth that in certain circumstances war might again be unavoidable – even for a pacifistic democracy.

The cumulative and enduring effect of this 'anti-war' phase with its savage criticisms of Haig and the conduct of the war on the Western Front, specifically the Somme, has made it almost obligatory for later writers and commentators to deal with the battle on terms established by the critics. This was vividly exemplified in the Second World War when the American Chief of Staff George Marshall was urging the speedy opening of a second front in Europe. 'It's no use,' Churchill's doctor Lord Moran replied, 'you are fighting against the ghosts of the Somme'.[15]

The chief official historian, Sir James Edmonds, perhaps unintentionally provided ammunition for critics of the Somme Campaign by concluding the first volume on the subject, published in 1931, with the end of the first day of operations – 1 July 1916. Edmonds' conception of his role and his ambivalent attitude to Haig continue to puzzle historians[16] but it seems clear that under pressure from senior participants in the campaign, notably General Sir Archibald Montgomery-Massingberd (who was Chief of Staff 4th Army in 1916, became Adjutant-General in 1931 and Chief of the Imperial General Staff in 1933), he was prepared to tone down criticism, suppress evidence and put his own idiosyncratic interpretation upon comparative casualty statistics. The result is a generally bland narrative which reaches no firm conclusion about Haig's intentions on the first day, and contrives to suggest that he consistently pursued a strategy of attrition which paid off: total Anglo-French casualties being reckoned at 623,907 and German at a round figure of 600,000. However, in the second volume, Edmonds contended that German casualties should be increased by 30 percent to allow for lightly wounded men not previously included. Later research, which is rarely used by popular writers, proved Edmonds' calculations to be demonstrably false.[17]

The irregular appearance of the official history volumes on the Somme served spasmodically to re-awaken controversy over Haig's generalship and particular episodes in the campaign, such as the decision to employ tanks for the first time on 15 September and to persist with the offensive into November despite dreadful conditions.

Captain B.H. (later Sir Basil) Liddell Hart's changing views on Haig and the Somme were greatly influenced by the 'credibility gap' between what he read in the official history and the more critical information which Edmonds leaked to him confidentially. As a convalescent subaltern in 1916, Liddell Hart had compiled a remarkably eulogistic account of the battle then still raging, and in *Reputations* (1928) he was still taking a moderate and balanced view of Haig. In *The Real War* (1930) his tone was more critical, but he did at least cover the whole campaign in outline, allowed that it had had some positive, albeit indirect, effects at Verdun and on other fronts, and ended by noting the severe strain suffered by the Germans – even if their heavy casualties were largely due to their commanders' faulty tactics.

Eight years later in *Through the Fog of War* he based his short critique entirely on the official history's account of the first day, devoting only one sentence to the following 140 days. He concluded that the mutual destruction in the battle was not a necessary contribution to the final issue, 'while even as an actual contribution it was not comparable to the blockade'. It was, in sum, 'the summit of strategic senselessness – until 1917'.[18]

As a result of his prolific output of books and articles, readable style and confident, critical tone Liddell Hart probably had more influence than any other historical writer in the 1920s and 1930s in shaping the reading public's notions about the British Army's inept performance on the Western Front and the unwisdom of its heavy commitment there.

There were, however, other contrary interpretations which were widely read, most notably C.R.M.F. Cruttwell's *A History of the Great War 1914–1918*, first published in 1934 but remaining in print in several later editions. Cruttwell, an Oxford don who had been seriously wounded in the war, took a more balanced and judicious view of the war as a whole than Liddell Hart. Though perfectly capable of acidic criticisms of British generalship and tactics, Cruttwell took a remarkably positive view of the Somme campaign. While allowing that the ground gained was not impressive, he argued that the British advance had put the enemy under intolerable strain. The retreat to the Hindenburg Line proved that the Germans could not spare the troops to man the extended line of November 1916. He concluded that the campaign, 'in spite of the grave tactical mistakes which opened it', had rendered a serious service to the Allies. 'In spite of the slaughter, the British army gained experience rather than discouragement, as the attack before Arras was to show in the coming spring.'[19]

In similar vein was Cyril Falls' *The First World War*, which was not published until 1960 but owes its genesis to the 1930s when the author was a member of the team of official historians. Falls admitted that British tactics in 1916 had been clumsy, but said this was mainly due to the amateur character of the Army whose instructors were too stiff and conventional. 'Yet for determination and devotion the army that fought on the Somme has never been surpassed.' While making due allowance for other contributing factors, Falls concluded that Haig and Joffre had indeed succeeded in wearing down the German Army as Ludendorff and others had admitted after the war.[20]

As saturation coverage of the Second World War declined and the approaching 50th anniversaries of the war of 1914–1918 caused a revival of publishers' interest in the earlier conflict, a new generation of historians rediscovered the Great War in which their fathers or even grandfathers had fought. Several were directly, and nearly all indirectly, influenced by Liddell Hart – by 1960 the doyen of British military historians with a firmly established and highly critical view of Haig and the conduct of war on the Western Front.[21]

Hence for these and other reasons springing from the more radical and anti-authority *Zeitgeist* of the decade, most of the new historians were inclined to debunk the conduct of the earlier war. Though concerned with 1914–1915 rather than the Somme, Alan Clark's title *The Donkeys* (1961) epitomised the fashionable approach to British generalship in the war.

There were of course historians who resisted what might be called the 'Liddell Hart orthodoxy', most notably for his courage, industry and sheer perseverance John Terraine, who began his personal counter-offensive with *Douglas Haig: the Educated Soldier* in 1963.

These opposing viewpoints clashed in the making of what was then the biggest ever British television documentary series – *The Great War* (1964). Terraine, who scripted the Somme and Passchendaele programmes, sought to put over a positive view of British generalship and the primacy of the Western Front, with the corollaries that heavy casualties had been unavoidable and had contributed significantly to eventual victory. Predictably the outcome was a clear victory for the medium over the message. Audience Research Reports showed that the terrible battlescapes and the sufferings of all participants (soldiers, civilians, animals) had reinforced earlier (pre 1939) views about the horrors of war and the waste of young manhood. A new generation was unable to assimilate the implicit revisionism embodied in Terraine's scripts. Thus in complete contradiction of his intentions this enormously successful series had reinforced the notion of the futility of the First World War.[22]

Of course the *Great War* series and the astonishing flurry of publications in the 1960s did not end the controversies over the Somme and Haig's generalship. Like his hero, Terraine never acknowledged defeat and continued an attritional barrage which, for all its duds, shortfalls, and misses, gradually ground down at least some of the opposition's defences. He deplored the obsessive concern of so many writers with the disastrous first day, preferring instead to stress the Army's endurance over the remaining 140 days of the campaign at what he considered to be an acceptable casualty rate (just under 3,000 per day), given that Britain was now beginning to bear the main burden of fighting the German Army on a strongly defended sector. The 'pay off' for Terraine lay in the Germans' propensity to counter-attack rather than yield ground (some 330 are listed), and the fact that the great majority of their 125 divisions on the Western Front were exhausted in the attritional battle on the Somme, obliging Ludendorff eventually to retreat to the Hindenburg Line. In sum, while not going so far as to claim that the Somme was a victory in itself, Terraine argues that it was a necessary battle in which an attritional strategy was deliberately pursued, resulting in a fatal drain on German manpower which contributed significantly to the eventual collapse in 1918.[23]

Two books from the 1960s specifically about the Somme deserve a brief discussion. Brian Gardner's *The Big Push* (1961) was an unambitious popular account relying on mostly familiar published sources. Gardner was sure that a historical verdict would be reached on the battle during the 1960s but hedged his bets as to whether it would be seen as a victory or a disaster. His illustrations and sketch maps clearly suggested the latter as did his concluding chapter heading 'Napoo!' – soldiers' slang for 'useless', or worse. Anthony Farrar-Hockley's *The Somme* (1964) was much more thoroughly researched, including interviews with survivors, and benefited from the author's first-hand knowledge of the Army's command structure and his distinguished combat experience. He provided excellent coverage of the long gestation of the battle, the first day and 'the long struggle' up to mid-September, but then rather skimped on the final stages.[24]

The 1970s witnessed the emergence of a new style of popular military history, the best of it exploiting the oral and written testimony of veterans, but also reinforcing the growing public obsession with the Somme as the archetypal 'futile' battle of the First World War. Martin Middlebrook's *The First Day on the Somme* (1971)[25] made original use of veterans' recollections to convey a vivid sense of what it was like without polemical intent. Although his coverage is wider than the title suggests, Middlebrook's technique was better suited to the detailed study of an episode rather than a broader account of a long battle, let alone the whole war. Similarly John Keegan confined himself to the first day of the Somme in demonstrating how to delineate *The Face of Battle* (1976). Subsequently there have appeared numerous detailed studies of particular episodes in the Somme campaign or the experience of particular units including: the Ulster Division on the first day, the 38th (Welsh) Division at Mametz Wood, the South Africans at Delville Wood and the Australians at Pozières. Many of these studies by enthusiasts are critical of strategy, tactics and the higher command while evincing admiration for the courage and endurance of the troops – one recent study of the fighting at Arras in 1917 is entitled *Cheerful Sacrifice*[26] – an uncomfortable notion in the 1990s. This genre, and especially a series about the Pals Battalions, is above all concerned to commemorate and celebrate the achievements of individuals and units, based on personal recollections and close study of the ground. This is a very different approach from the popular de-bunking mode of the 1960s.

One unexpected consequence of the treatment of the First World War in the 1960s was to resurrect the ghosts of the 1920s and early 1930s for a new generation which was anti-establishment, anti-authority and profoundly sceptical of the values of the 'officer class'.[27] Since then there have been encouraging signs that the Somme campaign is at last being approached as history – as distinct from a national disaster – and so properly placed in the full context of technological development, politics and strategy. Studies such as Shelford Bidwell's and Dominick Graham's *Fire-Power* (1982), Tim Travers' *The Killing Ground* (1987) and Robin Prior and Trevor Wilson's *Command on the Western Front* (1992), prove that it is possible to bring the full range of scholarly qualities successfully to bear even on such a controversial and emotion-saturated subject as the Somme campaign. Unfortunately there is still a vast gulf between the influence of these historians and the pervasive popular stereotype of 'Butchers and Bunglers'.[28] In a sense 'the early writers of the 1920s and 1930s took the Somme out of history' and converted it into a national myth.[29] Though still experiencing the occasional counter-attack, historians are now grappling with the task of restoring the Somme to operational and strategic history. Its place in cultural and social history is also being firmly established.

References

1. I am most grateful to Professor Ian Beckett for allowing me to make use of his unpublished lecture on the historiography of the Somme delivered at the Imperial War Museum in November 1986.
2. John Terraine, *The Smoke and the Fire* (Sidgwick and Jackson, 1980), pp. 108,205, 221–22. All the books referred to in this essay are published in London unless otherwise stated.
3. Brian Bond (ed), *The First World War and British Military History* (Oxford University Press, 1991). See especially the chapter by Alex Danchev '"Bunking and Debunking": the Controversies of the 1960s', pp. 263–88.
4. Beckett, op cit p. 2.
5. Stuart Sillars, *Art and Survival in First World War Britain* (Macmillan,1987), pp. 56–7.
6. Quoted in Sillars, op cit p. 71.
7. Peter Crookston 'Death of the Pals' in the *Sunday Times* Colour Supplement, 30 October 1988. See Martin Middlebrook, *The First Day on the Somme* (1971), Appendix 5 p. 330 for a list of battalions suffering more than 500 casualties on 1 July. Eight battalions had more casualties than the Accrington Pals.
8. Sillars, pp. 49–51.Beckett, p. 3. See also Roger Smither, 'A wonderful idea of the fighting: the question of fakes in the *Battle of the Somme*' in *Imperial War Museum Review* No. 3 (1988), pp. 4–16.
9. M. J. Williams, 'The Treatment of the German losses on the Somme in the British Official History' in *Journal of the Royal United Services Institute* (February 1966), pp 69–74. See also the chapters by David French and Keith Simpson in Bond op cit.
10. I am indebted to Robert Stevens for the following information on the Somme anniversary as reported in *The Times* and the *Daily Express*.
11. I should like to thank the British Film Institute for allowing me to see this film and Simon Baker for sending me a detailed synopsis, credits and other information. Dr Nicholas Hiley called my attention to the existence of this film.
12. See Correlli Barnett, *The Collapse of British Power* (Eyre Methuen, 1972), pp. 428–35, and Noel Annan, *Our Age: Portrait of a Generation* (Weidenfeld and Nicolson, 1990), pp. 66–76.
13. Douglas Jerrold, *The Lie about the War* (Faber and Faber: Criterion Miscellany – no. 9, 1930), pp. 22–23, 46–47.
14. Nicholas Hiley, 'The New Media and British Propaganda 1914–18' (unpublished paper) and review of Sillars' book, cited above, in *The Times Literary Supplement*, 16–22 September 1988.
15. F. C. Pogue, *George C. Marshall: Ordeal and Hope* (New York: Viking, 1968), p. 317.
16. See David French's chapter in Bond, op cit.
17. See M. J. Williams' article cited in n. 9 above and his earlier article 'Thirty Per Cent: A Study in Casualty Statistics' in *RUSI Journal* (February 1964), pp. 51–55.
18. B. H. Liddell Hart, *The Real War* (Faber and Faber, 1930), pp. 221–23, 267 and *Through the Fog of War* (Faber and Faber, 1938) pp. 257–58. See also Hew Strachan's chapter in Bond, op cit, for the contrasting careers and comparative merits as historians of Cruttwell, Liddell Hart and Falls.
19. C. R. M. F. Cruttwell, *A History of the Great War* (Oxford University Press, Second edition, 1964), p. 277.

20. C. Falls, *The First World War* (Longmans, 1960), pp. 177–78. Hew Strachan rates Falls' study higher than those of Cruttwell and Liddell Hart, particularly for its balance and objective judgement.
21. See my introduction pp. 6–7 in Bond, op cit.
22. Danchev's chapter in Bond, pp. 280–81.
23. Beckett op cit p. 8 provides an admirable summary of Terraine's main concerns and arguments.
24. A. H. Farrar-Hockley, *The Somme* (Pan paperback edition, 1964), pp. 242–53.
25. See Peter Simkins' discussion of Middlebrook's work and influence in Bond, op cit, pp. 302–03.
26. Jonathan Nicholls, *Cheerful Sacrifice: the Battle of Arras 1917* (Leo Cooper, 1990) – an excellent study despite its tendentious title.
27. In Bond, op cit, p. 287.
28. John Laffin, *British Butchers and Bunglers of World War One* (1988).
29. Beckett op cit, p. 11 'In a sense, the early writers of the 1920s and 1930s took the Somme out of history and slowly the historians are coming round to the problem of giving it back to history.'

4

Soldiers and Statesmen: British Civil–Military Relations in 1917[*]

Civil-military relations and the strategic direction of Britain's war effort have received very little attention so far in the centenary commemorations of the conflict. It is to be hoped that this very important aspect will be more fully covered when we reach the years 1916–1918.

The essential points made in this article, first published in 1968, still seem to be valid, but of course the historiography has expanded greatly and has, in particular, deepened our knowledge of the principal characters involved; notably Haig, Robertson, Henry Wilson and, above all, Lloyd George. Here I will only list three titles which provide an essential basis for students new to the subject. They are: David French, *The Strategy of the Lloyd George Coalition 1916–1918* (OUP, 1995); Jim Beach, *Haig's Intelligence. GHQ and the German Army, 1916–1918* (C.U.P., 2013); John Grigg, *Lloyd George: War Leader* (Allen Lane, The Penguin Press, 2002).

[*]   Reprinted from *Military Affairs*, Volume XXXII, Number 2, Fall 1968.

Relations between generals and politicians in Britain during the First World War could rarely be described as smooth or cordial, but in 1917 they probably sank to the nadir. Superficially friction appeared to result primarily from the clash of strong and inflexible personalities, but more serious in reality was the lack of adequate institutional machinery for the discussion and formulation of strategy. This weakness applied both to relations among the services and to contacts between the service chiefs and the government. That this fundamental handicap did not result in more serious clashes before the advent of Lloyd George as Prime Minister in December 1916 was due mainly to the general acceptance of a simple, straightforward strategy: the overriding task of the British Army was to support the French and secure a decisive victory on the Western Front. Only briefly and halfheartedly had Asquith's government given priority to an indirect or 'Eastern' strategy during the ill-fated Dardanelles campaign in 1915.

Consequently in the first three years of the war the military leaders – and Kitchener though Secretary of State for War was universally regarded as a generalissimo rather than a politician – built up a dominating position in the control of military policy. Considerable backing by the Press lords and by prominent Conservative politicians, widespread popular adulation, and, in the case of Sir Douglas Haig, the favour of the King all served to blur and even nullify in practice the constitutional theory that the soldiers' task was to execute the policy arrived at by the government. Indeed Asquith's Cabinet, with the notable exception of Winston Churchill, actually encouraged the generals' practical control of strategy by the scope it gave to Lord Kitchener, confining its role mainly to providing the men and resources required to wage a war of unforeseen magnitude.

The Third Ypres Campaign acted as a burning glass to focus the heat of civil-military discontent, because of several factors in combination. First, as the Somme and Verdun campaigns had already shown, the French were becoming desperately war weary and the dominant role was inexorably passing to Britain. Second, the removal of Joffre as French Commander-in-Chief at the end of 1916 deprived the allies of the one soldier who had possessed the prestige to act as an informal chairman and co-ordinator of the separate national armies. This meant that for much of 1917 there was even less co-ordination of effort on the various fronts than there had been in 1916. Although Lloyd George strove from the start of his premiership to achieve genuine unity of direction, his methods (particularly at the Calais Conference in February 1917, when he attempted to subordinate the British Army to the command of Nivelle) only served to prejudice Haig and Robertson (Chief of the Imperial General Staff) against accepting the experiment in any form. Third, 1917 brought a series of crises and disasters for the allies offset only by the distant prospect of American military intervention in Europe: there was the Russian February Revolution, Nivelle's tragic failure, the culmination of the submarine campaign against Britain's merchant shipping, and later in the year Passchendaele, Caporetto and Cambrai. Fourth, and most directly relevant to this study, Lloyd George, contemptuous of the military mind and appalled by its manifestation on the Somme, challenged the generals' basic assumption that the war could be won – and won only – on the Western Front. The result was ironical. After promptly reposing his trust in the inexperienced Nivelle to win a rapid victory on that front, Lloyd George and his newly formed War Cabinet then allowed yet another enormous British offensive to be mounted on 31 July and to continue inconclusively far into November.

It has been generally recognised that the Haig-Robertson partnership was crucial to the frustration of Lloyd George's designs during the planning and execution of the Third Ypres Campaign (May–November 1917). What has been less clearly demonstrated in detail is that the two soldiers, though at one in their constancy to the notion of the primacy of the Western Front and in their mistrust of the French and suspicion towards politicians generally, differed markedly in background and temperament.[1] Moreover during 1917 Robertson developed doubts about the soundness of Haig's course of action which only a strong sense of professional loyalty – and overwhelming mistrust of Lloyd George – enabled him to stifle. It is hardly too much to claim that Robertson's career was ruined by Passchendaele, whereas Haig, whose faith in his offensive never wavered, successfully resisted every attempt that was made to displace him. By focusing on the triangular relationship between Haig, Robertson and the Prime Minister, this study shows how the campaign came to be launched against strong misgivings, and why it continued so long without the full support of the War Cabinet. Lastly it will be shown how Lloyd George was far on the way to securing the removal of Robertson by the end of the campaign.

The failure of Nivelle's ambitious and over-publicized offensive by the end of April 1917 shattered the strategy agreed upon in December for a concerted offensive by all the allied armies, and left the British and French governments with very few strategic options. Nivelle's failure brought accumulated discontent and war weariness to the surface; mutinies affected nearly half the units in the French Army in May and June, and it became exceedingly doubtful that the French would be capable of another major offensive in the foreseeable future. Worse still it was becoming doubtful that Russia could even continue in the war. Britain had been forced to the brink of disaster by her merchant shipping losses. American intervention would have no significant effect on the war in Europe until 1918.

Thus a grim prospect faced the allied military leaders when they met in Paris on 4 May. The Western Front must be held, they agreed, but no decision could be expected there in 1917. A purely passive defense however, would be disastrous for morale and would correspondingly give new heart to the enemy. General Robertson summed up the service representatives' proposals as follows:

> It is no longer a question of aiming at breaking through the enemy's front and aiming at distant objectives. It is now a question of wearing down and exhausting the enemy's resistance, and if and when this is achieved to exploit it to the fullest extent possible. In order to wear him down we are agreed that it is absolutely necessary to fight with all our available forces, with the object of destroying the enemy's divisions. We are unanimously of opinion that there is no half-way

between this course and fighting defensively, which, at this stage of the war, would be tantamount to acknowledging defeat. We are all of opinion that our object can be obtained by relentlessly attacking with limited objectives, while making the fullest use of our artillery. By this means we hope to gain our ends with the minimum loss possible.[2]

Lloyd George on this occasion uncritically supported his generals. Evidently chastened by his misjudgment in supporting Nivelle so fervently, he unfortunately veered to the other extreme in doubting his ability to assess the qualifications and strategic judgments of the professional experts. The Prime Minister now declared that he had no pretensions to be a strategist and left that to his military advisers. He did not even wish to know the details of the plan of attack and urged the French government to treat their commanders along the same lines. It was hardly surprising that Robertson told Lord Esher, then a political representative at Paris, that this was 'the best conference that we have ever held'.[3] A British offensive in Flanders, already adopted in principle in 1916, would go ahead and the British would henceforth tend to dominate the direction of the war because of their growing naval, military and economic preponderance.

Within a few weeks, however, the War Cabinet began to doubt the wisdom of Haig's offensive, while Robertson strove to preserve agreement. The first problem was the reliability of French promises of support for Haig's attack which was generally agreed to be vital to his chances of success. Only on 2 June did Haig hear officially from French GQG of their armies' disciplinary problems, but the new French Commander-in-Chief, Pétain, was more specific on 7 June. Haig was not unduly perturbed because he had long believed that French will to win was ebbing. Pessimistic reports from Lord Esher and others had meanwhile had a greater impact in London. On 14 May Robertson put the War Cabinet's position clearly to Haig: the Cabinet would give him wholehearted support provided the French agreed to play their full part, but it could never agree to Britain's incurring heavy losses with comparatively small gains, the obvious result if the French reneged. Haig was confident that the French would be more forthcoming once they had settled their command problems.[4]

So it seemed, for on 18 May Pétain met Haig and promised that the French Army would fight and would support the British in every possible way. But was this credible even if Pétain spoke in good faith? Sir Henry Wilson, though disliked by many of his fellow generals as a political intriguer, was nevertheless an acute and well-informed analyst of French intentions. From his precarious post of liaison officer at GQG he poured out warnings to Haig and Robertson to the effect that the French Army was virtually in a state of collapse and must not be relied upon to support the British; indeed it was rather a question of gaining a military or diplomatic victory *somewhere* to keep France in the war.[5]

By the first week in June Wilson had correctly perceived that neither Foch (recently appointed Chief of the French General Staff) nor Pétain had the slightest enthusiasm for the ambitious plan formulated by Haig, anxious though they were that the British should persevere with limited attacks. Foch, according to Wilson, asked who it was 'who wanted Haig to go on a duck's march through the inundations to Ostend and Zeebrugge' He thought the whole thing 'futile, fantastic, and dangerous'; and Wilson agreed.[6] On 8 June Wilson personally expressed his fears of a French collapse to the War Cabinet. Pétain's difficulties were now undeniable since he had been unable to support Haig's successful preliminary offensive the previous day at Messines. Haig, incidentally, had not passed on the disturbing news conveyed by Pétain to the War Cabinet, presumably because he feared his attack would be cancelled.

The other chief cause of apprehension on the part of Robertson as well as the War Cabinet was the ambitious scope of Haig's plan of operations and his confident belief that the British Army could achieve decisive results. Haig was not so naive as to talk openly in terms of a 'breakthrough' as Nivelle had done, but his plan for a series of limited advances nevertheless added up to territorial gains of strategic importance that dwarfed anything so far achieved by the allies on the Western Front,[7] and which differed sharply from the offensive envisaged by most of the other representatives at Paris on 4 May.

Haig was in fact completely out of sympathy with the strategy of limited offensive action agreed upon at Paris. He remained convinced that the Somme had been a great victory (a victory confirmed in his view by the German retreat to the Hindenburg Line in the Spring of 1917) and, Nivelle's failure notwithstanding, he believed that the German Army was now so brittle and short of reserves that a sustained British offensive could win the war. Thus on 26 May he commented on a War Office forecast of drafts available: 'I feel sure that if the ranks of the British Army were only kept full up, that the British would win the war for the Allies. Indeed, our Army is the only one which has the heart and stamina to do so.' On 2 June he made the following typically optimistic diary entry: 'Extracts from German correspondence which we have recently captured are the most encouraging I have yet read; hunger, want, sickness, riots all spreading in the most terrible manner throughout the Fatherland...'[8] Further insight into Haig's sanguine temperament is provided by the following extract from a letter to his wife: 'Even if Russia did make a separate peace, that would not make a very serious difference to the rest of the Allies, because the situation of Germany already appears very desperate...'[9] This confidence, based on extremely optimistic intelligence reports provided by Haig's own staff at GHQ, was naturally strengthened by the brilliant, though deliberately limited, advance at Messines beginning on 7 June.

Robertson was far less optimistic and on 9 June he tried to impress his anxiety upon Haig. The latter's reaction deserves to be cited in full:

> I had a long talk with Robertson. He wished me to realise the difficult situation in which the country would be if I carried out large and costly attacks without full co-operation by the French. When Autumn came round, Britain would then be without an Army! On the other hand it is possible that Austria would make peace, if harassed enough. Would it not be a good plan, therefore, to support Italy with guns? I did not agree. Altogether I thought Robertson's

views unsound. I told him that I thought the German was now nearly at his last resources, and that there was only one sound plan to follow viz., without delay to:

1. Send to France every possible man.
2. Send to France every possible aeroplane.
3. Send to France every possible gun.[10]

The following day Haig mistakenly thought that Robertson was 'less pessimistic' after 'a night's reflection and Duncan's words of thanksgiving for our recent victory'. In fact, as Robertson's biographer has rightly commented, Haig was deluding himself that 'Wully' was as enthusiastic as himself on all aspects of the Third Ypres plan. He was not. Robertson's position obliged him to take a wider view of the war; he was less sanguine about French military support, more anxious about the Russian and other fronts, and above all far less convinced than Haig that the German Army was near collapse.

It was at this meeting or soon afterwards that Robertson nevertheless made the decision that enabled the Third Ypres Campaign to be launched. However great the risks entailed by Haig's plan, they were less dangerous, in the CIGS's opinion, than the alternatives such as the apparent French preference for a less aggressive policy or Lloyd George's monotonously reiterated proposal to shift the main effort to Italy. The combination of 'Wully's' ineradicable mistrust of Lloyd George and the habits of a lifetime of soldiering from the lowest to the highest position caused him to smother his doubts and manifest a touching loyalty to Haig. In June and July every ounce of Robertson's support would be needed by Haig to resist the challenge of Lloyd George and the War Cabinet. The politicians may be criticised for indecisiveness; they certainly did not allow the soldiers to carry their case by default.

Following Sir Henry Wilson's pessimistic report on French military capability the War Cabinet, on 8 June, set up a small committee to review British war policy as a whole. Its overriding problems were whether to confirm Haig's offensive, and to examine the main alternative of reinforcing the Italian front for offensive or defensive purposes. The Prime Minister strongly inclined to the latter course. In April he had been excited by reading the Emperor of Austria-Hungary's terms for a separate peace, conveyed to the French by the Emperor's brother-in-law, Prince Sixtus of Bourbon-Parma. The French Government had subsequently rebuffed this attempt at dynastic diplomacy, but Lloyd George continued to hope that its most obvious drawback, the exclusion of Italy, could be overcome.

The members of the War Policy Committee were Lloyd George, Curzon, Milner, Smuts and, for all practical purposes, Bonar Law. The subtle changes of mood and opinion of these statesmen, excepting the Prime Minister, makes it difficult to summarise their positions on British strategy in 1917. Broadly, however, Milner threw his influence increasingly behind the Prime Minister and Bonar Law did so to a lesser degree; Smuts, though he had reservations, tended to be the most sympathetic to the service chiefs, and Curzon was also inclined to back the generals against the Prime Minister. It is fair to add that none of them regarded the Somme as a victory or desired to see a repetition of it in Flanders in 1917.

The sense of urgency behind this review of policy is evident from the fact that 16 meetings were squeezed in between 8 June and 20 June, when the results of the inquiry were laid before the full War Cabinet. In the week before Haig was summoned to face Lloyd George as prosecuting counsel (Robertson testifies to the aptness of the judicial analogy), the CIGS attempted to moderate Haig's optimism. On 13 June he telegraphed advising the Commander-in-Chief to delete the appendix from his appreciation for the War Cabinet in which General Charteris, Haig's Chief of Intelligence, appeared to exaggerate the depletion of enemy reserves, and to ignore the likelihood of reinforcements being transferred from the Russian Front. On the same day Robertson wrote to warn Haig that 'there is trouble in the land just now... the L. G. idea is to settle the war from Italy', and added: 'What I do wish to impress on you is this: Don't argue that you can finish the war this year, or that the German is already beaten. Argue that your plan is the best plan – as it is – that no other would even be safe let alone decisive, and then leave them to reject your advice and mine. They dare not do that. Further, on this occasion they will be up against the French.'[11]

When Haig gave evidence to the War Policy Committee on 19 June it was the first time the Flanders plan had been revealed to civilians in detail. In Victor Bonham-Carter's apt words, 'They were taken aback. So much seemed to depend on faith rather than fact... '[12] For three days Haig and Robertson withstood a relentless examination from the Committee, particularly from the Prime Minister, who tirelessly strove to force the generals to acknowledge the dubious assumptions and likely dangers inherent in the plan.

The Prime Minister stated bluntly that 'none of his colleagues was sanguine of success'. What the Committee wished to avoid was 'a series of costly operations as a result of which we would have no more to show than after the Somme last year'. Everyone would realize we had failed if only the first objectives were taken, and 'What reason is there to believe that we can first drive the enemy back 15 miles and then capture a place 10 miles away?' It was pointed out that none of the three basic conditions for success were obtained, namely, overwhelming superiority of men and guns, the enemy so strongly attacked elsewhere as to engage all his reserves, or the enemy's morale already crumbling. Above all, Lloyd George pointed out, the element of surprise was lacking.[13]

The generals remained immovable. Robertson very ably marshalled the arguments in favour of a limited offensive on the Western Front and against any diversion of men or artillery to Italy. To the Prime Minister's charge that he had changed his attitude since 4 May, in that he now advocated an offensive in Flanders even without full French support, Robertson replied with a 13-page memorandum. In this he argued that he was *not* aiming at distant objectives, he had not before past offensives repeatedly given assurances of success, there was some evidence that the French would cooperate, and he would not support the continuation of the attack if it did not promise results. Where he (and Haig) differed fundamentally from the Prime Minister was on the latter's belief that it was 'a fatal error' to attack the enemy where he is strongest. Haig endorsed Robertson's strategic appraisal; he himself 'had no intention of entering into a tremendous offensive involving heavy losses. His plan was aggressive without committing us too far.' Elsewhere in his evidence, however, Haig declared, 'We have a very good chance of victory this year'; and it is not easy to see how this can be reconciled with Robertson's statement that the British tactics were identical with Pétain's: to attack on a wide front with limited objectives and so to wear down the enemy.[14]

The 'amateur strategists' in the War Policy Committee felt even less inclined to a direct confrontation with the generals after Admiral Jellicoe, the First Sea Lord, had declared on 20 June that he 'felt it improbable that we could go on with the war next year for lack of shipping', unless the Army was able to clear the Channel ports. Though Jellicoe's statement was fallacious and unduly pessimistic it nevertheless had a powerful impact.[15] The unwillingness of the civilians to take a firm stand without professional backing is painfully apparent in the Prime Minister's summing up on 21 June: 'His view was that the responsibility for advising in regard to military operations must remain with the military advisers. Speaking for himself, and he had little doubt that his colleagues agreed with him in this, he considered it would be too great a responsibility for the War Policy Committee to take the strategy of the war out of the hands of their military advisers... If after hearing his views... they still adhered to their previous opinion, then the responsibility for their advice must rest with them.'[16]

This decision by no means signified the War Cabinet's final approval of the Flanders offensive. The Prime Minister spent the next month vainly trying to ascertain precisely what support the French would give Haig, and he periodically irritated Robertson by reviving the Italian scheme. By the end of June, Pétain had begun to restore order after the widespread mutinies, but his own attitude remained pessimistic and uncooperative. Robertson reported this to Haig on 30 June 30 after meeting Pétain:

> I went to see him with the full intention of showing that the German is now in a bad way, and that we have a good chance of finishing him off if only we will stick to it. I felt that, the French being a little down on their luck, it would be a good thing if I showed myself to be fully satisfied and cheerful with respect to the present situation. But Pétain would listen to nothing of this nature. When I talked about the internal condition of Germany; the probable shortage of ammunition and food; the weakness in effectives; and the burden of Germany's allies he simply dissented or attached no importance to what I said... He insisted upon talking about Diplomacy, the necessity of detaching some of the enemy Powers, and the absence of any leader in France, and he drew sad pictures about the tired state of the French Army and more particularly the French Nation. In fact he talked like a man without a jot of confidence as to the future.[17]

Robertson passed on these impressions to the War Policy Committee and they were underlined by Henry Wilson, who thought the French would fight well if attacked but would not themselves attack effectively.[18]

Thus as the date for beginning the Flanders offensive approached Haig had good reason not to expect that degree of French cooperation which had been deemed essential in May. True, General Anthoine's First French Army, comprising six divisions, had been placed under Haig's command for the duration of the offensive, and Pétain had brought him more encouraging news in mid-July; but there could be no certainty that the French would launch vigorous assaults at selected points on their front to coincide with the British attack. As late as 26 July, Lord Esher, one of Haig's most fervent and loyal supporters, wrote to him from Paris, 'As I told you from the start of this Administration the French armies are not to run any big risks. The war is to be fed with small packets here and there, as children feed elephants with buns.'[19] The conclusion seems clear that, while Haig would be grateful for any French help he might receive, he was confident that the German Army was sufficiently weak to be defeated by the forces under his command in Flanders.[20]

The War Cabinet finally gave permission for the offensive to be launched only on 20 July, and then without enthusiasm. As Robertson informed Haig, 'We had a rough and tumble Meeting yesterday… The fact is that the Prime Minister is still very averse from your offensive and talks as though he is hoping to switch off to Italy within a day or two after you begin. I told him that unless there were very great miscalculations on your part, and unless the first stage proved to be more or less a disastrous failure – which I certainly did not expect it would be – I did not think it would be possible to pronounce a verdict on the success of your operations for several weeks.'[21]

Haig's disgust at the War Cabinet's hesitation and lack of confidence in him is understandable, but he underestimated the CIGS's difficulties when he criticised him for not squashing the Prime Minister's Italian scheme.[22] Indeed it is unlikely that Haig ever appreciated fully the doubts Robertson had had to stifle and the sacrifices he made in giving the Commander-in-Chief such unswerving support.[23] Had Robertson publicly voiced the reservations he privately expressed about the Flanders offensive there can be little doubt that Lloyd George would have been emboldened to force a showdown with Haig.

Whatever chance Haig may have had of reaching his first objective – the capture of the whole of the Passchendaele–Staden ridge – was dashed by torrential rain from the very first day of the attack. By mid-August the Prime Minister had already concluded there was virtually no hope of reaching the Channel coast; the problem rather was to prevent another 'Somme' from recurring. On 15 August Hankey noted that the Prime Minister was 'obviously puzzled, as his predecessor was, how far the Government is justified in interfering with a military operation'.[24] Lloyd George had in fact already revived the Italian project at an allied conference in Paris, but Foch, Cadorna and Robertson had all opposed him on the grounds that Haig's operation must not be halted at this stage. Foch however sowed the seed of disunity among the generals by proposing the creation of an Allied Staff in Paris. Robertson correctly foresaw in this project his own eclipse, and vituperated against Lloyd George: 'His [Lloyd George's] game will be to put up (the useless) Foch against me as he did Nivelle against you [Haig] in the Spring. He is a real bad 'un. The other members of the War

Cabinet seem afraid of him. Milner is a tired, dyspeptic old man, Curzon a gas-bag. Bonar Law equals Bonar Law. Smuts has good instinct but lacks knowledge. On the whole he is best, but they help one very little.'[25] The irregularity and disloyalty of such comments from the Government's chief military adviser to the Commander-in-Chief, technically his subordinate, requires emphasis but no elaboration. It was all too typical of the disrespect, even contempt, with which British generals tended to regard politicians during World War One.

Robertson had to bear the brunt of the War Cabinet's anxieties and misgivings when the Flanders offensive failed to yield significant gains, and he was increasingly worried by the manpower situation. While he continued to support Haig's belief that the Allies could not afford to return the initiative to the enemy on the Western Front, he became less and less optimistic about the 'decisive results' which the Commander-in-Chief still confidently expected.[26] Robertson had seen the terrible conditions at the Front in Flanders, and, according to the Military Correspondent of *The Times*, he retained no illusions. 'He thought that there was nothing for us but to go on. Haig thought that he was killing a lot of Germans.'[27]

Before August was out Lloyd George had initiated a devious strategy which would eventually drive a wedge between Haig and Robertson and force the latter to resign. Sir Henry Wilson, whose prospects had been temporarily blighted by Nivelle's fall in June and who, in his own favorite phrase was 'ready to make mischief', proposed a scheme for an inter-Allied Council to be over all the CIGS, and to draw up plans 'for the whole theatre from Nieuport to Baghdad'. According to Wilson, Lloyd George was 'distinctly taken'. Wilson reported that the Prime Minister was satisfied with Haig, but dissatisfied with Robertson. He was quite clear in his mind that the war was not being won along present lines; but he did not know what should be done, and he had no means of checking or altering Robertson's and Haig's plans though he knew they were too parochial. He said that he was not in the position, nor had he the knowledge, to bring out alternative plans and to insist upon their adoption, 'as it would always be said that he was overruling the soldiers'.[28]

Before this scheme could be developed, however, events in Italy seemed to promise a quick solution to the Prime Minister's dilemma. Cadorna's attack across the river Isonzo began auspiciously in mid-August and Lloyd George reacted with intense excitement in pressing for the transfer of guns from France to Italy.[29] Robertson and Maurice, the Director of Military Operations, were utterly opposed, but support for Lloyd George came from a surprising quarter – Foch – and a hundred guns were reluctantly transferred by Haig and Pétain. Predictably by the time they arrived the attack had already petered out. Haig and Robertson were furious with both Foch and Lloyd George, and the latter set off for Criccieth on 6 September suffering from neuralgia and overstrain. The Prime Minister was perhaps as near to a breakdown as at any time during the war.

In September and early October the meticulous set-piece offensives carried out by Plumer's Second Army in Flanders made limited and comparatively inexpensive gains, but then the rain began afresh and the campaign entered its last and most terrible phase, that properly referred to as 'Passchendaele'. As the casualty list mounted, the Prime Minister, with some support from Milner, attempted to displace Robertson and Haig. Lord Derby, the Secretary of State for War, warned Haig of this design while Churchill confirmed the Commander-in-Chief's belief that the Prime Minister had no faith that victory could be won on the Western Front. Derby and Carson, recently 'kicked upstairs' from the Admiralty to the War Cabinet, both promised Haig their support.[30]

Robertson's unenviable position, caught as he was between loyalty to a Commander-in-Chief whose sublime confidence in the value of the Flanders offensive he far from shared, and a War Cabinet in whose judgment he had no confidence at all, is evident in his letter to Haig on 24 September:

> The Prime Minister has been away during the last fortnight and his mind has consequently been very active. I have had to knock out a scheme for operating in the Aden hinterland involving the employment of not less than a division. I have also had to destroy one for landing 10 divisions at Alexandretta, all of which would have had to come from you. Further, I have had to fight against sending more divisions to Mesopotamia. Generally, all round, I have been quite successful, although the expenditure of energy which ought to have been otherwise employed has been a little greater than usual. The whole Cabinet are anxious to give the Turk as hard a knock as possible this winter.[31]

Robertson never doubted that the war would eventually be decided by a military victory on the Western Front, but his position obliged him to take a broader strategic view than Haig. He informed the latter, as delicately as he could, that Russia's defection had allowed Germany to reinforce the Turks and a small reserve ought therefore to be built up in the Middle East. Furthermore, whereas Haig apparently deduced from Russia's collapse that it was more than ever necessary to him to clinch the victory in Flanders in 1917, Robertson calculated – correctly – that victory in the West would not be achieved before Germany had transferred a significant number of divisions from the East, i.e., by the Spring of 1918. This calculation he tactfully put to Haig on 27 September:

> My views are known to you. They have always been 'defensive' in all theatres but the West. But the difficulty is to prove the wisdom of this now that Russia is out. I confess I stick to it more because I see nothing better, and because my instinct prompts me to stick to it, than because of any good argument by which I can support it. Germany may be much nearer the end of her staying power than available evidence shows, but on the other hand certain countries in the Entente are not much to depend upon, and America will require a long time (to make ready).[32]

After the miscarriage of the scheme to reinforce Italy, the Prime Minister seems to have abandoned the hope of halting the Flanders campaign (Plumer's successes increased the problem of timing) and he could find no obvious replacement for Haig.

Rather surprisingly nothing more is heard of Haig's and Robertson's concession in June to halt the offensive if it did not quickly yield substantial gains. The minutes of the War Cabinet contain hardly any critical references to the campaign; on the contrary on 16 October it congratulated Field Marshal Haig 'on his continuous, persistent, and dogged advance of four and a half miles in conditions of great difficulty'.[33] Indirectly, however, Lloyd George continued the struggle against his two leading generals; men in whom he had ever less confidence but did not feel strong enough – perhaps mistakenly – to remove. At Boulogne on 25 September an Anglo-French Conference (without the two Commanders-in-Chief) agreed in principle that the British would take over more line from the French during the winter. Haig believed Robertson had betrayed him at this meeting by ignoring a promise that no such agreement should be reached without his being present.[34]

Early in October Lloyd George plainly demonstrated his lack of confidence in Robertson by inviting Lord French and Sir Henry Wilson to prepare papers giving their views on future British strategy. Robertson rightly dismissed the medical analogy of calling in independent specialists. Not only was the analogy inexact, but French had good reason for hostility to Haig, who had ousted him as Commander-in-Chief in 1915, while Wilson was the heir apparent to Robertson's post.

For the moment Lloyd George had overplayed his hand. Robertson offered Lord Derby his resignation and the latter at once told Curzon. Curzon then informed Hankey that if the Prime Minister drove out Robertson, 'Robert Cecil, Balfour, Derby, Carson and he himself probably would leave the government, which would then break up'. The next day, 11 October, Hankey walked round St James' Park with Lloyd George before the War Cabinet met. 'I repeated Curzon's warning in very straight terms and he (Lloyd George) took the hint very quickly. I told Curzon what I had done and he said I had rendered a very considerable public service.'[35] The War Cabinet then decided that Robertson should see the French and Wilson papers first, and the latter rejoiced, somewhat prematurely, that 'the PM has found out that he has not got the Cabinet with him after all'.

Various complications delayed the appearance of the papers until the last week in October. French in particular devoted most of his memorandum to criticising Haig and Robertson, but neither produced a reasoned alternative to continuing to give priority to the Western Front. Both, however, stressed the necessity for a Supreme War Council to co-ordinate Allied strategy. This enabled Lloyd George to revive his long cherished scheme, and a military disaster now played into his hands.

Ironically it was not so much Passchendaele that forced the allies to take joint action, but the rout of the Italians at Caporetto, beginning on 24 October. Not only was Robertson now ordered to dispatch divisions from Flanders to Italy, but practical arrangements rapidly went forward for setting up a Supreme War Council. The War Cabinet approved the scheme on 2 November and appointed Sir Henry Wilson as the permanent military representative. A plenary conference of the Allies met at Rapallo on 6 November. Robertson had been told little of these momentous developments, and when the creation of the Supreme War Council was discussed on 7 November he ostentatiously walked out of the room, asking Hankey to record his action in the minutes.

In part this was the emotional response of a choleric general who had never forgiven Lloyd George for his devious attempt to subordinate the British Army to Nivelle at the Calais Conference in February. Robertson's angry gesture epitomizes the tragic lack of trust or loyalty between soldiers and statesmen in Britain in 1917. Behind this personal hostility and mutual lack of understanding lay a deeper factor; neither Haig nor Robertson was at this stage prepared to risk subordinating Britain's independent strategy to an Allied council. In view of France's political instability and military weakness in 1917, this was an understandable if narrow view.[36] Robertson also appreciated at once that his military career was at stake. If Lloyd George could henceforth legitimately regard Wilson as his chief professional adviser, and if the latter could transmit orders to Haig, then both Robertson and Lord Derby would be redundant. The Prime Minister moved slowly and cautiously in clarifying the relationship between the CIGS and the permanent military representative, but on 7 November the vital step had been taken. Wilson was brought in without disrupting the Government, and the Haig–Robertson axis was weakened. When Robertson was eventually pushed into resignation in February 1918 after a series of most complex maneuvers by the Prime Minister, Wilson succeeded him as CIGS and Haig raised not a finger to try to save his loyal supporter.[37]

Friction between soldiers and statesmen is almost inevitable in a great and protracted war, and it would therefore be pointless to criticize civil–military relations in Britain during 1917 against some unattainable standard of amicable co-operation. The other principal belligerents certainly fared no better in the War, and Germany in particular fared a good deal worse. What was regrettable was that, in the absence of universally accepted institutions such as the later Chiefs of Staff Committee and the subcommittees of the War Cabinet, cooperation between generals and politicians reached such a low ebb that an enormous offensive, Third Ypres, could be undertaken without mutual confidence, and could be continued for so long when even the Chief of the Imperial General Staff had developed serious doubts about its effectiveness. Lack of trust among Britain's war leaders was exacerbated by the poor degree of co-ordination achieved among the allies after three years of war; indeed the two problems were interrelated as was exemplified by Lloyd George's maneuvers at the Calais Conference. It is of course far from clear that a better system of consultation would have prevented Third Ypres altogether, but it does seem likely that some of the problems, ambiguities and contradictions would have been clarified. The War Cabinet, for example, ought to have been in a position to decide whether Haig's or Robertson's intelligence staff was nearer the truth; and there ought to have been a more critical analysis of Haig's optimistic and Jellicoe's pessimistic predictions.

What actually happened was that, in the absence of firm control of strategy by the War Cabinet, Haig's single-mindedness and boundless self-confidence enabled him to resurrect and implement the long-standing project of a Flanders offensive, but in circumstances that made its success unlikely from the start. Here Robertson's support was invaluable. He remained an unrepentant 'Westerner', regarding all other fronts as of secondary importance, but he never wholly shared Haig's belief that the allies could win the war in Flanders in 1917. It is interesting to speculate whether Lloyd George might have won over Robertson to his side by the exercise of his almost irresistible charm, perhaps playing on their common achievement in rising to the top from humble origins. In reality the CIGS proved obdurate, their relationship went from bad to worse, and Robertson's professional allegiance to Haig was correspondingly strengthened. The assorted and frequently badly thought-out strategic schemes put forward by members of the War Cabinet were also easily demolished by the CIGS and did not increase his respect for 'amateur strategists'. Robertson, contrary to Lloyd George's unfair comments in his *War Memoirs,* was in fact a competent strategist, but his horizons were limited. In particular he was too insensitive to political pressures and problems to comprehend the enormous difficulties confronting Britain in 1917. By contrast, Sir Henry Wilson, though guilty of some staggering errors of prophecy in his time, did at least take a broad view of the war and was nothing if not politically adroit. If less able than Robertson as a professional strategist – and it is a debatable question – Wilson's talents made him eminently suitable as chief military adviser to Lloyd George.[38]

However one assesses the results of the Third Ypres Campaign for the future course of the war, it can scarcely be denied that Britain's war effort in 1917 was severely handicapped by the bitter conflicts among the military and civilian war leaders. Certainly many of the chief actors, including Lloyd George, were determined that, so far as better institutional machinery could ensure, a similar situation must be prevented from recurring if another great war arose. To what extent practical lessons were learnt it is difficult to say with precision, not least because of Winston Churchill's personality, his unique experience of war and his strong parliamentary position from May 1940 onwards. Considering, however, the speedy creation of the Chiefs of Staff Committee in the 1920s, the revival and expansion of the Committee of Imperial Defence, and the appointment in 1936 of a Minister for Co-ordination of Defence, it seems just to conclude that Churchill owed a significant element of his strength in 1940 to Lloyd George's experience in 1917.

References

1. A balanced account is given in Victor Bonham-Carter, *Soldier True: The Life and Times of Field Marshal Sir William Robertson* (1963), pp. 196–321. For a vivid contrast in the temperaments and behaviour of Haig and Robertson see Brigadier General E. L. Spears, *Prelude to Victory* (1939), pp. 141ff. See also B. H. Liddell Hart, *Through the Fog of War* (1938), pp. 39-–7 and 110–15.
2. Field Marshal Sir William Robertson, *Soldiers and Statesmen 1914–1919* (1926), II, p. 235.
3. Robert Blake (ed.), *The Private Papers of Douglas Haig, 1914–1919* (1952), p. 228; and Bonham-Carter, *op. cit.,* p. 241.

4.   Blake, *op. cit.* pp. 230–31. In mid-May Pétain replaced Nivelle as Commander-in-Chief and Foch became Chief of the General Staff.
5.   *Ibid.,* p. 232; Major-General Sir C. E. Callwell (ed.), *Field-Marshal Sir Henry Wilson, His Life and Diaries.* (1927), I, 354–59 passim. On 20 May Wilson wrote to Haig, 'He (Pétain) reminded me that you had asked him to express an opinion on your project, but this he would never do, but he said to me that, with the amount of assistance he could give our Cabinet were setting you an impossible task.' *(Haig Diaries,* Vol. XVI). I am indebted to Earl Haig and the Ministry of Defence for permission to study the photocopy of the original diary made by the Historical Branch of the Committee of Imperial Defence. Extracts quoted in this article are not reproduced by Blake.
6.   Callwell, *op. cit.,* p. 359. The entry makes it clear that Foch was opposed to the whole enterprise and not just to the proposed coastal advance through the inundations near the mouth of the Yser.
7.   See for example his *Instructions for Army Commanders,* 5 July 1917 (O.A.D. 538); *Haig Diaries,* Vol. XVIII. The first object was to gain the Passchendaele ridge; the second, the line Thourout–Couckelaere; the third, the line Thourout–Ostend and then to push on towards Bruges.
8.   *Haig Diaries,* Vols. XVI and XVII. See also Blake, *op. cit.,* pp. 233–34.
9.   Sir Douglas to Lady Haig, 15 May 1917, *Haig Papers,* Vol. 147 (National Library of Scotland).
10. Blake, *op. cit.,* pp. 236–37; Bonham-Carter *op. cit.,* p. 257.
11. Blake, *op. cit.,* p. 239. See also Bonham-Carter *op. cit.,* p. 399, note 22.
12. Bonham-Carter, *op. cit.,* p. 259.
13. War Office Papers Cab 27/6–8, Minutes of Committee on War Policy, meetings on 12 June and 21 June, 1917.
14. *Ibid.,* Minutes of 20 June and 21 June; for Robertson's *Notes on the Prime Minister's Memorandum Regarding Future Military Policy* dated 23 June 1917 see the *Robertson Papers,* I/17/2. (Centre of Military Archives, King's College, London). Part of Robertson's statement to the Committee on War Policy is printed in Bonham-Carter, *op. cit.,* pp. 260–62.
15. See Captain S. W. Roskill, 'The U-boat Campaign of 1917 and Third Ypres', *Royal United Service Institution Journal,* November, 1959, pp. 440–42. Haig's Chief of Intelligence, General Charteris, noted in his diary, 'No one believed this [Jellicoe's] rather amazing view, but it had sufficient weight to make the Cabinet agree to our attack going on.' *At GHQ* (1931), p. 233.
16. Minutes of Committee on War Policy, 21 June.
17. Robertson to Haig, 30 June 1917, *Robertson Papers,* I/23/33.
18. Minutes of Committee on War Policy, 3 July.
19. Esher to Haig 26 July 1917, *Haig Papers,* Vol. 214, File f.
20. 'In this Army we are convinced we can beat the enemy, provided units are kept up to strength in men and material. Our opinion is based on actual *facts* viz: the poor state of the German troops, high standard of efficiency of our own men (etc.)… An occasional glance at our daily intelligence summaries would convince even the most sceptical of the truth of what I write. Moreover I have been in the field now for over three years and know what I am writing about.' Haig to Robertson, 13 August 1917. *Haig Diaries,* Vol. XIX.
21. *Robertson Papers,* quoted by Bonham-Carter, *op. cit.,* p. 265.
22. Blake, op. cit., p. 246.
23. General Whigham, Robertson's Deputy, felt impelled to write privately to Haig in mid-August telling him of the mounting pressure against Robertson and of the loyal way he was defending Haig's plans. This drew a friendly reply from Haig, but he again criticised Robertson's Intelligence Branch for issuing such pessimistic estimates. See Bonham-

Carter, *op. cit.*, p. 281. Blake omits some important material between 9 August and 28 August 1917.

24. Lord Hankey, *The Supreme Command 1914–1918* (1961), II, p. 693.
25. Robertson to Haig, 9 August 1917. Blake, *op. cit.*, pp. 251–52. For a contrasting view of Milner see A. M. Gollin, *Proconsul in Politics* (1964), pp. 443 ff.
26. For example, 'I think that, *if we can keep up our effort*, final victory may be won by December.' *Haig Diaries*, Vol. XIX, entry for 19 August 19 1917.
27. Colonel Repington, *The First World War, 1914–1918* (1920), II, pp. 228–31.
28. Callwell, op. cit, II, p. 10.
29. Hankey, op. cit., II, pp. 693–97.
30. Blake, op. cit., pp. 254–55.
31. Robertson, *Soldiers and Statesmen*, pp. 253–54.
32. *Ibid.*, p. 255. See also Robertson to Haig, 15 and 24 September, *Haig Diaries*, Vol. XX.
33. Cab 23/4. The recipient correctly interpreted this as a political manoeuvre, see Blake, *op. cit.*, p. 261.
34. Blake, op. cit., p. 256. See also Bonham-Carter, op. cit., p. 288.
35. Hankey, op. cit., pp. 712–13.
36. On August 13 Haig had written to Robertson. 'I fear the old man (Foch) is done; but in any case the idea of organising an Allied Staff in Paris is quite unsound, *even if a really good French Staff Officer were in existence.*' [My italics] *Haig Papers*, Vol. XIX.
37. The fullest account of how Lloyd George achieved Robertson's resignation without breaking up the government is in Gollin, *op. cit.*, pp. 467–95. For Haig's reactions to Robertson's fall see Blake, *op. cit.*, pp. 286–88. It may be that by the end of 1917 Haig's opinion of Robertson as strategist had fallen. Certainly Esher, who tended to tell Haig what he wanted to hear, felt free by 23 November to write most critically of Robertson as CIGS, listing five ways in which he had conceived his functions too narrowly. It is also noteworthy that in a letter to Haig on 7 June Esher put Wilson only 'a fraction of a second behind' Haig in 'that school wishing, before all else to defeat the enemy'. Robertson and Lloyd George he put together some way behind. *Haig Papers*, Vol. 214, File f.
38. The tendentious title apart, Bernard Ash gives a vivid and generally convincing account of Wilson's highly political career in *The Lost Dictator: A Biography of Field Marshal Sir Henry Wilson* (1968).

Part II
The Inter-War Decades

5

The 'Anti War' Writers and their Critics

This essay was prepared for the Leeds International 1914–18 Commemoration Conference which was held in September 1994. It was the first time I had written at length about the ambivalence of the term 'anti-war' as applied to the literature of the 1920s and early 1930s.lt was evident from reading these authors and discussing them with my MA students that nearly all combatants regarded war in general as abhorrent, but they were not opposed to Britain's role in the First World War and were determined to stick it out until victory was won. How could you be 'anti-war' in a political sense if you had displayed gallantry in battle and had been awarded the Military Cross? It was also important to show that some of the memoirs by former officers, such as Guy Chapman and Charles Carrington, took a positive line about their military experience but were certainly not in favour of war or militarism. Finally, for students of this subject, it is essential to examine some of the best-known war books of other countries such as the anti-war polemics of E. M. Remarque's *All Quiet on the Western Front* and the ecstatic nationalism of Ernst Jünger's *Storm of Steel*. These authors and the vast subject of the First World War's cultural and political legacy are brilliantly explored in Modris Ekstein's *Rites of Spring* (1989).

This essay is concerned to challenge both the cohesion and representativeness of the 'anti-war' writers who are so much discussed by literary and cultural critics such as Paul Fussell and Samuel Hynes, but there are problems of identification and terminology. One has only to mention the best-known 'anti-war' memoirs, poetry and plays to see that they contain many inconsistencies, ambiguities and paradoxes, while it would be grossly unjust to label their critics 'pro-war', and even 'patriotic' seems inadequate. Ultimately, perhaps, the distinction to be drawn is between those writers whose view of the First World War is negative (with 'futility' as their watchword), and those who stress its positive features and legacy, despite full awareness of the destruction, suffering and heavy casualties.

The paradox has long been recognised that some of the best anti-war satirists were not pacifists or conscientious objectors but brave, efficient and even zealous subalterns, such as Siegfried Sassoon, Robert Graves and – to a lesser extent – Wilfred Owen, who voluntarily returned to the front after recovering from wounds or illness despite the fact that they had become disillusioned about the justice of the war. Recently, in his study *Taking it like a man: suffering, sexuality and the war poets*, Adrian Caesar has argued that these three writers (and Rupert Brooke) were not really anti-war at all in the usual interpretation of that term because a great deal of their mental turmoil and the resulting frustration and anger were due to sexual problems deriving from their education and repressive home environment. To a degree their war experience was only incidental to their personal 'hang ups'. More positively they needed the war to obtain personal freedom and to seek love and consolation through suffering.

> The poet must emulate the soldiers' suffering in order to be worthy of their love...
> Any potential critique of the politics of the war is subordinated to the personal, emotional and erotic implications of suffering.

Caesar suggests that Sassoon's poetry in particular covertly supports war by providing positive consolations based on the idea that suffering is good.[1]

These famous 'anti-war' writers also believed that protest against the war depended upon participation in it. Owen, especially, hated 'washy pacifists' as much as 'whiskered prussianists'. His readers are asked to pity the suffering soldiers, but also told that they cannot understand or pity unless they too go and fight. Contrary to the myth, then, these anti-war poems become in subtle ways war poems – war is celebrated as well as detested. Ample evidence is quoted by Caesar to prove that Owen enjoyed his second spell of active service in France but wished this to be concealed from friends and readers who thought he was having a bad time. Caesar's conclusion is that the four poets studied have come to 'represent' the First World War through partial readings which have highlighted a compassionate denunciation of war, whereas he believes their complex and equivocal attitude to war and suffering has exerted a dangerous influence.

This liberal-humanist reception of the texts works finally to accommodate the grotesque and enables societies to wage further wars in the name of England, Christ and freedom. The sentimental attitude prevails.[2]

Sassoon did, of course, make a famous public protest under the guidance of pacifist friends, including the Morrells and Bertrand Russell. His anti-war declaration, published in *The Times* on 31 July 1917 read in part:

> I believe that this War, upon which I entered as a war of defence and liberation, has now become a war of aggression and conquest. I believe that the purposes for which I and my fellow soldiers entered upon this War should have been so clearly stated as to have made it impossible to change them and that, had this been done, the objects which actuated us would now be attainable by negotiation.[3]

He expressly stated that he was not protesting against the conduct of the war, but only the deception practiced by the politicians. One might comment that the conduct of the war *was* open to criticism, but Britain's political objectives could certainly not have been achieved by negotiation in 1917. Robert Graves, who saved his friend from a court martial, believed that Sassoon's action met with approval at the regiment's Liverpool depot, but his colleagues at the front deplored it, telling him that they had to stick it out until Germany was beaten, and lamenting his association with pacifist 'croakers' at home. Sassoon did return to active service and later admitted that his protest had been a mistake.

The political naivety of Sassoon's protest highlights the perennial difficulty – or near-impossibility – of the front-line combatant understanding what the war is 'about' and how it is progressing from the government's viewpoint. But it also illustrates the specific problem of presenting Britain's political and strategic objectives in the First World War. Most historians would probably now agree that there were compelling reasons for entry into the war in 1914, and very little chance thereafter of a negotiated peace without victory on acceptable terms. Unfortunately, from the viewpoint of justifying to the people a long, attritional conflict, Britain's war aims were essentially negative and defensive; namely to prevent German domination of central and western Europe. However, even allowing for the excesses of anti-Hun propaganda and the exaggeration of enemy atrocities, the vast majority of the troops and the civil population seem to have believed that the cause was just and that the struggle must continue until a clear victory was achieved. A victorious conclusion to the war was far from certain at the time of Sassoon's protest, and even in mid-1918 still seemed far-distant, so that the maintenance of resolute military morale and the almost complete absence of mutinies presents a very different picture from that outlined by Sassoon and others who would like to have 'stopped the war'. Where Sassoon and other soldier-critics, such as C. E. Montague, were on firmer ground was in their understanding that home-front propaganda for grandiose, abstract war aims, such as 'crushing German militarism' did not impress front-line combatants, who were more concerned with the practicalities of unit pride, comradeship and survival against a tough and generally respected enemy.[4] In short there was more empty rhetoric and militaristic sentiments on the home front than in the trenches. Much of what has commonly been accepted as 'anti-war' writing really refers to this antagonism and mutual lack of empathy between the home and military fronts.

Sassoon's failure to address the complex issues of military strategy, foreign policy and diplomacy in 1917 is understandable; far less so is the almost complete avoidance of these matters by the post-war writers who shaped the anti-war 'myth' which had become deeply rooted by 1930. Samuel Hynes, though primarily interested in 'the myth' as a cultural phenomenon, does at least appreciate why military historians and generals are intensely irritated by it; namely that it renders the whole war effort meaningless.

> If the myth-making authors... were right, then the war had no history, in the sense of a story expressing the meaning of events, but was anti-historical, apocalyptic, an incoherence, a gap in time.[5]

There is no need here to develop in detail the historian's response to this enormous defect in the anti-war literature, which has already been castigated with typical verve and pugnacity by Correlli Barnett.[6] The anti-war writers, he points out, failed to tackle the hard questions such as the German occupation of Belgium and northern France which largely determined allied strategy. Instead they poured out their emotional revulsion at the dreadful conditions and heavy casualties with impressive power and cumulative effect. It remains puzzling nonetheless as to why the middle-class reading public responded so approvingly to this superficial emotional revulsion as 'the truth' about the war. Some explanations will be advanced at the end of this essay, but a full analysis would require a long account of the class system, reading habits and the pre-war liberal cast of mind regarding peace and war. What really causes historians intense annoyance is that influential literary experts, such as Paul Fussell, not only continue to accept the anti-war myth as 'the truth' about the war, but also provide an inadequate, erroneous and contradictory historical context.[7]

One of the main contentions in this essay is that much of what passes for anti-war literature written after 1918 was really provoked by the shattering of war-time idealism and disappointment with the results of victory in the early post-war years. This viewpoint was forcefully expressed by Charles Carrington (under the pseudonym Charles Edmonds) in *A Subaltern's War*, published in July 1929 avowedly to counter the prevailing literary fashion of disillusionment with the war. He described 1919 as 'the maddest year of all' in which the spell which had bound the soldiers for such a long time was broken.

> Disillusion came in with peace, not with war; peace at first was the futile state. In war a man at least did know what he was at... but peace seemed to lead nowhere: it was anti-climax.[8]

If the events between 1914 and 1919 were to be characterized as sheer futility, why had he and his comrades been such fools as to take part in them? The answer was self-evident: there had been absolutely no other course open to plain, honest men.

An early post-war publication which set a fashion for war memoirs and by its title provided a key word for much that followed was C. E. Montague's *Disenchantment* (1922). One suspects that the apposite title is invoked by many commentators who have not read the book. Montague was untypical of the 'anti-war' writers in terms of his age and background. Educated at the City of London School and Balliol College, Oxford, by 1914 he was a distinguished leader-writer for the *Manchester Guardian* and 47 years old. Montague's idealism was so intense that he dyed his grey hair and lied about his age to gain entrance to the army. His polemic is beautifully written but clearly reveals why he was more thoroughly disenchanted than much younger and more robust volunteers such as Carrington, Guy Chapman or Graham Greenwell, who entertained fewer illusions about the nature of military service and combat. Montague's sympathy throughout is with his fellow volunteers whose early idealism was rapidly eroded by the Regulars, by bloodthirsty chaplains, mendacious politicians, civilian war-mongers, profiteers and shirkers. He is also scathing, however, about the lack of 'brain-power' and the amateur incompetence of the staff and higher command. But his book seems to have been inspired mainly by outrage at the harsh terms imposed on Germany in the Treaty of Versailles which, he said, was an insult to the dead. In rhetoric reminiscent of Thomas Carlyle at his most dyspeptic, Montague contended that Prussia:

> Beaten out of the field, had won in the souls of her conquerors' rulers; they had become her pupils; they took her word for it that she, and not the older England, knew how to use victory.

England, in short, had won the fight and lost the prize by becoming militaristic and vindictive.[9]

Sergeant (later Professor) R. H. Tawney shared Montague's idealistic approach to war service but believed that the soldiers' idealism had endured, while that on the home front diminished, because only if those ideals were valid could their sacrifices be justified. This explains the sense of alienation experienced by many returning troops, their reluctance to discuss the war, and the frequently expressed regret that the 'home' they had found in their regiment and in the trenches was not replicated when they returned to Britain.[10]

Another famous book title routinely but dubiously cited as an anti-war classic is Robert Graves' *Goodbye to All That* (1929). Graves avowedly exploited the current publishing fashion to write a pot-boiler when he was desperately short of money, embellishing and embroidering his war experiences so as to make the maximum impact. Significantly, the compiler of the excellent regimental history of the Royal Welch Fusiliers, (J. C. Dunn (ed), *The War the Infantry Knew*), rejected Graves' proffered contributions on the grounds that they were heavily infiltrated by fiction.[11]

In any case Graves' title was accurate: he was saying goodbye to all that; including the stuffy conventions of pre-war society, war-time hysteria and immorality on the home front; and personal problems at the time of writing, including a marital crisis and being grilled by the police on suspicion of attempted murder. Finally, despite his criticisms of the regular officers' snobbery, Graves was extremely proud of his war service with the Royal Welch Fusiliers and remained so throughout his long life. In 1930 he expressed surprise that his memoirs were being included in the category of anti-war literature.[12]

By this date (1930) the anti-war myth was firmly established, in the sense that books, plays and poetry which were critical of the war experience in various ways were deemed to represent 'the truth' while other works, including a patriotic, and even 'gung-ho' film series, about the Somme and other campaigns produced by the British Film Institute in the late 1920s were severely handled by the critics.[13]

There is no need here to list the spate of publications which established the anti-war conventions between 1928 and 1931. The evidence for their popularity is undeniable. For example, R. C. Sherriff's play *Journey's End* was reprinted 13 times in 1929, and in that year alone sold 45,000 copies. Edmund Blunden's *Undertones of War* was reprinted three times in one month, and Frederic Manning's *Her Privates We* four times in a month. Wilfred Owen's poems by contrast had not yet had a wide impact: only 730 copies of the 1920 edition were printed and a second edition of a similar number sold poorly. Rupert Brooke, by contrast, remained enormously popular: by 1930 his *Collected Poems* had sold 300,000 copies.[14]

For all their differences in style and emphasis, a common viewpoint emerged from the 'trench memoirs': of idealism turning into sour disenchantment; of the terrors of battle and the obscenity of death and mutilation, and all for no comprehensible reason; the suffering and sacrifice had been futile.

Samuel Hynes conveys a clear idea of how this interpretation developed and summarises the myth as follows:

> the idealism betrayed; the early high-mindedness that turned in mid-war to bitterness and cynicism; the growing feeling among soldiers of alienation from the people at home for whom they were fighting; the rising resentment of politicians and profiteers and ignorant, patriotic women; the growing sympathy for the men on the other side, betrayed in the same ways and suffering the same hardships; the emerging sense of the war as a machine and of all soldiers as its victims; the bitter conviction that the men in the trenches fought for no cause, in a war that could not be stopped.[15]

The single work which presented the most poignant expression of the myth and probably exercised the widest influence was Erich Maria Remarque's book (and subsequent film) *All Quiet on the Western Front* (1929). The novel was launched with calculated publicity in Germany and was received there and in other countries, including Britain and the United States, with enormous enthusiasm. It rapidly became one of the best-sellers of all time. It was repeatedly referred to as 'the greatest of war novels', and in semi-religious terms as 'the Bible of the common soldier'. Above all, it told 'the truth about the war'; which was that it had been an irrational, nihilistic slaughter; that its protagonists and victims had no sense of purpose; and that it had been fought in vain. This message seemed congenial to the liberal left and socialists in Europe and the Anglo-Saxon world, but was denounced by fascists for whom war was an essential part of their outlook. The Nazis banned it as pacifist Marxist propaganda and burnt all the copies they could lay their hands on.

As Modris Eksteins astutely observes, the novel was more a reflection of the post-war than the wartime mind, telling 'the truth' not so much about the war as about Erich Maria Remarque in 1928. The author exploited the prevailing view of the war to make a fortune, but his admirers and critics were no more objective. His first person narrative epitomized the widely-held assumption that only on the level of individual suffering could the war have meaning. The war was a matter of individual experience rather than collective endeavour. Art had become more important than history. Historians up to that date (and, some would argue, to the present), had allegedly failed to meet the challenge of explaining and describing the horrendous realities of the war.[16]

In the British case it is difficult to claim that the anti-war myth was countered by 'pro-war' writers. True, Henry Williamson became a fascist, but his First World War novels, notably *The Patriot's Progress* (1930) is anything but a pro-war tract in that its hero, John Bullock, is portrayed as an archetypal victim. Britain, it seems, produced no equivalent of Ernst Jünger with his mystical and nationalistic reverence for war. Jünger, for example, likened the human race to a primeval forest:

> From whose dark and misty depths emerged the cry of victims ripped out of their nests by... beasts of prey. To live meant to kill... Man would never overcome war because it was greater than he was, and woe to him if he tried to escape from its grasp, for it was in war that men fulfilled themselves most completely... War was a creative force. It made men and their times what they were... Territories and war aims were mere symbols necessary to get men to die. War was an eternal rite in which young celebrants strove after moral perfection. In the performance of this rite death was unimportant.[17]

At least it should be noted that Jünger practised what he preached, being outstandingly brave as a platoon and company commander and suffering 14 wounds. [Despite his celebration of the supreme experience of death in battle, he is still alive and approaching his hundredth year when this is written.] Indeed, it is hard to think of any British author who approaches war in Jünger's ecstatic manner. Nevertheless, as Robert Wohl acutely observes, some intellectuals who later recalled the First World War mainly in terms of horror, fear and brutalization also experienced it as an opportunity, a privilege and a revelation: Ambivalence towards the war is the main characteristic of the best and most honest of the war literature.[18]

There is more than a hint of the Romantic reaction in the young Graham Greenwell, whose incredibly frank letters to his mother were first published in 1935 under the title *An Infant in Arms*. Greenwell aroused some reviewers' distaste by the admission in his preface that 'I look back on the years 1914–1918 as among the happiest I have ever spent', sentiments he had expressed in a letter home in December 1918.[19] This was clearly a politically incorrect line to make public in the mid-1930s but by no means unique. The late Field Marshal Earl Alexander told the present writer with, one suspects, only slight exaggeration that he had 'enjoyed every minute of the war. It was great fun'. But then he was a *beau sabreur*, not an intellectual or a writer.

The most overt, combative and polemical riposte to the outpouring of anti-war literature was Douglas Jerrold's pamphlet *The Lie About the War* which appeared in February 1930. Jerrold had served with the Royal Naval Division in the war and had written its history, also that of the 36th (Ulster) Division and other books about the war. In reviewing 16 war books Jerrold's main aim was to show that the war was not futile or meaningless but rather a great tragedy because it was a great historical event. It had accomplished many good things politically while even for individuals its effects were by no means all negative. His most palpable hits on his literary targets were, first, that the authors were unusually sensitive and imaginative individuals whose obsession with the ghastly nature of combat was unrepresentative of the vast majority of ordinary soldiers. Secondly, and as a corollary, these writers travestied the variety of war experience by portraying it as four years of ceaseless, sanguinary attrition, thereby creating in the minds of the public 'a love of peace foolishly based on a barren fear of useless suffering'.[20] Thirdly, and most important, Jerrold pointed out that the authors under review ignored the wider purposes and meaning of the war by focusing on individual experience. These wider purposes are seldom apparent to the private soldier in a trench, but war is *par excellence* a competition between large disciplined groups. Jerrold's critique received support from his fellow official historian Cyril Falls, whose more comprehensive review, *War Books* (1930), also argued that the war made sense politically, and that most accounts had grossly caricatured the common experience by, for example, omitting any reference to periods of rest and games.

Charles Carrington had written a plain, objective account of his battle experiences as a young officer just after the war but did not publish it until July 1929 (as *A Subaltern's War*) in an effort to counter-act the over emotional and pessimistic tone of the anti-war books then receiving so much attention. Then, and for the rest of his life, he remained a sharp critic of the 'disenchantment' school, contending that he and his fellow volunteers had known from the outset that they faced a terrible ordeal but were determined to see it through. His epilogue, provocatively entitled 'An essay on militarism', was really an eloquent riposte to the caricature of front-line experience as one of unrelieved suffering, fear and deprivation. Such accounts deny both the soldier's capacity for an inner life and also his capacity for intense happiness despite, or even because of, appalling physical conditions:

Further, it is not honest to deny the existence of happiness which was actually derived from the war. First, the horrors and the discomforts, indescribable as they are, were not continuous. The unluckiest soldiers, whose leave was always stopped, who never had a 'blighty' wound, still spent only a comparatively few days in the face of the enemy, and of these only a few were of the most horrible kind. Their intensity, when they came, sharpened the senses and made the intervals correspondingly delightful.[21]

Secondly, young men like adventures, even those where their life is put at risk. This is an imaginative challenge to all historians over 40. Thirdly, there was comradeship, 'richer, stronger in war than we have ever known since'. Carrington's rather harsh remarks about 'comfortable folk who hate war because it shakes them out of their routine and whose motto is "Safety First"', became more strident in his later book *Soldier from the Wars Returning* (1964), but he still maintained a robust defence of the motives, values and positive experience of the 1914–1918 generation of soldiers.

Frederic Manning was by temperament an aesthete, a classical scholar and poet, whose chronic ill-health also unfitted him for a soldier's life. He served in the ranks in the battle of the Somme and eventually obtained a commission; but he proved to be an incompetent officer, frequently inebriated, and was fortunate to avoid a court martial by being allowed to retire.[22] It seems pointless to try to place Manning in a pro-or-anti-war category, but his war fiction *The Middle Parts of Fortune* (originally published in a bowdlerised edition as *Her Privates We* in 1930), is unsurpassed as an account of soldiering; about (in Michael Howard's words):

> the scrounging, drilling, yarning, gossiping, gambling, drinking and woman-izing which has always constituted the great bulk of military experience.

If this novel did nothing else, it provided graphic evidence that 1 July 1916 was not a typical day on the Western Front.

Although Manning clearly imparts some of his own qualities to his enigmatic hero, Bourne, he achieved artistic detachment by describing the experience of a group of soldiers. Despite his personal inadequacies, Manning also conveys the idea of combat as a supreme test of character in which those who come through achieve a lasting sense of liberation and self-knowledge. As he wrote to William Rothenstein :

> I found that I felt most free in precisely those conditions when freedom seems to the normal mind least possible – an extraordinary feeling of self-reliance and self-assertion.[23]

Guy Chapman records a similar sense of liberation, exaltation, and almost divine energy in recalling an escape from extreme danger in which many of his comrades had been killed in 1917. He reflected (in the 1970s) on:

how much less alive I am than I was then... What is missing is the sense, fleeting, beyond price, of living in every nerve and cell of one's body and with every ghostly impulse of one's mind. I am grateful to have had it.[24]

Numerous other memoirists of the First World War combated or countered the 'disenchanted' school. Their books, many reprinted in recent years, are treasured by military historians but not so well known by the general public, especially to younger generations brought up on the assumption that the 'war poets' and Graves are authoritative sources for the meaning of the war. In addition to Graham Greenwell, mentioned earlier, Sidney Rogerson's *Twelve Days*, about the 2nd West Yorkshire Regiment during a quiet period in the Somme campaign, was originally published in the unpropitious year 1933. Rogerson praised the courage, resolution and, not least, the cheerfulness of ordinary soldiers against those who had recently portrayed the war as one long nightmare:

> The bemused survivor is slightly irritated to find his experience exploited by the marrow-freezing agents of peace for all time... But this post-war propaganda, piling corpse on corpse, heaping terror on futility, seems bound to fail from every point of view. In its distortion, the soldier looks in vain for the scenes he knew.[25]

There has surely been no more honest or moving evocation of the fascination of war than that reluctantly admitted by Guy Chapman:

> Once you have lain in her arms you can admit no other mistress. You may loathe, you may execrate, but you cannot deny her. No lover can offer you defter caresses, more exquisite tortures, such breaking delights. No wine gives fiercer intoxication, no drug more vivid exaltation. Every writer of imagination who has set down in honesty his experience has confessed it. Even those who hate her most are prisoners to her spell. They rise from her embraces, pillaged, soiled, it may be ashamed; but they are still hers.[26]

Chapman, a humane scholar and certainly no militarist, also wrote of the life-long spell which the war had exerted over him. Apart from meeting his wife (the novelist Storm Jameson), Chapman reflected in his autobiography that his battalion was the only wholly good thing in his life:

> To the years between 1914 and 1918 I owe everything of lasting value in my make-up. For any cost I paid in physical and mental vigour they gave me back a supreme fulfilment I should never otherwise have had.[27]

Among the many other writers who have expressed similar positive views about the war's enhancing effects on the rest of their lives may he mentioned R.H. Tawney, Vivian de Sola Pinto, Lord Reith, Sir Maurice Bowra, Harold Macmillan and P.J.

Campbell – but the list could be greatly extended. True, with the important exception of Tawney, these authors were all officers, but the more recently published memoirs or letters of Norman Gladden, George Coppard, Frank Dunham and others provide evidence that the other ranks were far from inarticulate, and could also recall their war service with pride.

Why, then, have these positive and often moving testaments in defence of the British war effort failed to overshadow the anti-war literature and images in the public consciousness? First, no amount of honesty and eloquence can counter 750,000 deaths, their names recorded in every village church. Secondly, the desolate battlescapes depicted by Paul Nash, C. R. W. Nevinson and others have created an indelible image of what the Western Front was 'really like'; no one wants to be told, for example, of the dry and dusty spell during the Passchendaele campaign. On the Western Front it was always raining, when it was not snowing, and men and horses were always knee-deep in mud. Thirdly, the war poets, Remarque and the popular memoirists, such as Vera Brittain (*Testament of Youth*), appeal strongly to the emotions with their accounts of wasted lives, a lost generation and the soldiers as victims or martyrs in a pointless war. On the last aspect, Adrian Caesar does well to remind us that Owen's and Sassoon's soldiers were also killers; indeed Sassoon himself was unusual for an officer in the enthusiasm he displayed in despatching Germans.[28]

Fourthly, the beneficial results of Britain's unprecedented war effort were hard to discern either at home or in international relations by the early 1930s. Moreover, for those like C. E. Montague who had cherished illusions of a better world, the bitter post-war reaction was exacerbated by excessive promises of the 'war to end wars' and of a 'land fit for heroes'. Here perhaps is the sharpest divide in post-war attitudes between the majority who had simply fought doggedly to defeat Germany and thus preserve their homes and way of life; and the minority like Montague for whom the conflict only made sense if regarded as a crusade to secure a better world.

Finally, influential sections of the educated middle classes (i.e., readers of the 'quality' newspapers and of the literature discussed here) seem to have reacted very strongly in the 1920s against war in general and against the British Army and its leaders in particular. There was a long 'open season' for journalistic attacks on incompetent generals (if there were competent ones the critics were not interested) and 'Colonel Blimps', exemplified by Major-General J. F. C. Fuller's savage satires; while his fellow military reformer, Captain B. H. Liddell Hart, advanced the seductive theories that Britain could and should have avoided a total commitment to mass, Continental warfare, and that Germany had been defeated by the blockade rather than the wasteful attrition on the Western Front.[29]

The anti-war myth spawned in the late 1920s and early 1930s is still very influential, notably in setting the agenda and tone for anniversaries and other commemorations of the First World War (for example in the annual television programmes on the Somme and the Armistice).

In addition many facets of the myth were resuscitated and given a new lease of life during the 1960s at the time of the 50th anniversaries.[30] Books such as Alan Clark's

The Donkeys (1961), Leon Wolff's *In Flanders Fields* (1958), and Joan Littlewood's play *Oh! What a Lovely War* (1963) gave a tremendous boost to the myth of the bloody, muddy conflict, incompetently conducted and ultimately futile – in that it set the scene for an even more titanic struggle against Germany. On the other hand, the same decade witnessed a new phase of serious historical interest in the war led by John Terraine and later developed by academic scholars including Tim Travers, Dominick Graham, David French, Trevor Wilson and Robin Prior. But the tendency to present the whole complex conflict in terms of 'butchers and bunglers' remains strong.

It does not require any great intellectual or moral effort to be 'anti-war', and the First World War is an easy target from almost any standpoint. Nevertheless, the literary-cultural anti-war myth as outlined in this essay must be challenged on at least three counts which need only be briefly recapitulated here.

First, despite the fact that the war was a terrible tragedy if evaluated in Clausewitzian terms as an instrument of policy, it was nevertheless fought about great national and international issues. Furthermore, albeit unpredictably and at great cost, it did bring about enormous political changes affecting individual states and empires and the relationship between them. In the light of available information and assumptions, the British government had little option but to enter the war in August 1914, and it is very hard to see how a 'peace without victory' could have been honourably negotiated at any point in the next four years.[31]

Secondly, this essay supports the line taken by Carrington, Barnett and others that the anti-war writers were not at all representative of the vast majority of civilians in uniform who experienced active service. Indeed it is salutary to remember that the generation which grew up in the 1920s and 1930s was not deterred by the pervasive, 'disenchanted' legacy of the First World War from fighting the second.[32]

Finally, the phrase 'anti-war' and the collection of ideas and assumptions which constitute the 'myth' as discussed earlier, are far too sweeping and imprecise to encourage serious study and understanding of the First World War. Quite the contrary they inhibit fresh thinking by their assumption of the moral high ground. To take just one aspect: much of the most bitter criticism during the war and through the 1920s was (justifiably we may feel), directed at the failings on the home front rather than at the reasons for fighting or the conduct of operations. Paradoxically, as Adrian Caesar has reminded us, the 'anti-war' label has become attached to soldier poets, writers and artists whose attitudes to the war were ambivalent if not actually supportive, whereas the true civilian anti-war campaigners receive little public attention.

It is difficult to find a firm basis on which to challenge the anti-war myth; indeed the endeavour is about as rewarding as disputing the merits of apple pie or motherhood. Nevertheless, even in the prevailing climate of opinion in Britain in the 1990s, it ought to be possible to gain a sympathetic hearing for patriotism, the military virtues and the seductive attraction of combat; all to be found in the writings of Douglas Jerrold, Charles Carrington, Frederic Manning and Guy Chapman. Perhaps in the course of the twenty-first century those who shape British public opinion will come to accept the First World War as history (like the earlier Great War against Napoleonic

France), rather than in predominantly literary terms as a black hole or national trauma – a gap in history – redeemed and rendered meaningful for them only by disenchanted memoirs and the poetry of pity.

References

1. Adrian Caesar, *Taking it like a man : Suffering, sexuality and the war poets* (1993), pp. 97–8.
2. Ibid, pp.104, 158, 162, 233.
3. Robert Wohl, *The Generation of 1914* (1980), pp. 262. Samuel Hynes, *A War Imagined: the First World War and English Culture* (1990), pp. 175-80.
4. Modris Eksteins, *Rites of Spring. The Great War and the Birth of the Modern Age* (1989), pp.175–6. See also Michael Howard's introduction to Frederic Manning, *The Middle Parts of Fortune* (1977 edition).
5. Hynes, pp. 166–67, 215, 455.
6. Correlli Barnett, *The Collapse of British Power* (1972), pp. 433–34.
7. See Robin Prior and Trevor Wilson, 'Paul Fussell at War' in *War in History* Vol I. No I. (1994), pp. 63–80.
8. Charles Edmonds, *A Subaltern's War* (1929), pp. 206–08.
9. C. E. Montague, *Disenchantment* (1929, Phoenix library edition), pp. 188–89. Hynes, pp. 307–10.
10. Hynes, pp. 118–19.
11. Keith Simpson (ed), *The War the Infantry Knew* (1987), p. XXXI
12. Robert Graves, *Goodbye to All That* (1957 edition), Prologue. Hynes, pp. 427–30.
13. Hynes, pp. 446–47. Also my own comments on the Somme film in 'The Somme in British History' (unpublished paper, 1992).
14. Barnett, op. cit. pp. 428–29. Hynes, p. 302.
15. Hynes, p. 439.
16. Eksteins, pp. 285–99.
17. Wohl, pp. 58–9.
18. Ibid p. 219.
19. John Terraine's introduction to Graham H. Greenwell, *An Infant in Arms* (1972 edition), pp. IX–XIX.
20. Douglas Jerrold, *The Lie about the War* (1929), p. 46. Hynes, pp. 451–54.
21. Charles Edmonds (Carrington), *A Subaltern's War* (1929), pp. 194–95.
22. Jonathan Marwil, *Frederic Manning: an Unfinished Life* (1988).
23. Ibid p. 179.
24. Guy Chapman, *A Kind of Survivor* (1975), pp. 158–59.
25. John Terraine quoting Rogerson in his introduction to Greenwell, op cit p. XIII.
26. Guy Chapman, *A Passionate Prodigality* (1933). The quotation is from the second edition (1965), p. 226.
27. Guy Chapman, *A Kind of Survivor* (1975), p. 280.
28. Caesar op. cit. p. 144. 'On one occasion he ignored a written order… in order to occupy and hold a German trench – alone. Sassoon had badly wanted to kill a German at close quarters', Wohl, p. 97.
29. See for example, J. F. C. Fuller, *Generalship: Its Diseases and their Cure* (1933), *The Army in my Time* (1935), and *Memoirs of an Unconventional Soldier* (1936). B. H. Liddell Hart, *The British Way in Warfare* (1932).
30. See the editor's introduction and Alex Danchev's 'Bunking and Debunking: the controversies of the 1960s' in Brian Bond (ed), *The First World War and British Military History* (1991), pp. 1–12, 263–88.

31. See, for example, the robust conclusions of Trevor Wilson in *The Myriad Faces of War* (1986), pp. 848–53. For a recent statement of the case that Britain could and should have remained neutral in 1914 see Niall Ferguson, 'Were we right to fight the Great War?', *Sunday Telegraph*, 31 July 1994.
32. Wilson, p. 852.

6

The Army between the Two World Wars

In the brief space available I could only cover a few salient aspects of the British Army in the 1920s and 1930s, such as its low political priority, difficulty in finding enough soldiers to provide imperial garrisons, especially for India, enforced reliance on obsolete equipment, and failure to develop mechanised forces which its theorists had championed in the 1920s. Drawing on my earlier book *British Military Policy between the Two World Wars* (O.U.P., 1980) I contended that the Army's almost comatose state for much of this period was only in part due to its internal defects and complacency, and rather more to governmental reluctance to confirm a Continental commitment until a few months before the outbreak of war in 1939.

Clearly, then, there is a need for a social history of soldiering in these decades but, to my knowledge, this remains a gap in the historiography. Readers interested in this aspect could do worse than start with Spike Mays' *Fall Out the Officers* (1969) and Frank Richards' *Old-Soldier Sahib* (1936) with its extremely incorrect views on how to treat the natives in India. I attempt an impressionistic sketch of the Army's character and ethos in these decades in the second chapter of my book mentioned above.

A graph of the British army's fortunes between 1918 and 1939, as indicated by annual budgets and strategic priorities, would suggest a story of political neglect after the unprecedented national effort during the First World War. The line would plunge steeply from the Armistice, when there were over 3.5 million troops on the British establishment, to the end of 1920, when there were only 370,000. Another sharp drop was affected in 1922 when the Geddes Axe drastically reduced both numbers and expenditure, and thereafter the army's annual budget fell steadily every year from just over £43.5 million in 1923 to just under £36 million in 1932. The renewed threats from Japan and Germany in the early 1930s scarcely affected the army for several years, and even the start of rearmament proper in 1935 brought only meagre increases in funding. Only in 1938, with a defence loan of nearly £36 million supplementing a budget of £87 million, can the army be truly said to have begun preparing for war.

At least by 1923 the worst of the inevitable post-war upheavals were over and the army, reduced to its pre-1914 establishment and dependent on voluntary enlistment, was settling down again to the humdrum routines of home security and imperial policing. Kipling's bitter lines about the public's indifference to 'Tommy Atkins' once a great war was over were more than ever appropriate in the disillusioned mood of the 1920s. Lacking either the traditional esteem of the Royal Navy or the novel appeal of the Royal Air Force, the army soon felt itself to be the 'Cinderella service' – criticized in the press, always short of men despite continuing high unemployment and increasingly dependent on obsolescent weapons and equipment.

In the aftermath of the First World War the British Empire reached its maximum extent, with the enormous additional responsibilities of mandated territories in the Middle East, and occupation duties in the former Ottoman empire and the Rhineland. The largest commitment, India, required approximately 70,000 British troops, but there were also sizeable garrisons in Egypt, Iraq and Northern Ireland. Despite being overstretched in terms of manpower, the War Office had a vested interest in the 1920s in maintaining the army's policing role in the Middle East and on the North-West Frontier against the RAF's claims to perform this function more effectively and more cheaply. As the limitations of policing dissident tribesmen from the air began to attract both operational and moral criticism, so the role of ground forces expanded. By the late 1930s, for example, the growing Arab rebellion in Palestine had drawn in the infantry component of almost two divisions; the North-West Frontier saw a series of costly punitive expeditions; and substantial mechanized forces were dispatched to Egypt to guard against the Italian threat from Libya. Greatly reduced reserve forces meant that the army was harder pressed to meet these commitments than before 1914.

It is not therefore surprising that, as the horrific experience of war receded, to be replaced by the onerous problems of peacetime soldiering, the feeling should grow that the unprecedented war effort of 1914–18 had been unique, even an aberration. No less an authority than the Chief of the Imperial General Staff (CIGS), Sir George Milne, endorsed this view in 1926 when he described the recent war as 'abnormal'. At present, he added, the army could not even mobilize a single corps; it was most unlikely ever again to be required to fight a European war. The phrase 'never again' was frequently used about such a nightmarish prospect; politicians implied scornfully that they would not send troops to 'the trenches', and even the use of the term 'Expeditionary Force' was deplored in government discussions and official reports.

In extenuation of official neglect of the army, it must be stressed that until the appearance of the threat from Nazi Germany it had no obvious European enemy – the United States and Japan as theoretical antagonists being almost entirely naval concerns. War with Britain's recent ally, France, was scarcely credible, and was in any case mainly a contingency for the RAF. Consequently in the later 1920s and early 1930s the army's war-gaming was primarily concerned with a Soviet threat to India through Afghanistan. In these circumstances, and in view of acute domestic social and economic problems, the government's informal imposition of a Ten-Year Rule from 1919 with regard to defence expenditure was eminently sensible. All three services were to plan on the assumption of no major war for the next 10 years and the army was specifically advised that no expeditionary force would be required for such a purpose. However, in the mid-1920s the Rule was put on a moving basis and was not abandoned until1932 on the urgent pleas of the Chiefs of Staff.

Therefore, in its early years especially, the Rule simply acknowledged the fact that no funding was available for military expansion and very little for technical innovation or training. While it may have contributed to the Army's introspection, social snobbery and conservatism – later to be epitomized by David Low's caricature 'Colonel Blimp' – it certainly did not cause those negative features of peacetime soldiering. It did, however, give the Treasury the whip hand over expenditure and cause considerable irritation in numerous disputes over penny-pinching which Colonel J. F. C. Fuller and other satirists gleefully exposed. The much more serious faults of the Rule were that it was maintained for several years too long, allowed the domestic arms industry virtually to disappear, and rested on the dubious assumption that Britain would have the will-power, industrial capability and, above all, time to rearm once an enemy (or as it turned out three potential enemies) had appeared.

The dispatch of the Shanghai Defence Force in 1927 made public what was already well known to the army's leaders; namely, the difficulties entailed in mobilizing even a division shorn of a considerable amount of its guns, vehicles, and heavy equipment. Only the previous year, during the General Strike, the CIGS had referred to the nightmare of an overseas crisis necessitating the dispatch of available regular infantry units coinciding with widespread industrial disorder at home. On more than one occasion he stated officially that the army was 'completely out of date' and was unfitted to respond to any contingency in Europe.

Soldiering in these unpropitious conditions could be dull and frustrating. Given also the slow promotion system and the tendency of senior officers to hang on as long as possible in service, it is not surprising that many imaginative, progressive-minded officers either left the service or lost some of their enthusiasm. Even later well-known generals like Wavell, Dill and Ironside were affected by these adverse conditions. Field Marshal Chetwode's farewell address as Commander-in-Chief in India in 1934 was perhaps the most devastating indictment of the military profession in this era by an insider, including the reflection that: 'The longer I remain in the Service, the more wooden and the more regulation-bound do I find the British officer to be.' Liddell Hart, Fuller and others made equally scathing remarks of the army at home.

Against this gloomy background, however, it is possible to be favourably impressed by the progressive spirit and ideas displayed by a minority of zealous professional officers, especially in the 1920s, when reforms and innovations could be discussed fairly objectively without the need to focus on a particular enemy. Thus Fuller and Liddell Hart were only the most famous of a band of middle-ranking officers and ex-officers who established international reputations with a spate of publications critical of the conduct of the recent war and advocating a variety of reforms. Journals such as that of the Royal United Services Institute and the *Army Quarterly* suggested a ferment of proposals for reform, not least in the annual prize essay competitions setting a specific contemporary issue for discussion. At the Camberley Staff College, a dynamic Commandant such as Ironside recruited top-class instructors such as Dill and Fuller who were eager to disseminate the tactical lessons of the First World War.

Above all, it remains a matter of astonishment that the numerically declining and underfunded British army should have continued its pioneering efforts on tanks and mechanization generally from the First World War through to the early 1930s. In particular the trials and manoeuvres between 1927 and 1931 of mixed and, eventually, wholly mechanized units communicating by radio set the standard which the larger European armies would not emulate for several years. In 1927, for example, the first experimental manoeuvres were handicapped by the miscellaneous nature of the available tanks, armoured cars, and other vehicles and by the lack of radio communication between the tanks. Non-existent anti-tank guns were notoriously represented by flags. Nevertheless the manoeuvres impressed observers with the potential mobility and striking power of armoured formations. Despite numerous mechanical problems and the deliberate handicapping of the mechanized forces to prevent demoralization of the traditional arms, considerable progress had been made by 1931 when Brigadier Charles Broad carried out a brilliant demonstration on Salisbury Plain by moving 180 tanks in dense fog with 'an almost inhuman precision' by radio control. This seemed to herald a new era of armoured and mechanized formations, including air co-operation, in which horsed cavalry and marching infantry would have no part. On the theoretical side, Broad had already, in 1929, published the official booklet *Mechanized and Armoured Formations* (better known from its cover colour as 'The Purple Primer'), and three years later Fuller would bring out the influential *Field Service Regulations, Part III*, which analysed the likely nature of combat between armoured forces. By the early 1930s, however, Milne and his successor as CIGS, Montgomery-Massingberd, had made it clear that they favoured the gradual mechanization and motorization of all arms, including the conversion of the cavalry to light tanks or armoured cars, rather than concentrating on the expansion of the small Royal Tank Corps (only four battalions in 1932) as the basis for larger armoured formations. There was undoubtedly a conservative and even reactionary aspect to this War Office policy which generally prevailed through the 1930s and it was bitterly criticized by Fuller, Liddell Hart and other proponents of armoured warfare; see, for example, the latter's *Memoirs*, volume one, (1965) for a detailed account of Britain's surrender of her lead in what was soon to be termed the *blitzkrieg* style of warfare.

Various explanations can be offered for what in retrospect was to seem an egregious error in rearmament policy. First, the War Office's financial resources for weapons development of all kinds remained meagre, and the facilities for tank-building almost non-existent. Successive CIGSs took the view that limited resources must be thinly spread across all the arms of the service rather than concentrated on tanks. More open to criticism was the weak design and development section of the General Staff concerned with tanks, and also the protracted uncertainty about which tank models to put into production and for what combat roles.

But by far the most important inhibiting factor, in this author's view, was the government's continuing hesitation about the continental role of the army until almost the eve of the Second World War. Tanks did not fit comfortably into the Cardwell system for garrisoning the Empire by the routine alternation of infantry and cavalry units, and they were bound to be given a very low priority so long as deterrence through air and sea power dominated the government's, and not least the Treasury's, defence policy. Anti-aircraft guns and air defence generally received a much higher priority than tanks. Only an earlier political undertaking to send an Expeditionary Force to the Continent would have opened the possibility of creating a more tank-orientated army, and even then it is difficult to envisage the appearance of *panzer*-style armoured divisions in the anti-war, disarmament-orientated Britain before the spring of 1939. In the defence review completed in December 1937, for example, the estimated savings on tanks would exceed all other army economies added together. In that year too the War Office actually underspent its allocation for warlike stores by nearly £6 million due to lack of industrial facilities and indecision over designs and long-term orders. Generals such as Ironside and Burnett-Stuart, or journalists like Liddell Hart, who opposed the continental commitment, should have perceived the close link between the army's projected role and the low priority given to the creation of armoured divisions.

A little more needs to be said about the place of the army in the National Government's conception of defence policy because this is crucial to an understanding of the service's slow development throughout the 1930s. In November 1933 the government set up the Defence Requirements Committee (DRC), composed of the Chiefs of Staff and representatives of the Treasury and the Foreign Office, to report on the three services' worst deficiencies with a programme to remedy them over the next five years. This was therefore emphatically not the first step in rearmament; indeed such a policy was expressly denied until 1935.

The General Staff proposed, and the DRC accepted, a total of £40 million for the army based on a calculation of what the War Office could actually spend, given the run-down of the arms industry, rather than on a realistic appraisal of needs. Colonel Pownall, then on the Secretariat of the Committee of Imperial Defence (CID), reckoned that to produce an Expeditionary Force of four regular divisions with an adequate reserve of Territorial divisions would need about £145 million over five years. In addition £30 million was required to implement the Defence of India Plan.

As the generals anticipated, it was the proposal to prepare a modest Expeditionary Force (smaller than that available before 1914) equipped to fight on the Continent which aroused ministerial opposition. The attack was led by the Chancellor of the Exchequer, Neville Chamberlain, behind whose ruthless logic it is possible to detect an emotional revulsion against the attritional nature and heavy casualties of the First World War, coupled with a fear that if the War Office's proposals were accepted they would lead to a repetition of the trench stalemate. Curiously, politicians who had fought in the war, including Churchill, Eden, Duff Cooper, and Macmillan, took a more robust view about the need to prepare an army for a possible European campaign than those who had not, such as Chamberlain, Hoare, and Simon.

The nub of the Chancellor's case was that the Maginot Line rendered the French frontier impregnable so the real problem was Belgium. If her ground defences were strong they would be overcome by German airpower; if not a British Expeditionary Force could not possibly prevent a German breakthrough. Since Britain could not afford to rearm all three services the Chancellor favoured concentrating on the navy and air force which he believed (unlike the army) would exercise a deterrent effect; the army should be left to concentrate on its extra-European role, apart from its contribution to the air defence of Great Britain (ADGB).

Despite Pownall's sarcastic diary entry to the effect that the Chancellor's ideas on strategy 'would disgrace a board school', they generally prevailed, even though the Chiefs of Staff preserved at least a facade of unity in arguing consistently that an ability to put a small army on the Continent should be a vital component of Britain's defence policy. The army's allocation from the DRC was halved to £20 million; and although the continental commitment was never expressly ruled out, very little was done to provide the training, equipment, weapons, and, particularly, ammunition to enable even the first two divisions to take part in a European war. Worse still, as the fear of a knock-out blow from the air increasingly alarmed the electorate, the Territorial Army was largely diverted to the role of anti-aircraft defence. In this period (1934–5) the army probably reached the nadir of its fortunes in the inter-war years and, despite the valiant efforts of its minister Lord Hailsham, its demands were largely overruled just when the shortages resulting from the Ten-Year Rule needed to be tackled. As Hailsham remarked, the army had been cast as 'a Cinderella of the forces'.

As if the army's existing problems were not enough, two crises in the Mediterranean theatre in the mid-1930s added to the strain in terms of manpower and equipment, and strengthened the views of soldiers and politicians who believed that a military commitment in Europe should be renounced. First the Abyssinian crisis of 1935–6 raised the possibility of war with Italy in which the army's responsibilities would include the defence of Egypt and the Mediterranean bases. In September 1935 three battalions were dispatched from England to Malta and an extra brigade to Egypt. Later reinforcements to Egypt included a battalion of light tanks, a company of medium tanks, and a mechanized brigade of the Royal Artillery. These reinforcements helped to form the nucleus of the desert army which excelled against the Italians in 1940, and it is easy to understand how senior soldiers, such as General Ironside, could view their role as an alternative to that of a continental campaign against Germany.

The second crisis concerned the persistent, if sporadic, rebellion of the Palestinian Arabs from April 1936 onwards. The security of Palestine was regarded as hardly less important than that of Egypt for Britain's Middle Eastern and imperial strategy. It provided an essential staging post for Britain's air routes to India and the Far East; it was viewed as a buffer zone for the defences of the Suez Canal; and in Haifa lay the terminus of the pipeline for vital oil supplies from Persia and Iraq. After a year or so of comparative quiet, full-scale rebellion broke out again in the summer of 1938 and continued into the autumn, thereby creating a serious distraction and dispersion of trained battalions which could be ill spared. Colonel Pownall's diary entry for 29 August 1938 evokes the problem as viewed by the General Staff:

> sending troops to Palestine is like pouring water onto the desert sands – they are immediately absorbed, the thirsty sand cries for more and one never gets a drop back. At the end of September they'll have 11 [infantry] battalions and a cavalry regiment... two of our colonial divisions in effect... God, what a mess we have made of this whole Palestine affair!

By this time the Cabinet appeared to have discounted any army contribution to a European ally at the outset of war. In confirming the revised strategic priorities proposed by the Minister for the Co-ordination of Defence, Sir Thomas Inskip, in December 1937, the army's responsibilities were listed in the following order: the provision of anti-aircraft defences at home; followed by the reinforcement of imperial garrisons; the dispatch of the field force to 'an Eastern theatre'; and, last of all, 'co-operation in defence of the territories of any allies Britain might have in war' though it was unlikely that much could be done under this last heading. Inskip at least showed awareness of the risk his proposals entailed. But as Michael Howard commented, 'What was generally termed a policy of "limited liability" in Continental warfare had now shrunk to one of no liability at all.'

Apart from the diehards on the General Staff, who understandably feared that, if war occurred and the ill-trained and underequipped field force was dispatched to a shambles, they would be held responsible, the army's European role had few supporters in the months before the Munich crisis. The Royal Navy's and the RAF's interest in a continental commitment had declined for different reasons; Sir Maurice Hankey had withdrawn his influential support, and with the replacement of Duff Cooper by Hore-Belisha in May 1937 even the War Minister ceased to fight the army's corner on this vital issue, the latter being a believer in the impregnability of French defences and therefore in the feasibility of 'limited liability' for the British army.

During Hore-Belisha's first year at the War Office he was preoccupied, above all other reforming projects, by Britain's pathetically inadequate ground defences against the *Luftwaffe's* anticipated attempt to strike a knock-out blow. Duncan Sandys, MP, had made trouble for him on this issue, and the Munich crisis demonstrated that London was for all practical purposes defenceless. Nevertheless, Hore-Belisha drew a different lesson from the crisis. For all the government's declarations to the contrary, he now believed that the field force *would* be dispatched to France in the event of war. He was appalled at the prospect. Quite apart from the lack of tanks, guns, and reserves of ammunition, the troops would have had no winter clothing in 1938. This was a state of neglect almost comparable with the condition in which the army had been sent to the Crimea. Almost immediately Hore-Belisha began a courageous and very unpopular campaign in the Cabinet, though he was soon to receive valuable support from the Foreign Secretary, Lord Halifax, to give the European commitment first priority so as to loosen the iron grip of the Treasury. To resurrect the programme refused two years previously would cost about £200 million – a seemingly impossible goal in view of the other services' existing programmes.

It is unnecessary here to cover in detail the complex process which led to the government's *volte-face* and reluctant acceptance of a continental commitment for the regular army divisions in February 1939 beyond stressing that Hore-Belisha played a leading part in it. This was acknowledged by his arch-critic (in the privacy of his diary), Major-General Henry Pownall, in 1938–9 Director of Military Operations and Intelligence at the War Office. On 20 February he recorded 'a great victory'; namely the launch of an adequately funded programme to equip the field force properly for a continental role, though this still only applied to the first four regular divisions and four Territorial divisions. Pownall saw a demonstration of new weapons at Aldershot and was 'much comforted'. 'The Army,' he noted, 'really is coming to life again, no longer a "depressed class".' He envisaged the creation of a really high-class modern army – small but efficient and well equipped.

This ideal was not to be realized because it ran counter to Pownall's conflicting and prophetic insight that, unless Britain lost a short war, she would be forced to mobilize national resources and eventually to clothe, arm, and accommodate a national army on a large scale. Hore-Belisha began this movement in March 1939 when, partly as a publicity stunt to exploit the recent rush of volunteers to the Territorial Army, he raised the establishment to war strength (170,000) and, by a proverbial stroke of the pen, doubled it to the goal of 340,000. This alarmed some of Hore-Belisha's Cabinet colleagues as heralding a commitment to a new mass war in the trenches of France. But in the short term it created enormous administrative problems due to shortage of drill halls, equipment, uniforms, and, most seriously, instructors many of whom would have to be taken from regular units.

In the following month Hore-Belisha performed the bravest action of his political career in forcing Chamberlain to accept a measure of compulsory service in peacetime despite repeated pledges to the contrary. The War Minister was responding to French pressure for *un effort du sang* and to permit at least a portion of the anti-aircraft defences to be manned round the clock against a threat from the *Luftwaffe* which did not actually exist. But beyond these needs, Hore-Belisha wished to strengthen overseas garrisons and the field force – as the former Expeditionary Force was now termed.

Coming so soon after the nominal doubling of the Territorial Army, the arrival of 200,000 conscripts for six months' training created unimaginable chaos in the summer of 1939; what one War Office critic moderately described as 'a proper granny's knitting'. He also admitted that it was preferable to get the worst of this confusion over before war began. On the debit side, however, critics like Liddell Hart pointed out that the War Office had apparently abandoned any hope of creating a small, high-quality mechanized field force and seemed bent on conscripting a vast, immobile, and underequipped conscript army suited only to a static attritional war like that of 1914–18.

In the summer of 1939 strenuous efforts were made to foster close Anglo-French relations and to co-ordinate inter-Allied arrangements at all levels so as to avoid the friction which so many British senior officers in 1939 could recall from the First World War. Amicable arrangements were made concerning the French ports to be made available to the field force, its assembly area to the north-west of Amiens, and its place in the line on the French left – all almost uncannily reminiscent of 1914. The two governments agreed on the composition and role of a Supreme War Council and on the British Commander-in-Chief's place in the French chain of command, but no permanent joint staff organization was ever achieved.

As a consequence of inter-service rivalry throughout the inter-war period, the field force would sail to France with only the meagre air support of the air component, consisting of two bomber reconnaissance squadrons, six army cooperation squadrons, four fighter squadrons, and two flights of a headquarters communications squadron. The two services were about equally to blame for the lack of an agreed tactical doctrine for close air–ground co-operation. The RAF's leaders were adamant that the bomber was not a battlefield weapon: it would be wasteful and inefficient to employ bombers in 'penny packets' under the orders of army commanders on tasks which could be more suitably carried out by artillery. This was probably the operational issue on which there had been least progress since 1918, and where recent practical experience – particularly on the North-West Frontier of India – had been completely neglected in Britain.

In view of the late acceptance of a continental commitment, followed by the enormous influx of untrained Territorials and conscripts, no amount of hard work and improvisation could equip and train the field force for a European campaign in less than 18 months. A review of the regular infantry divisions of the field force in July 1939 revealed, for example, that there were available only 72 out of 240 heavy anti-aircraft guns and 144 out of 240 anti-tank guns. The field artillery regiments had not yet received any of the new 25-pounder guns. In August a War Office spokesman admitted that only 60 infantry support tanks were available against a requirement of 1,646. There had been no large-scale manoeuvres for several years as part of the economy drive; hence even the regular divisions lacked basic tactical skills. The mobilization and movement to France of the first four regular divisions in September 1939 went off remarkably smoothly, but they were inadequately trained and short of every type of equipment, especially tanks, guns, and ammunition. The vast citizen army assembling in Britain lacked even the equipment for realistic training.

It is often claimed that the field force was the only national contingent to go to war in 1939 'fully mechanized'. True, the army no longer depended on horse transport, but a more accurate term would be 'motorized' and even then military vehicles had to be supplemented by large-scale requisitioning from civilian firms. In his *Memoirs*, Field Marshal Montgomery described, in September 1939, how the countryside of France was strewn with broken-down vans and lorries from his 3rd Division. He concluded a long list of deficiencies with the damning verdict that 'we sent our Army into that most modern war with weapons and equipment which were quite inadequate'.

By the end of September 1939 more than 160,000 soldiers and airmen with over 23,000 vehicles and a vast tonnage of stores and supplies had been safely landed in France. By mid-October I and II Corps (the first four divisions) had occupied the Franco-Belgian frontier defences on the allotted British sector between Maulde and Halluin. This was no mean achievement for an army which only a year previously had been assigned to an extra-European role against inferior opposition. Unlike their predecessors in 1914, however, the soldiers in 1939 were not immediately swept into a costly encounter battle and were in fact to have more than six months to prepare themselves before the blow fell. Shattering though the experience of battle was to be in May 1940, it must be considered fortunate from the viewpoint of the British army that the *blitzkrieg* was not launched earlier. A high price had to be paid in this and subsequent campaigns for the political indecision of the 1930s. It makes no sense to criticize the character and ethos of the British army in the inter-war period without taking full account of the social and political environment in which it struggled to maintain its traditional professional standards.

7

Leslie Hore-Belisha at the War Office, 1937–1940

Hore-Belisha's political career has long been in need of a full, scholarly reappraisal to replace R. J. Minney's somewhat partisan account (see note 6), but biographers have been deterred by the meagreness of surviving private papers. My long essay benefited from close association with Liddell Hart and a thorough study of his enormous archives. I also enjoyed a unique advantage through editing the diaries of Lieutenant General Sir Henry Pownall (see note 16) with their uninhibited revelations of the General Staff's attitudes to the War Minister, both in peacetime, and during the early months at war in 1939. The reader unfamiliar with this subject – and perhaps chiefly associating Hore-Belisha with the orange beacons on pedestrian crossings which bear his name – may be astonished by three remarkable themes. First, the deplorable state of the Army in 1937 when a definite commitment to prepare for Continental war was still far off. Second, the strength of political and military opposition and obstructiveness towards Hore-Belisha as regards his character, methods and proposed reforms. Thirdly, the tragi-comic circumstances of his downfall: cornered by his enemies over the largely irrelevant 'Pill-Box' affair; ruthlessly removed from the War Office by the Prime Minister who had just given him his full verbal backing; and denied an honourable transfer to the Ministry of Information essentially because he was a Jew.

When Neville Chamberlain succeeded Stanley Baldwin as Prime Minister in May 1937 he rather surprisingly promoted Duff Cooper to the Admiralty and replaced him with the successful Minister of Transport, Leslie Hore-Belisha. Chamberlain clearly expected the latter, who was energetic, ambitious and only 43 years old, to shake the War Office out of its notorious inertia and conservatism, but there is also evidence to suggest that he expected Hore-Belisha would be a more suitable instrument than the rebellious Duff Cooper to implement the government's 'limited liability' role for the army.[1]

> The army had suffered even more than the other two services from the 'locust years' following the First World War, and it received the lowest priority when a cautious programme of rearmament began in the mid-1930s. When Hore-Belisha entered the War Office the army's fortunes were at their nadir: its role was uncertain, its equipment mostly obsolete and its production base almost non-existent. Perhaps worst of all was the atmosphere of pessimism and despondency which was beginning to affect even the more progressive-minded officers and would-be reformers. Consequently, despite the handicaps of being a Jew and having a military record lacking in social distinction (Hore-Belisha had attained the rank of major in the Royal Army Service Corps in the First World War), the advent of this dynamic personality to the War Office on 28 May was widely welcomed. For example, General Ironside, newly appointed to Eastern Command, noted in his diary on 29 May, 'We are at our lowest ebb in the Army and the Jew may resuscitate us. I hope that he hasn't been ordered to cut us down, and yet surely we can be cut down in our overhead expenses.' And the next day Ironside added, 'I lay awake in the morning and thought of Hore-Belisha. He will probably be our saving. He is ambitious and will not be lazy like some of the others were. He starts in when things are at their worst and will have to show results?'[2]

'Flamboyant' is the first adjective that springs to mind in describing Hore-Belisha. He was an outstanding orator and had been the first post-war president of the Oxford Union. He had an almost oriental love of splendour in his personal surroundings and was utterly unpractical in simple matters such as shaving, packing and driving. He was fertile in imagination; eager for new ideas; and zealous in pushing through reforms – as he had proved in his successful campaign to reduce traffic accidents. In personal relations he was a man of contradictions: though demanding and sometimes inconsiderate, he was capable of inspiring affection and devotion among those who worked closely with him. On the other hand he could be irritating and even infuriating to people not in sympathy with him. He was habitually unpunctual and could be rude and overbearing. He could display intolerance towards generals and civil servants with minds slower than his own, and he had the reprehensible habit of asking soldiers and junior officers what they thought of their seniors. He was sensitive about his Jewish race and middle-class background, and – perhaps by way of compensation – had great faith in the importance of publicity and self-advertisement. Though sensitive to criticism, particularly in the press, he sometimes tended to be naively complacent regarding the loyalty and friendship of fellow politicians and generals.[3] Lastly, since serving as a Financial Secretary to the Treasury from 1932 to 1934, he had become very much a 'Chamberlain man': this allegiance stood him in good stead on taking office, but as a National Liberal in a government and Parliament dominated by Conservatives it meant that his political position was extremely vulnerable.

Initially Hore-Belisha knew very little about the army and its problems but, as his great Liberal predecessor at the War Office R. B. Haldane had proved, this need not necessarily be a disadvantage. Unlike Haldane, however, Hore-Belisha characteristically chose to look outside the War Office and the General Staff for an independent view of the whole field of necessary military reforms. For his chief, though always unofficial, mentor he selected Captain B. H. Liddell Hart, the brilliant and influential defence correspondent of *The Times,* to whom he had been introduced by Duff Cooper. Since Liddell Hart has devoted virtually the whole of the second volume of his *Memoirs*[4] to what both men came to regard as their 'partnership', it is only necessary to mention here that the War Minister relied on this prolific, progressive and unorthodox source of advice to an astonishing extent during his first nine months or so in office. Liddell Hart was extremely well informed; he probably entertained a more comprehensive and radical programme for reform than any inhabitant of the War Office; and his strategic thinking on the role of the army was at that time in close accord with the government's. Inevitably, however, there was much professional prejudice against him from the outset, and not exclusively, one must record, on the part of conservative generals. For the more reactionary it was sufficient to note that Liddell Hart was a journalist who had only attained the rank of captain in the First World War. Others naturally resented his powerful advocacy of the doctrine of 'limited liability' for the army, and his pressure in the newspapers for the promotion of mechanised warfare experts such as Hobart and Pile. But the fundamental reason for hostility to him was the General Staff's understandable resentment at a rival source or advice without responsibility so close to the War Minister. In justice to Liddell Hart it should be stressed that he would have welcomed the legitimising of his position as a member of a formally constituted research group, but it seems that Hore-Belisha did not insist on this innovation and it was successfully resisted by Liddell Hart's own appointee as Deputy Chief of the Imperial General Staff, Sir Ronald Adam.[5]

Within a few weeks of taking office Hore-Belisha encountered the same tight financial constraints on military expenditure which had greatly exasperated his predecessor. In February 1937 the government had approved a defence budget of £1,500 million to be spent by all three services over the next five years. A Treasury Inter-Service Committee carefully scrutinised the separate programmes and frequently referred proposals, no matter how urgent, if they involved an outlay in excess of the ration allotted. As Hore-Belisha sadly recorded in his diary on 13 July 1937:

> My proposal for the provision of war equipment, war reserves and maintenance for four Territorial divisions [£43 million] was turned down today... I argued

with Simon [Chancellor of the Exchequer], but he was quite firm that at present there should be no increase in the cost of the Army's programme. I pointed out that the Army's programme was behind that of the Navy and Air Force... It was a disheartening business for the War Office.[6]

By the late summer of 1937, in close collaboration with Liddell Hart, he had worked out a far-reaching programme for army reorganisation the keynote of which was the reduction of infantry units, particularly in the garrison of India, in order to save funds for increased mechanisation. But these initial proposals met with so much obstruction and outright opposition that Hore-Belisha became convinced that a wholesale replacement of the senior generals at the War Office must precede more constructive reforms. By August 1937 he had discovered that General Sir Harry Knox, the Adjutant General, was 'his chief obstacle and the main reason why Duff Cooper failed'. The CIGS, General Sir Cyril Deverell, possessed some fine soldierly attributes but was reduced to blustering incoherence by Liddell Hart's radical proposals as purveyed to him by Hore-Belisha. He refused to consider reducing the garrison of India, simply declaring, 'I've been there 12 years and I tell you that you cannot reduce it.' When Hore-Belisha asked the CIGS what changes he would advise if it were decided that there should be no expeditionary force, Deverell answered that he 'would not alter the present arrangements one iota'. By mid-November, therefore, Hore-Belisha had decided that he would like to remove Deverell and replace him with a much younger man, the recently appointed Military Secretary, Lord Gort.[7]

Before making sweeping changes in the Army Council and military commands Hore-Belisha took care to enlist the support of the Prime Minister, particularly as he had already decided to remove one member of the Army Council, Sir Hugh Elles, the Master General of Ordnance, and replace him with a Director General of Munitions Production. In this move he had the backing of Gort. Among the objectives which Hore-Belisha listed in a letter to the Prime Minister on 1 November were:

1. The elimination of the 1914–18 mentality, which persists in regarding the whole role for which the Army is being prepared as a repetition of its task in the last war.
2. The elimination of the attitude towards any new development, such as Mechanization and Anti-Aircraft defence, as taking away money needed for the new '1914–1918' Army.
3. The elimination of the India obsession, which refuses to allow objective examination of the proper disposition and organization of our Imperial Forces.
4. The elimination of the sentimentality which regards appointments and promotions as governed by the comradely principle of 'Buggins's Turn'.[8]

Even after he had received the Prime Minister's consent to the dismissal of Deverell and Knox, the War Minister remained extremely nervous, stressing to Liddell Hart that he was risking his career. After the 'purge' had been carried out on 1 December without much adverse comment Hore-Belisha was exultant. He told Liddell Hart that the latter had given him the courage to do it and they were 'a great combination'.[9]

Lord Gort, a fighting general *par excellence*, somewhat reluctantly became CIGS, with Sir Ronald Adam as his deputy, Hore-Belisha's idea being that the former would supply the drive and the latter the brains. Major General Clive Liddell (no relation to Liddell Hart) succeeded Knox, and Archibald Wavell, whose taciturnity had deprived him of a good chance of becoming CIGS, was transferred from Palestine to Southern Command. This looked like a promising team to rejuvenate the War Office and reform the army.[10] Within a few weeks, however, Liddell Hart received disturbing reports that Gort was 'soft-pedalling on radical proposals' and displaying resentment at the journalist's close relationship with the War Minister. Even Adam showed distinct signs of coolness towards him. Worse still, there were rumours that Hore-Belisha was hated in the Cabinet. His advertising and obvious ambition were resented; his recruiting figures were suspect, and it was feared that he would leave his colleagues in a mess.[11]

Meanwhile the vexed question of the role of the army, which had been allowed to drag on unresolved since 1934, was coming to a head in the autumn of 1937. The army's order of priorities as between home defence, imperial garrisons, defended bases and providing an expeditionary force for employment in the empire or in Europe determined its financial allocation and consequently affected every aspect of reform. Moreover, if the Continental commitment was renounced or placed last, the army was likely to suffer in competition with the other services for scarce production facilities and skilled labour.

Hore-Belisha entered office with no pronounced strategic views and with a much keener interest in improving the terms of service and living conditions of the other ranks. He was therefore a willing convert to Liddell Hart's ideas on 'limited liability', particularly as the latter stressed that streamlining of obsolescent arms would secure economies that would permit the creation of two mechanised divisions.[12] In October, at the Prime Minister's urging, Hore-Belisha read the chapter on the role of the army in Liddell Hart's latest book, *Europe in Arms*, which argued that if Britain was obliged to make a military contribution to a Continental ally (i.e. France) it should take the form of a small, high-quality mechanised force. This reading probably only served to reinforce the impressions which the War Minister had derived from his recent attendance at the French autumn manoeuvres. He was enormously impressed by the Maginot Line, which, he was informed, required only 100,000 men to garrison, leaving a large reserve for the field army. 'When the French realise that we cannot commit ourselves to send an Expeditionary Force,' he noted on his return, 'they should be all the more induced to accelerate the extension of the Maginot Line to the sea.' He told Liddell Hart that the French agreed with the latter's arguments in articles in *The Times* that two mechanised divisions would be far more valuable as a British reinforcement than four infantry divisions.[13] Both men evaded the real issue, which was that without a definite *political* commitment there would be neither mechanised nor infantry divisions ready to send in an emergency.

Hore-Belisha's memorandum on the role of the army, which was presented to the Cabinet early in December 1937, was entirely Liddell Hart's draft, even to the phrasing. The War Minister, though grateful, was understandably becoming sensitive to the accusation that he was a mere mouthpiece for an *eminence grise*.[14] When, on 22 December 1937, the Cabinet considered Sir Thomas Inskip's proposals for the defence programme as a whole, there was no serious challenge to a definitive statement which placed a possible Continental commitment last in order of the army's priorities. If an expeditionary force had to be sent overseas in a crisis its most likely destination henceforth was deemed to be an 'Eastern' theatre, i.e. the defence of Egypt against an Italian attack from Libya. What chiefly pleased ministers about Inskip's proposals for the army, given their profound emotional aversion to a Continental commitment, was the prospect of considerable savings on stores and equipment. There would be, for example, a saving of some £14 million in capital cost on the field force. Operations against a second-class opponent outside Europe would require a lower scale of reserves, particularly in the provision of tanks and heavy guns. Hore-Belisha concurred in these reductions because he accepted that the overriding priority was the development of anti-aircraft defences at home. Like other ministers, he did not at this time give sufficient weight to Inskip's warning that:

> If France were again to be in danger of being overrun by land armies, a situation might arise when, as in the last war, we had to improvise an army to assist her. Should this happen, the Government of the day would most certainly be criticised for having neglected to provide against so obvious a contingency.[15]

In the early weeks of 1938 Hore-Belisha drove an unwilling General Staff to draw up a new organisation for the army in the light of its revised priorities. The General Staff, and in particular the CIGS, Lord Gort, and his new director of Military Operations and Intelligence, Major General Henry Pownall were less than enthusiastic about this task because they believed the 'limited liability' policy to be both illusory and dangerous: war with Germany on the Continent was becoming ever more likely and an expeditionary force must be prepared in advance; it would be criminal to send out troops ill trained and under-equipped; and in practice – whatever politicians might say in peacetime – it would be impossible to limit Britain's liability to a hard-pressed ally in war. On 28 February, only a month after taking office, Pownall was moved to record one of many diatribes against the War Minister in his diary:

> He has an amazing conceit, thinking himself in the direct line of descent with Cardwell and Haldane in matters of Army organisation. He knows nothing about it – even in his service in the RASC he seems to have acquired no military knowledge at all – and he doesn't seem to listen and he will not read what is put before him. Impossible to educate, thinking he knows when he doesn't know, impatient, subject to a lot of improper outside influence, ambitious, an advertiser and self-seeker – what can we do with him? And to think that he classes himself

with Haldane as a reformer!! It would be funny if it were not so lamentable and dangerous.

Senior War Office officials also resented being harangued by Hore-Belisha to accelerate the rearmament programme when in fact, as a consequence of the army's revised priorities, they had been ordered by the Treasury to cut expenditure by £82 million over the next two years. Pownall recorded sourly that Hore-Belisha 'has no idea of how to get people to work for him. Ginger is sometimes needed by everyone, but we shall get no further if he limits himself to cracking the whip.'[16]

Unfortunately this metaphorical 'cracking of the whip' was becoming, in the spring of 1938, a substitute for practical reforms as the War Minister's energy appeared to diminish after the early burst of activity.

Several explanations may be suggested for this change of tempo. First, Hore-Belisha remained acutely conscious of the risks he had taken in 'purging' the high command and had literally worked and worried himself into a state of exhaustion. Secondly, the army's low priority in rearmament and the virtual abandonment of a Continental commitment afforded the minister very little political leverage in the Cabinet – where the War Office's difficulties seldom elicited much sympathy anyway. Thirdly, as the Liddell Hart *Memoirs* make abundantly clear, the new military team at the War Office – even those like Gort and Adam whom Liddell Hart regarded as friends and allies – were bitterly opposed to Hore-Belisha's association with an outsider. They became obstructive towards new proposals, suspecting, often correctly, that they derived from Liddell Hart. For his part, Hore-Belisha was increasingly disappointed at the lack of reforming zeal shown by his new team, particularly Gort, but knew that another purge was impossible. After all the press publicity about dynamic 'new brooms' he was clearly stuck with them. This surely explains why he gradually allowed the partnership with Liddell Hart to dissolve in 1938, though, unfortunately for both men, the generals remained convinced that the minister was still 'in a journalist's pocket'.

Though Hore-Belisha's difficulties at the War Office were increasing, his public reputation remained high. He was adept at gaining press coverage for the army and himself, and in a rather drab period his flamboyant figure was a gift to the cartoonists. His first Army Estimates speech, on 10 March 1938, was a personal triumph. His cautious exposition of the army's revised priorities was almost universally applauded, since very few politicians – or soldiers – relished involvement in another European war. Even Hitler's absorption of Austria (the *Anschluss)* on the very day of Hore-Belisha's speech failed to ring warning bells regarding Britain's military unpreparedness.

But Hore-Belisha's popularity derived mainly – and deservedly – from his passionate endeavours to make the army a more humane, honourable and respected profession. The army, as he neatly put it, should be 'a part of the nation, not apart from the nation'. In his first year in office he could justly boast of improvements in recruiting, the removal of numerous petty restrictions on the soldier's liberty and better terms of service. There would, for example, be progressive increases in pay, special proficiency pay, and increased family allowances. He displayed great concern for the soldiers' health and diet, and secured maximum publicity from the appointment of Sir Isadore Salmon, MP, managing director of J. Lyons & Co., as honorary catering adviser to the army.[17] These measures, and Hore-Belisha's obvious relish in visiting military establishments, where he chatted and drank beer with ordinary soldiers, won him a national reputation as 'the soldier's friend'. His habit of by-passing formalities inevitably created some enemies among officers who felt snubbed, while his critics unfairly alleged that he was only out for cheap personal publicity. For the moment, however, he was riding high.

In the late summer of 1938, however, Hore-Belisha's handling of the Sandys affair, or 'Sandys storm', cast doubt on his political judgement. Duncan Sandys, a young Conservative MP and son-in-law of Sir Winston Churchill, was a second lieutenant in a Territorial anti-aircraft unit. He obtained from the adjutant disturbing information about the inadequacy of the air defences, including full details of the emergency plan for the defence of London, which were highly secret. Towards the end of June he informed Hore-Belisha that he intended to raise the matter in a parliamentary question unless the War Minister could contradict the information, which of course he knew to be impossible. Instead of talking to Sandys himself, Hore-Belisha consulted the Prime Minister and accepted his advice that Sandys should be interviewed by the Attorney General. The latter unwisely threatened the MP with the Official Secrets Act. Within a few days the affair had got out of hand, the House of Commons setting up both a select committee and a committee of privileges while Hore-Belisha was establishing a military court of inquiry. Gort was furious with Hore-Belisha for exposing him unnecessarily to the hostile questioning of the three Labour members of the select committee, one of their first questions being 'I suppose you dislike politicians?'. Gort's veracity was also queried, and it was wrongly assumed that he favoured severe punishment for Sandys and his informant. The select committee eventually reported on 28 September, during a more momentous crisis: it criticised Sandys for the provocative way he had raised the issue, the Attorney General for his inept handling of Sandys, and Hore-Belisha for failing to postpone the court of inquiry once parliamentary proceedings had begun.[18]

Liddell Hart warned Hore-Belisha as early in the Sandys affair as 3 July that he had made a bad mistake in alienating Churchill, and had also, in effect, delivered himself into the hands of the General Staff. In the autumn he was disturbed to find that the War Minister appeared complacent about the effects of the Sandys case and also naively assumed that Gort was loyal to him. Pownall's running commentary on the affair in his diary shows that Liddell Hart's anxiety was well founded. Pownall was probably correct in concluding that Hore-Belisha and Sandys could easily have avoided a showdown had they not been intent on achieving one.[19]

Though its importance was somewhat obscured at the time by the Sandys case, the late summer of 1938 witnessed the culmination of one of Hore-Belisha's most significant and, lasting, reforms, namely the radical restructuring of the system of officer appointments, promotions and tenure of posts. The officer career structure had been badly affected by the rapid demobilisation of the mass armies after 1918, and by the protective attitudes and military 'trade unionism' caused by subsequent reductions. In short, the officer corps became top-heavy as senior officers of First World War vintage stayed on to earn a maximum pension; key appointments were filled on the principle of Buggins's turn; promotion in the middle ranks was distressingly slow; and discontent was exacerbated by the deplorable practice of placing officers on half pay between appointments. Prompted by Liddell Hart. – and this must be noted as one of *his* greatest achievements as an indirect reformer – Hore-Belisha introduced the following measures:

1. Reduction of the retiring age of generals and lieutenant-generals from 67 to 60, and of major-generals from 62 to 57.
2. Reduction of command and staff appointments from a four- to a three-year tenure.
3. Abolition of the system of half pay.
4. Introduction of time-promotion, so that officers should be promoted captain after eight years' service and major after 17.

On 5 August the *London Gazette* contained the names of nearly 2,500 officers in 20 closely printed pages. It was the largest single list of promotions in British military history.[20]

Although the Munich crisis did not cause Hore-Belisha to rebel against Chamberlain's policy to the point of resignation, as it did Duff Cooper to his eternal credit, it did alert him to the dreadful fact of the army's impotence and first caused him to question the feasibility of the 'limited liability' policy. His contemporary diary entries make clear his unease at Chamberlain's personal diplomacy, which had the effect of 'bereaving Czechoslovakia of its power to exist'. He realised too that Britain was powerless to implement her guarantee to the rump of Czechoslovakia, and feared that the proposed solution 'might only be a postponement of the evil day'. While he accepted that pressure on Czechoslovakia to yield territory in order to prevent war was unavoidable, given the state of British defences, he drew the moral that Britain must now rearm vigorously.[21]

The Munich crisis also caused Hore-Belisha's reputation to plummet in that the mobilisation of the anti-aircraft defences revealed to a wider public what was already common knowledge in official circles, namely the capital's virtual defencelessness against air attack. The War Minister was only to a small extent culpable, but he had given hostages to fortune by exaggerating the number of anti-aircraft guns available. Hore-Belisha responded to criticism by demanding 600 more 3.7in. guns and 1,000 two-pounders in defiance of General Staff advice. In November Sir Edward Spears, MP, circulated a brochure of complaints about the anti-aircraft deployment to a number of fellow members which Pownall took to be an effort to shake Hore-Belisha out of office.[22]

Political discontent with Hore-Belisha's performance at the War Office culminated in a widely publicised 'Junior Ministers' Revolt' in mid-December, whose ringleader was R. S. Hudson, Secretary of the Department of Overseas Trade. Hore-Belisha was particularly distressed to find his trusted Parliamentary Under Secretary, Lord Strathcona, among the malcontents. Rather like a medieval peasant rising, the revolt was ill organised and lacking in clear objectives. Chamberlain quashed it by dismissing Strathcona and reassuring Hore-Belisha that he had done extremely well; indeed, that he considered him the best Secretary of State for War since Haldane. Hore-Belisha told Liddell Hart a few months later that his fate had trembled in the balance. Chamberlain had spoken smooth words but was not to be relied upon. Hore-Belisha had 'pulled a gun on him' by making it clear that if he fell the Prime Minister would also be involved, especially over his rejection of Hore-Belisha's proposal to set up a Ministry of Supply, which had been one of the charges of the War Minister's critics. Hore-Belisha realised by early 1939 that Churchill, whom he admired, was the rising leader, and was now sorry that he had antagonised him.[23]

Early in December 1938 the role of the army again came under review and the General Staff impressed on the War Minister that if war broke out in western Europe the expeditionary force would certainly be dispatched, despite its unpreparedness, and there would be a first-class scandal. Gort pointed out that the army's share of the £2,000 million defence allocation was only £277 million and of this only £78 million was intended for the field force. Hore-Belisha, already depressed by his failure to secure a Ministry of Supply or any real increase of tempo in rearmament, skilfully presented the army's viewpoint to his generally unsympathetic Cabinet colleagues, omitting the strategic arguments for a Continental commitment which they hated to hear. By early January 1939, however, Hore-Belisha had abandoned his pretence that he was not challenging government policy on the army's priorities, and now argued openly that the concept of limited liability must be abandoned.

On 2 February the War Minister recorded a major success: the Committee of Imperial Defence approved the provision of complete equipment and reserves for the four regular divisions of the field force and also for the first four of the 12 Territorial divisions. Even at this stage the Cabinet insisted on some petty economies by postponing planned dates of embarkation (hence reducing the standard of stores and reserves), and by slightly lowering the state of readiness of the Territorial divisions. Hore-Belisha's valiant fight was, however, rewarded by an additional £55 million for the regular field force. Shortly after the Cabinet had finally approved the preparation of a small field force for European war in mid-February, Pownall visited Aldershot, where he was much comforted to see a demonstration of new weapons at last beginning to appear in bulk. 'The Army,' he recorded proudly, 'is coming to life again, no longer a "depressed class".'[24] For this improvement, though belated and still on a modest scale, Hore-Belisha deserved much of the credit.

In presenting his second Army Estimates, on 8 March 1939, Hore-Belisha found himself defending a role for the field force virtually identical to that so courageously but vainly advocated by his predecessor, Duff Cooper. The War Minister now admitted that the position regarding a Continental commitment had changed drastically since the previous March. Although, he stressed, there was no binding commitment to

France, if Britain *did* become involved in war her effort would not be half-hearted or based upon any concept of limited liability. In describing what was in truth still only a *potential* field force, Hore-Belisha indulged in characteristic hyperbole. Whereas, he said, the BEF created by Haldane before 1914 had comprised only six regular infantry divisions and one cavalry division, the force which he was organising would consist of four regular infantry and two armoured divisions supported by 13 Territorial divisions, making a grand total of *19* divisions. The War Minister gained considerable political capital and kudos from his impressive reference to 19 divisions, but the General Staff was well aware that several of them scarcely existed except on paper.

Hore-Belisha was on firmer ground in announcing further reforms designed to make the army better fed, better housed, better educated, better paid and, not least important, better trained, with trade qualifications for civil employment after leaving the service. The practical success of his social reforms was manifest in the increased flow of recruits both for the ranks and for commissions.[25]

In the moment of triumph, with the press on the whole applauding his Estimates speech, Hore-Belisha wrote to express his gratitude to Liddell Hart for inspiring so many of his reforms. He ended with a light-hearted word of advice. 'Stick to your last and don't become that most confused personality, known as a politician.'[26] He was shortly, however, to embark on a campaign to lay the basis for a greatly expanded army which would dismay his former mentor. In March and April 1939 Hore-Belisha was primarily responsible for introducing two measures which, in stark contrast to previous assumptions of a small but mechanised army, envisaged a national force approaching the scale of the First World War and consisting largely of poorly equipped infantry divisions.

The first of these dramatic decisions was announced to both Houses of Parliament on 29 March. On the previous day Halifax impressed on Hore-Belisha that it was imperative to give some clear sign of Britain's determination to resist aggression. The War Minister now favoured some form of compulsory service, but the Prime Minister had recently repeated his pledge that conscription would not be introduced in peacetime. On the spur of the moment, and without consulting the Army Council, Hore-Belisha suggested doubling the Territorial Army so as to take full advantage of the recent upsurge in volunteering. Chamberlain jumped at the proposal and agreed that it should be announced immediately. The plan was to increase the peace establishment of the TA from 130,000 to its war strength of 170,000 and then double it to set a target of 340,000. This would be achieved by allowing all units to over-recruit beyond their establishment to provide the cadres for duplicate units. This was a spectacular piece of window-dressing but its practical implications were staggering. The existing drill halls were nowhere near adequate in number or capacity; there was a great shortage of equipment, uniforms and weapons; and perhaps worst of all, the force could not be trained without drawing the bulk of the instructors from already hard-pressed regular units. The service chiefs accepted this *fait accompli* philosophically, but they were not amused.[27]

In April 1939 two very different pressures forced Chamberlain to accept the necessity for some form of conscription. French pressure for such a manoeuvre as a touchstone of British determination to resist Germany had grown steadily since December 1938. The other source of pressure was domestic, namely the government's obsessive fear of a devastating attack from the air and its wish to guard against this threat by manning at least a portion of the anti-aircraft defences round the clock. Chamberlain suggested that the Territorials might keep their normal daily jobs and man their guns and searchlights at night for periods of three to six months, but the General Staff advised that this was absolutely impracticable and Hore-Belisha agreed. He decided that conscription was the only solution to the anti-aircraft manpower problem, bearing in mind that the War Office was simultaneously trying to reinforce the overseas garrisons and build up the field force. He became exasperated to the brink of resignation by Chamberlain's prevarication and certainly risked his political career by forcing the issue. At the end of April the government introduced the Military Training Bill and rapidly forced it through Parliament despite fierce opposition from the Labour Party. Its main provision was that 200,000 conscripts (politely termed 'militiamen') would be embodied for six months. After three months' initial training, batches of 20,000 would take over the air defence duties for three-month periods. The remainder not required for air defence would be trained, where possible, with regular army units. Conscripts would be employed only on home defence duties in peacetime. Despite immense difficulties in finding uniforms and tents the first batch of 30,000 militiamen reported for duty on 15 July.[28]

In the short term the introduction of conscription served only to exacerbate rather than solve the War Office's problems of raising divisions for war, since it set impossible targets for all kinds of equipment, uniforms, weapons and accommodation. In political terms the gesture doubtless helped to cement the belated Anglo-French entente, but there is no evidence whatever that it deterred Hitler: on the contrary it may even have encouraged him to attack Poland while his western opponents were still disorganised. It is, however, arguable – and Pownall penned this opinion – that some form of compulsion was unavoidable and it was preferable to get the worst of the chaos over before the outbreak of war.[29] From this viewpoint, and it is a plausible one, Hore-Belisha performed one of his greatest services as War Minister by pushing through the measure when he did against the bitter opposition of the Prime Minister and some of his Cabinet colleagues. It is noteworthy that even Sir John Simon, who had resigned as Home Secretary in 1916 in opposition to conscription, became convinced in April 1939 that Hore-Belisha's case was unanswerable.[30]

By the summer of 1939 the atmosphere at the War Office had become extremely strained as frantic preparations were made to organise and equip a field force for the Continent while simultaneously laying the foundation for a national army of First World War magnitude. In these conditions harmonious relations between the War Minister and his principal professional advisers were essential, but, with a few notable exceptions such as General Adam, they deteriorated rapidly as war approached. Gort and Pownall especially resented Hore-Belisha making high level appointments without consulting them, particularly his recall of General Ironside from Gibraltar to become Inspector General of Overseas Forces and – it was widely assumed – commander-in-chief designate of the field force. Pownall suspected, probably wrongly, that Hore-Belisha was looking for an opportunity to give Gort an overseas command in order to get him out of the War Office, while Gort was now so hostile towards his political master that he shunned him as much as possible, employing Adam as his deputy. On his part Hore-Belisha now realised too late that Gort was simply not intelligent enough to be CIGS, but there was little if any personal animosity on his side. Hore-Belisha's military assistant at this time, Major General J. C. Haydon, believed that the War Minister and his CIGS were so different in outlook that a genuine partnership was impossible:

> On the one hand, Gort was very conservative, inclined to be rather rigid and austere, reserved and completely *English* in his attitude. He was absorbed by his soldiering and – apart from the sea – I do not know that he had many other serious interests or enthusiasms in life. I do not think he ever really understood politicians.
>
> In contrast, Hore-Belisha was 'continental' in outlook; a fluent French speaker, inclined to be flamboyant; at times rather ebullient. Essentially a warm character, ready to expand and be at his entertaining best when in the company of those he knew to be friends. He possessed an acute sense of the value of publicity which he enjoyed while Gort abhorred it.

Against Pownall's jaundiced view, however, Haydon did not believe that Hore-Belisha sought publicity purely for himself. Haydon perceived the tragic aspect in the unhappy relationship between two fervent patriots who were temperamentally incompatible.[31]

One unfortunate consequence of this disharmony at the highest levels of the War Office was that the appointment of the commander-in-chief of the field force and his senior staff officers was deferred until the day on which war was declared. Ironside had such good reason to expect the appointment that he went to Aldershot and began to assemble his personal staff. General Sir John Dill, however, also had strong claims to the post. In the event Hore-Belisha by-passed both and selected Gort: a decision congenial to both men but, in Haydon's view, one determined by merit rather than personal considerations. The War Minister had long admired Ironside's dynamism and outspokenness and, despite his reputation for intrigue and indiscretion, pressed for his appointment as CIGS. There was some opposition to Ironside's appointment in the newly constituted War Cabinet, but with Churchill's support he was approved. In retrospect these choices were soon to appear ill-judged. Gort was an adequate commander in some respects but Ironside would probably have been better. Gort took Pownall with him as his chief of staff and so deprived the War Office of the two men familiar with the plans for the field force. Ironside struggled manfully to do his duty as CIGS, but, incredibly, he had never before served in the War Office and by his own admission was not suited to the task. He too began to record contemptuous opinions of Hore-Belisha in his diary. Dill, who was widely regarded in the army as the obvious and almost ideal choice for CIGS, had to be satisfied for the time being with a corps command in France.[32]

Though he became a member of the War Cabinet, Hore-Belisha's reputation was not enhanced during the opening weeks of hostilities. This was partly due to the fact that there was now less scope – or opportunity for publicity – in improving the soldiers' comfort and welfare, which had been his real burning interest. His grasp of such matters as military organisation and strategy had never been his strong point and he had relied heavily upon Liddell Hart's guidance in these areas. It was also unfortunate for him that the army – in contrast to the Royal Navy, now once again under Churchill's dynamic leadership – seemed to be doing very little. The anticipated *Luftwaffe* assault on London had not occurred, while, from the public's viewpoint, the Allies appeared to be deplorably passive on the western front while Poland was being overrun.

The episode which provided the pretext for Hore-Belisha's enemies to close in for the kill, namely the notorious 'pill-box affair', seems doubly ironic in retrospect. First, it is clear from the detailed accounts of two senior officers who accompanied him on his tour of the field force, Francis de Guingand and John Kennedy, that Hore-Belisha was genuinely trying to help Gort.[33] Secondly, at the very time that the frontier defences became a fatal bone of contention between the War Minister and the generals, Gamelin was persuading the Supreme War Council that in event of a German attack in the west the Allied left wing, including the field force, would abandon its lines and advance into Belgium.

On 18 and 19 November Hore-Belisha was taken on a conducted tour of the British front. He was favourably impressed by the troops' good spirits but correctly perceived that the Allied defences were weak, as indeed General Dill, commanding 1st Corps, confirmed. Gort treated Hore-Belisha to his peculiar brand of schoolboy humour, making him climb a muddy bank and keeping him shivering in a howling gale while he explained in exhaustive detail First World War actions fought in that area. When they at last got inside a château Gort flung open a window, and when they emerged into the rain he shouted jovially, 'Isn't it a grand day!' The fastidious politician was given bully-beef sandwiches and ribbed so unmercifully about them by Gort that even Pownall was embarrassed. Hore-Belisha bore all this stoically and without complaint, but he did come away with the impression that the defences were being constructed too slowly and in the wrong way. As he confided to Brigadier Kennedy:

> There ought to be hundreds of pill-boxes, every hundred yards if necessary. Pakenham-Walsh [the Chief Engineer of the field force] had an enormous file with six designs in it, and no pill-boxes have been built except two, although they have been in that position a month or more.

On his return the War Minister informed the Army Council of his disquiet about the scarcity of pill-boxes and the slow rate of progress; and at a second meeting on 24 November he mentioned that some Dominion representatives who had been to

France had criticised the inadequacy of the defences to the Prime Minister. As de Guingand's contemporary note reveals, Hore-Belisha became somewhat obsessed by the pill-box issue, 'but his whole attitude was one of endeavouring to help rather than one of criticism'.[34] In handling the affair, Hore-Belisha made some inept and tactless moves which might have irritated a more benevolently disposed commander-in-chief than Gort. But, given Hore-Belisha's prompt gesture of repentance, the matter could easily have been amicably resolved had he not been dealing with such hypersensitive and bitter opponents as Gort, Pownall and Pakenham-Walsh. These officers resented any criticism at all, since they believed they were doing their best in adverse conditions which the War Minister had totally failed to grasp. But his particular 'crimes' (in Pownall's term) were that he had inaccurately presented the facts to the Army Council, discussed the matter in Cabinet after Ironside had left, sent a *verbal* reprimand to Gort through a subordinate officer (Pakenham-Walsh), and dispatched the CIGS to inspect the defences on the authority of the War Cabinet. Perhaps most galling of all to GHQ was Hore-Belisha's mistaken impression that the French were setting an example in the construction of pill-boxes and could serve as a model for the British.[35]

At the end of November Ironside visited the field force to assess the justice of Hore-Belisha's criticisms. Initially he probably had some sympathy with them, but he found GHQ and the front-line commanders seething with rage at the War Minister's charges and returned wholly converted to Gort's viewpoint to report adversely on Hore-Belisha to the King and the Prime Minister. Earlier, at Hore-Belisha's first mention of the subject, the CIGS had ominously warned him to be careful how he dealt with his C-in-C. 'He was put in by the King and must not be monkeyed about.'[36] On 2 December Hore-Belisha wrote to Gort in emollient terms assuring him that no criticism had been intended and that the incident was now closed. This olive branch was ignored.[37]

Whether or not Gort actively encouraged him or merely acquiesced, it is now clear that his chief of staff, Henry Pownall, acted as the 'hatchet man' who was determined to cut Hore-Belisha down. In late November Pownall visited London and poured his poisonous views of Hore-Belisha into the receptive ears of Lord Hardinge, the King's private secretary, P. J. Grigg, the new PUS [Permanent Under Secretary] at the War Office, Sir Horace Wilson, head of the civil service, and Sir Maurice Hankey, formerly Secretary of the CID and the Cabinet and now a member of the War Cabinet. After Ironside's visit Pownall wrote to Grigg to ensure that the CIGS would have to report to the Prime Minister, and persuaded Lord Munster (Gort's ADC and no friend of Hore-Belisha's) to ensure that the King became involved. Some idea of the venom of Pownall's sustained diatribe against the War Minister in his diary can be gathered from the following extract:

Tiny [Ironside] talks of 'not kicking a man when he's down', it's no good being Old School Tie with H-B, you have to fight him with his own weapons. One crushes a snake even if it does happen to be on the ground.

Pownall then dispatched a list of Hore-Belisha's 'Major Crimes' to Grigg and to one of the King's ADCs. Early in November the King visited GHQ and, according to Pownall, said he realised that Hore-Belisha must go. At dinner the King actually asked Pownall who should replace Hore-Belisha at the War Office, and his suggestion of Malcolm MacDonald seemed to meet with royal approval. Finally, in mid-December, the Prime Minister visited GHQ and Pownall impressed on him that the generals lacked confidence in the War Minister. 'I have no doubt,' wrote Pownall on Chamberlain's departure, 'that the Prime Minister will have H-B out of the War Office at the earliest opportunity. Let us hope that that will come soon.'[38]

On 14 December, just before leaving for France to visit GHQ, Chamberlain saw Hore-Belisha and asked him if he had confidence in Gort and Ironside. According to Hore-Belisha's diary note Chamberlain said, 'I had only to tell him if I wanted to make a change.' Hore-Belisha altruistically answered that he had faith in both generals. After his visit to France the Prime Minister summoned Hore-Belisha to another interview on 20 December, told him that feeling against him was still strong at GHQ, and advised him to be careful because some people were out to make trouble for him. Hore-Belisha pressed vainly for details and rather naively concluded that he had made a good impression, noting, 'The Prime Minister was extremely nice and ended by saying that he had complete confidence in me, adding, "You have great courage and do not mind being criticised".'[39]

It seems, however, that Chamberlain was perturbed by Hore-Belisha's air of complacency and failure to take the hint of his unpopularity, and subsequently decided, towards the end of December, that it would be advisable to transfer him to another office in order to appease the generals. Chamberlain wished to mitigate the blow to Hore-Belisha's pride by offering him the Ministry of Information, a particularly important assignment just then and a move which would not necessarily appear as a demotion. On 1 January Lord Halifax told his private secretary, Sir Alexander Cadogan, of the proposed change and the latter noted, 'This blinding – and exquisitely funny. I hadn't time to get my breath, but on thinking it over, came to the conclusion that Jew control of our propaganda would be a major disaster.' On 3 January Cadogan described the plan as 'catastrophic', and the next day he advised Halifax to suggest to the Prime Minister that H-B be got rid of altogether. 'He will get the worst of both worlds if he merely shifts him.' Halifax accepted Cadogan's advice and told Chamberlain shortly before he was due to see Hore-Belisha on 4 January that the Foreign Office objected to having the latter at the MOI. It would have a bad effect both because Hore-Belisha was a Jew and because his methods would detract from British prestige. Chamberlain was placed in an awkward position, because he had already offered the War Office to Oliver Stanley. An hour before his appointment with Hore-Belisha he accepted Halifax's advice and decided to offer him the Board of Trade – a definite step down from the War Office.[40]

A painful interview took place in which the Prime Minister was unable to give the astonished Hore-Belisha a clear explanation for his apparent *volte face*. Churchill had flown to France that morning, and Hore-Belisha, regarding him as a friend, telephoned him for advice. He was shattered to learn that Chamberlain had revealed his proposed changes to Churchill that morning. Hore-Belisha consequently rejected Churchill's advice to take the Board of Trade and composed a dignified letter of resignation dated 5 January.[41]

According to Cadogan's diary Chamberlain was worried about the resultant press and parliamentary 'pother over Horeb', and blamed Halifax, saying he would not have set things in motion had he realised at the start that he couldn't offer Hore-Belisha the MOI. But according to Iain Macleod's biography, Chamberlain was relieved when Hore-Belisha refused the Board of Trade. Ironside, though not, it seems, directly implicated in Hore-Belisha's fall and surprised at the news, recorded a reaction that was common among the generals:

> Changing horses in mid-stream is always a bad thing, but I must say that I had a feeling of intense relief on the whole. The man had utterly failed in war to run his show and we should have had a disaster. He is much better out of it.[42]

Hore-Belisha decided to make a dignified rather than a combative resignation speech in the interests of national unity. For a few weeks the newspapers buzzed with speculation about the causes of his sudden fall until the controversy was eclipsed by far more important events in Scandinavia and France. He was puzzled at the way he had been ousted from office, so soon after receiving emphatic assurances of the Prime Minister's confidence in him, but was mercifully unaware of the range and bitterness of the opposition. He correctly suspected that Gort and his influence at the Palace, rather than Ironside, had been responsible for his fall; and, when he told Liddell Hart that he thought Pakenham-Walsh was also hostile, Liddell Hart pointed out that Pakenham-Walsh was a friend of Churchill, whom he had advised in preparing his *Marlborough* volumes.[43] This was just one instance of Hore-Belisha's unhappy knack of making enemies in influential positions.[44]

An impartial judge must surely conclude from the cool perspective permitted by the passage of 40 years that although Hore-Belisha had made mistakes and revealed limitations, he was much 'more sinned against than sinning'. His removal as an immediate result of the tragi-comic pill-box affair now seems all the more unjust when we know that it virtually ended his political career, for apart from a brief tenure of the Ministry of National Insurance in 1945 he was never again to hold high political office. He died suddenly in France in February 1957 with his great political ambitions largely unfulfilled.

Hore-Belisha was both lucky and unlucky in the timing of his tenure of the War Office. Lucky because he was appointed at just about the time when the likelihood of war began to arouse the public to the army's utter unpreparedness and so provided an impetus to challenge the generals' inertia and the Treasury's stranglehold. On the other hand, nearly 20 years of neglect could not be remedied overnight, and the War Minister was inevitably – though unjustly – blamed when shocking weaknesses were exposed, as in the anti-aircraft defences in the scares of September 1938 and April 1939.

Secondly, as this chapter has stressed, Hore-Belisha's political base was extremely weak. As an unorthodox, flamboyant National Liberal he cut a strange figure in Chamberlain's largely Conservative government and was essentially dependent on the Prime Minister's personal support. There were always political cliques opposed to him, as the 'Junior Ministers' Revolt' revealed, and he added to his enemies while at the War Office by his personality, methods and measures. His use of Liddell Hart as an unofficial adviser was, on balance, a definite benefit for the army, but it was probably more responsible than any other factor for the bitter antagonism which he stirred up on the part of many senior officers. In the end he was left pathetically exposed to enemies in the army, the civil service and the Foreign Office. Considerable royal influence was also brought to bear on behalf of Lord Gort by the latter's friend, Lord Hardinge. It is hard to avoid the conclusion that even had the pill-box incident not occurred, or been smoothed over, Hore-Belisha could not have survived much longer at the War Office.

In retrospect it is clear that Hore-Belisha staked his reputation as a military reformer on the new team of senior officers which he appointed to replace the 'old guard' in the winter of 1937. Some of his (and Liddell Hart's) best selections could not be fitted in; others became tired and ill or lacked drive; and others became antagonistic. Yet it would be quite wrong to leave the impression that he was incapable of working amicably with all senior soldiers. Quite the contrary; as the recollections of Generals Adam, de Guingand, Haydon and Kennedy all show, he could inspire loyalty and devotion in those who worked very closely with him. As Sir John Kennedy wrote:

> I had never seen the side of his character that caused him to be disliked by so many soldiers…
>
> He was extremely kind to me; for all his fads and affectations, I never found him anything but easy to deal with. And I am in no doubt that the Army was deep in his debt.[45]

Hore-Belisha's outstanding achievement lay in improving the conditions of service for officers and other ranks and in bringing the army and the nation closer together. Disgruntled generals accused him of trying to 'democratise the army', but as he interpreted it that was surely a charge to be proud of. So long as Hore-Belisha held office the army was seldom out of the news, and after his downfall he was long remembered with affection by thousands of ordinary soldiers and their families. For these accomplishments, and for creating the foundations of the national citizen army of 1939–45, his name is deservedly linked with Haldane's as an outstandingly successful War Minister.

References

1. Brian Bond, *Liddell Hart: a Study of his Military Thought*, (London: Cassell, 1977), p. 108.
2. R. Macleod and D. Kelly (eds.), *The Ironside Diaries, 1937–1940*,(London: Constable, 1962), p. 24.
3. J. R. Colville, *Man of Valour: Field Marshal Lord Gort, V.C.*, (London: Collins, 1972), p. 74, and F. de Guingand, *Operation Victory*, (London: Hodder & Stoughton, 1947), pp. 19–23. For revealing comments on Hore-Belisha's character and tastes see Robert Rhodes James (ed.), *Chips: the Diaries of Sir Henry Channon*, (London: Penguin Books, 1970), pp. 34,152, 193, 224, 279–83,289.
4. B. H. Liddell Hart, *Memoirs*, II, (London: Cassell, 1965). All references are to this volume.
5. Liddell Hart papers, Centre for Military Archives, King's College, London, 11/H-B 1937/59 and 11/H-B 1938/91.
6. R. J. Minney, *The Private Papers of Hore-Belisha*, (London: Collins, 1960), p. 35, and see also N. H. Gibbs, *Grand Strategy, I*, (London: HMSO, 1976), p. 65.
7. Liddell Hart papers, 11/H-B 1937/14, Talk with Hore-Belisha, 21 August 1937. Liddell Hart, *Memoirs*, pp. 11, 43, 55.
8. Minney, p. 66.
9. Liddell Hart papers, 11/H-B 1937/114, 115, 118, 120, 127.
10. Colville, p. 81.
11. Liddell Hart, *Memoirs*, p. 82.
12. See Bond, *Liddell Hart*, chapter 4.
13. Minney, pp. 56–9; Liddell Hart, *Memoirs*, p. 30.
14. Liddell Hart, *Memoirs*, p. 75.
15. Gibbs, *Grand Strategy*, pp. 467–71.
16. Brian Bond (ed.), *Chief of Staff: the Diaries of Lieutenant General Sir Henry Pownall, Vol. 1,1933–1940*, (London: Leo Cooper, 1972), p. 136, and diary entry, 28 March 1938. All published quotations are from vol. I. The original diaries may be consulted in the Centre for Military Archives, King's College, London.
17. Minney, pp. 93–6; Colville, p. 91.
18. Minney, pp. 122–28; Colville, pp. 97–9.
19. Liddell Hart papers, 11/H-B 1938/146, 147, 152. Bond (ed.), *Chief of Staff*, pp. 151–54, 165, and Pownall diary entries, 20 June-18 July 1938, *passim.*
20. Liddell Hart, *The Defence of Britain*, (London: Faber, 1939), pp. 326–33. Minney, pp. 131–32.
21. Minney, pp. 138–46.
22. Bond (ed.), *Chief of Staff*, pp. 147–48,165–66. Diary entry, 7 November 1938.
23. Minney, pp. 161–64. Liddell Hart papers, 11/H-B 1939/3. See also Iain Macleod, *Neville Chamberlain*, (London: Muller, 1961), p. 284.
24. Gibbs, pp. 508–13. Minney, pp. 170–72. Colville, pp. 119–21. Bond (ed.), *Chief of Staff*, pp. 172–75,186–90.
25. Minney, pp. 173–82. Liddell Hart, *Memoirs*, pp. 223–24.
26. Minney, p. 184.
27. *Ibid.*, pp. 187–88. P. Dennis, *Decision by Default*, (London: Routledge & Kegan Paul, 1972), pp. 197–200. Lord Ismay, *Memoirs*, (London: Heinemann, 1960), p. 93. Bond (ed.), *Chief of Staff*, pp. 200–02.
28. P. Dennis, pp. 193–95, 211–25. Minney, pp. 191–98, 204–07.
29. Bond (ed.), *Chief of Staff*, p. 202.
30. Minney, p. 197.

31. Liddell Hart papers, 11/H-B 1939/11. Papers of Major General J. C. Haydon, Imperial War Museum 77/190/2c, Haydon to J. R. Colville, 29 January 1970. Colville, pp. 137–38. Bond (ed.), *Chief of Staff*, pp. 209–10.
32. Minney, pp. 229–31. Colville, p. 134. *Ironside Diaries*, pp. 93–4. Haydon papers, Haydon to Colville, 29 January 1970.
33. Liddell Hart papers, 11/H-B M/34, Note by F. de Guingand, and F. de Guingand, *Operation Victory*, pp. 38–42. Sir John Kennedy, *The Business of War*, (London: Hutchinson, 1957), pp. 33–9.
34. Liddell Hart papers, 11/H-B M/34.
35. Minney, pp. 257–64. Colville, pp. 157–65.
36. *Ironside Diaries*, pp. 164–67.
37. Liddell Hart papers, 11/H-B M/34 – a copy of Hore-Belisha's letter to Gort dated 2 December 1939 is appended to de Guingand's note.
38. Bond (ed.), *Chief of Staff*, pp. 256–68.
39. Minney, pp. 266–69.
40. I. Macleod, *Chamberlain*, pp. 285–86. D. Dilks (ed.), *The Diaries of Sir Alexander Cadogan*, (London: Cassell, 1971), pp. 241–44.
41. Minney, pp. 269–73.
42. *Cadogan Diaries*, pp. 243–44. Macleod, *Chamberlain*, p. 287. Colville, pp.163–65. *Ironside Diaries*, p. 194.
43. Liddell Hart papers, 11/H-B 1939/2, 8, 9.
44. Colville, p. 77, describes how Hore-Belisha antagonised the British military attaché in Paris, Colonel F. G. Beaumont Nesbitt, first by receiving the French War Minister, Daladier, while in his bath, and second by asking Beaumont Nesbitt's opinion of senior officers. In November 1939 the military attaché told Brigadier John Kennedy that it was good for his soul to meet Hore-Belisha occasionally; he disliked him so much that it was a very good exercise in self-control. See Kennedy, *The Business of War*, pp. 33–34.
45. Kennedy, *The Business of War*, pp. 149–51.

Part III
The Second World War

8

Britain's Field Force in France and Belgium, 1939–1940

The aim of this paper, originally prepared for a conference at Edinburgh University in 1995, was to show that there was much more of interest in the soldiers' experience of the 1939–1940 campaign in France and Belgium than its dramatic culmination at Dunkirk. In the 20 years that have elapsed since the conference, my impression is that authors and publishers are still obsessed with 'the Great Escape', largely at the expense of the preceding acts of the drama.

Here are just a few of the features which were highlighted as a result of my research. For the majority of British combatants it was the *Luftwaffe*'s almost total command of the skies which made the strongest impression. Chaos resulted when communications in every sense broke down; in physical terms the pathetic crowds of refugees packing the roads goes far to explain why orders were slow to arrive or could not be executed. The terrible weariness and hardship caused by the disorganised retreat were exacerbated by days of very hot weather during which water was often lacking. Two events which occurred a few days before Dunkirk that are generally remembered are the massacres of British prisoners by SS units at Le Paradis and Wormhoudt. Lastly, this account sketches the very varied experience of soldiers within the Dunkirk perimeter: a few recorded acts of indiscipline and selfishness but many more of gallantry and self-sacrifice.

The British Army's experience of war in France in 1939 and 1940 was strange and its culmination unexpected; months of inactive 'Phoney War' were followed by a sudden harsh awakening to the realities of *blitzkrieg*. Alan Bennett's play *Forty Years On* captures something of the public's ambivalent reactions to a tragi-comic campaign :

> Moggie: We're not winning in France are we?
> Hugh: Well, if we are, the sites of the victories are getting nearer and nearer.
>   Though why you expect me to know I can't imagine. I'm only in the Ministry
>   of Information and we're always the last to know.
> Nursie: It must be terribly difficult retreating. Fancy having to walk backwards
>   all that way![1]

The experience of the greater part of this inglorious campaign has been eclipsed in the historiography by its dramatic culmination in the evacuation from Dunkirk and the myths associated with that providential escape from even worse disaster. Most of the soldiers involved knew that it had been a catastrophe, yet the survivors were welcomed back as heroes. It was all very confusing.

The campaign had begun promisingly in September 1939 with the efficient shipment of the five regular divisions to France. These were all reasonably well-equipped and trained though defective in some crucial respects such as supporting aircraft and tanks. Major-General Bernard Montgomery's 3rd Division was probably the best, though even so in his *Memoirs* he was scathing about its weapons, miscellaneous transport and general preparedness for modern war.[2] A further eight Territorial Army divisions arrived in France between January and the end of April 1940. These were in general hastily improvised, with imported drafts from other units to complete establishments, short of regular officers and of varying quality. The best-trained was probably Major-General G. Le Q Martel's 50th (Northumbrian) Division, which was unique in being composed entirely of Territorial units; Lord Gort having wisely decided that each Territorial brigade should be given a stiffening of one regular battalion. A few regular officers later expressed resentment at this association, believing that they had been let down by ill-disciplined and under-trained Territorials who retreated too easily. Three of the Territorial Divisions – unofficially designated 'Labour Divisions' – were not equipped or trained to fight, but they were tragically swept into the maelstrom of the retreat and virtually annihilated. As a recent study sombrely concludes: no second line brigade survived after its first serious contact with the enemy; and none of the second line divisions imposed any significant delay on the German advance.[3] The sad fact was that the Field Force had not been equipped or trained for a fast-moving European war against a first class opponent and could not be fully ready in 1940. It was heavily dependent on the French high command and its strategy, and on fighting a static, defensive war not so very different from that of 1914–18.

Although the published sources for this campaign are vast, they are mostly deficient in dealing with the experience of war, especially from the viewpoint of the other ranks. The official history was published too soon after the event by an amateur, regimental historian and needs rewriting, but remains useful as a chronicle. David Divine, Richard Collier and others have published vivid popular accounts of Dunkirk, though Gregory Blaxland's history is much broader in scope and benefits from his personal experience as a subaltern in the Royal East Kent Regiment. Nicholas Harman injects a refreshingly critical approach, but his tone is polemical and his use of sources somewhat casual. Ronald Atkin's more recent study is based on an admirably wide range of interviews and personal recollections: it could scarcely be bettered as an impressionistic, descriptive survey but is less strong in putting the campaign in historical perspective.[4] There are numerous colourful and useful published memoirs by participants, including Ewan Butler and Selby Bradford, Bruce Shand, Anthony Rhodes and Christopher Seton-Watson, but most deal with the campaign of 1939–40 only as a first episode in their war – or indeed in their whole military career.[5]

As regards written but unpublished recollections, letters and diaries, the Imperial War Museum holds a huge collection which has been sampled for this paper. A few of these documents are of outstanding general interest, but many are understandably too detailed, personal and limited in scope. Some soldiers simply did not have a very interesting war or, if they did, lacked ability with the pen. Again, not surprisingly, a high proportion were from the support services (Royal Signals, Royal Army Ordnance Corps, Royal Army Service Corps etc) where there was a good standard of literacy, but these men mostly describe life in the rear areas where little combat was witnessed.

Of more direct relevance to the present theme was the Imperial War Museum's sound recordings project on Gort's Army. This extremely useful and under-exploited source consists of expertly-conducted, carefully structured interviews which follow a consistent pattern and consequently permit comparisons. Most of the interviews are also available in typescript. A few regimental histories have also been consulted, and these indicate a fascinating and under-explored field of local as well as national military history.

Here only some of the most striking facets of campaign experience can be discussed. First, let us look briefly at training during the months of phoney war. Realistic preparations for war were severely restricted by meagre resources and the urgent priority given to digging and fortifying a defensive line along the British sector of the Franco-Belgian frontier. Extremely severe weather in the early months of 1940 further restricted mobile exercises; in part because it was feared that vehicles and tanks would leave tracks which would be observed by German spotter planes.

The historians of the Coldstream Guards characteristically describe this as 'a dreary period of digging and wiring (in a dismal industrial area of France), interspersed with route marches, weapon-training and battlefield tours'. There were few incidents worth recording in the War Diary.[6] Private Victor Gilbey, of the Oxford and Bucks Light Infantry, was typical of many soldiers in experiencing very little range-shooting and no inter-arms training beyond the battalion. H. W. Dennis' battalion (the 1st East Surreys in 4th Division) only carried out humdrum and monotonous manoeuvres along the border. There was plenty of weapons drill, but no firing. Major F. P. Barclay (a company commander in 2nd Royal Norfolk Regiment) summed up his battalion's experience as 'Equipment poor and late in delivery. Training all right but too orthodox, e.g., movement at night neglected. Our commanders were too rigid in their attitude. They did not learn enough about enemy tactics'. Private George Andow was a Matilda tank crew member in 4th Royal Tank Regiment but he did very little training in tanks during the Phoney War. His memoirs describe many days of idleness and whiling away the time in cafes.[7]

It was not easy to provide off-duty entertainments during the dreary winter months. There is ample evidence available on life in barns and billets (very few tents were used), relations with local civilians, the limited attractions of Army cinemas and ENSA shows, and the greater ones of liquid and other forms of relaxation. Thus we find Gunner Alfred Baldwin grousing that the other ranks' living conditions and food were poor but his officers did not seem to care. The 1st East Surreys were driven to the brink of mutiny when billeted in a filthy carbon factory at Helluin and then were threatened with barrack damages for moving machinery in the interests of comfort. Yet the same witness (H. W. Dennis) who spoke some French, enjoyed good relations with local people and actually spent Christmas with a French family. Major D. F. Callander described his men (1st Cameronians) as 'very rugged indeed'. They had quite a high V.D. rate and were very hard to handle when drunk. He reveals that about six soldiers were staked out each night, suspended above the ground, as a punishment, even in extreme cold. As is well-known, Major General B. L. Montgomery was nearly sacked for a breezy memorandum advocating the setting up of licensed brothels, so that any soldier in need of 'horizontal refreshment' could ask directions from the military police.[8]

Apart from a few units which were given a chance to see some modest action in the French sector, there was widespread boredom over the 'sitzkrieg' and even eagerness for the 'balloon to go up'. In a typical entry, Major Barclay wrote that his battalion (2nd Norfolks) were raring to go after the months of waiting.[9]

This campaign was notable for the pervasive obsession with spies and 'fifth columnists', who were said to be contacting the enemy in ingenious ways, for example by hanging out washing in semaphore fashion, shining lights at night for enemy aircraft and even ploughing give-away patterns in the fields. Doubtless there were some cases of treachery (and prevalent fears were exploited by the Germans), but many innocent people (or lesser offenders like Belgian deserters) were manhandled, imprisoned or shot. Near Tournai, on 19 May, Captain J. H. Patterson (RAMC) ordered his CSM to inspect a suspicious column of nuns. The CSM examined especially their feet, hands and chins and reported they were definitely female. Suspects checked by Field Security Police were treated with much less tact. With only one officer and 10 NCOs per division to screen about 500 suspects a day tempers became frayed. Anthony Rhodes records a chilling conversation with the divisional provost officer responsible for providing firing parties for anyone deemed guilty. His notion of justice was 'teutonic' and there was no appeal against his decisions.[10]

The most striking single aspect of the sources consulted was that combat was experienced overwhelmingly as an air war in which the *Luftwaffe* enjoyed almost complete dominance. Many witnesses admit to fear and panic caused by strafing and dive-bombing, and there is almost universal grumbling and bitterness about the RAF's minimal role. Several participants saw few or no German ground troops but only glimpsed an occasional low-flying pilot. Here are just a few of the numerous comments on this aspect.

At Warlus on 21 May Major Ian English's battalion of the Durham Light Infantry was attacked by *Stukas* – the troops were numbed and morale plummeted. However, the survivors soon became habituated to this form of attack in which noise was the most upsetting factor. In the same action near Arras Private Andow admits that he and his fellow crew members were frightened out of their wits and hid under their tank. Signaller S. L. Rhodda was among those who saw no German troops, and Private Victor Gilbey first encountered them as late as 27 May. Corporal E. O. Manley, in 92nd Field Regiment Royal Artillery, felt abandoned during the retreat and cursed England for causing this humiliation. At Vimy on 20–22 May he recorded that 'most of the lads are pretty demoralised and disgruntled at the lack of RAF support'. Major Callander later admitted that he had felt bitter about the absence of the RAF. On 26 May Captain Patterson counted hundreds of enemy aircraft so that 'the sky was black with them', but he was charitable towards the poor showing by the RAF. On reaching England the troops in his train screamed at RAF personnel in another train ('Where have you been'), but the latter only cheered.[11]

When the German onslaught began early on 10 May 1940, the Field Force's leading formations advanced quite efficiently to the line of the river Dyle in Belgium as agreed with their allies, and for a few days the line was held with deceptively little enemy action. Once the retreat began, however, due to the German breakthrough further south, confusion and even worse soon occurred. Only a static or slow-moving campaign had been planned and communications (in all senses) soon collapsed under the unexpected strain. There had been sufficient motor transport for a planned advance but not for an improvised retreat on roads congested with refugees. There was soon an acute shortage of fuel. The British had relied almost entirely on the Belgian public telephone system which now collapsed. Radio communications had been restricted for security reasons and now proved useless, as did field telephones. Thus orders could not be transmitted with any confidence and, in effect, confusion reigned. Typical of many Territorial units' experience was that of 1st Buckinghamshire Battalion, which formed part of 145 Brigade, 48 (South Midland) Division. The battalion was based in Aylesbury and contained a high proportion of local men led by their civilian employers. They mobilized and trained near Newbury before sailing to Le Havre in mid-January 1940. Then they moved up to the dreary mining area of Wahagnies where the men were mostly billeted in farm buildings and spent most of their time digging what proved to be useless anti-tank ditches and marching on pavé roads. On 12 May the battalion moved up by lorry to the battlefield at Waterloo where there was desultory skirmishing with German infantry. After the retreat began, four days were spent defending the Canal line and units began to get mixed up; in a night march the transport and weapons were separated. The Colonel collapsed through overstrain and had to be replaced; his successor was killed a few days later as was also the adjutant. By 25 May the battalion had been pulled back to provide the sole defence of Hazebrouck whence GHQ was about to depart. On 27 and 28 May the battalion, whose scattered outlying companies lost touch with headquarters in the town centre, put up a valiant defence against an armoured division attacking from the west. With ammunition running out in a hopeless battle between infantry and tanks at close range, and with cellars crammed with wounded men the new commander, Major Elliot Viney, had little option but to surrender. From a fighting strength of about 600, 100 were killed or missing and between 200 and 250 taken prisoner. Approximately half the battalion, mostly from companies on the perimeter, escaped back to England.[12]

The metaphorical 'fog of war', which enveloped 1st Buckinghamshire Battalion as it moved back from Waterloo to its nemesis at Hazebrouck, affected all units of the Field Force in varying degrees. To the inevitable friction resulting from inter-Allied misunderstandings and contradictory orders, there was added the appalling and pitiful chaos caused by huge crowds of refugees. But when every allowance is made for these hazards of war, many other ranks and junior officers were surely right to complain that they were never adequately 'put in the picture'. This was a lesson that Montgomery took to heart: trust the troops and try to keep them informed about your plans and what is happening.

Private A. F. Johnson, a driver with 101 Company RASC, was among those relieved to find the Royal Navy in charge when he reached the coast at La Panne. He had not seen his section officer for 11 days. 'Ignorant troops are a liability,' he wrote. 'Muddle and incompetence reigned.' Gunner Alfred Baldwin was more scathing: not only were his battery officers absent; even the sergeants forgot what they were supposed to do. He could not understand why the sergeants did not gather their own gun crews and bring them to the beach as a party. There were only 16 men in Gilbey's section after it had destroyed its transport and it marched the final nine miles to La Panne. But in his experience the military police kept firm control on the beaches.[13] Thus, though there were honourable exceptions, we have to imagine not an orderly retreat in disciplined units, but rather a myriad of small ad hoc groups, all too often without their officers, marching in irregular, spasmodic stages towards the sea, sustained by a vision of evacuation to 'Blighty'.

For the most part the weather during the retreat was sunny and very hot. Exhaustion from constant, bewildering movement and lack of sleep was bad enough, but some groups also suffered from lack of food and, even worse, water. For example, S. L. Wright's battalion of the Green Howards had had no food for 48 hours and so reached Dunkirk as 'a starving, disorganised mob'. Major Cocke's signals company in II Corps found lack of water to be its most acute deprivation. One desperately thirsty RASC driver, Stan Smith, thought he had found relief in a store of lemonade, only to find he was drinking shampoo and hair oil – it was a barber's shop! Other groups liberated cellars full of wine, to the detriment of their marching stamina.[14]

Nearly all accounts stress the troops' utter exhaustion, caused by lack of sleep, and uncertainty, punctuated by moments of terror. Major English calculated that he had

had 10 hours of sleep in the first week (from 10 May), and only seven in the second. He summed up his experience as:

> Almost total disorganization and chaos really, mainly due to total lack of infor-mation about the enemy. Constant movement and lack of sleep reduced one's efficiency to about half. Everyone was just so tired.

On the retreat from the Dyle, 2nd Battalion Coldstream Guards had fought a hard battle at Pecq, and by the night of 23 May had only two officers per company on duty. When ordered to keep marching overnight, Captain Pilkington recorded:

> Weariness came down like a board on our heads. As I marched my eyes kept closing, and I knew that I was walking about like a drunkard. After a little, nausea overcame me, and I fell out for a few minutes. When we halted for a 10 minutes' rest I lay flat on the cold wet road and found a few minutes relief.[15]

German conduct of the campaign was marred by two appalling massacres of British prisoners, as well as several smaller-scale atrocities and others narrowly averted by the intervention of senior officers. On 27 May in a hamlet inaptly named Le Paradis some 90 men of the Norfolks surrendered to SS troops of 2nd Infantry Regiment *Totenkopf* Division. They were kicked, beaten and led into a paddock to be mown down by two heavy machine-guns. The wounded were finished off with bayonets, but two miracu-lously survived to publicize the incident, one getting his account published as *The Vengeance of Private Pooley*. As a consequence the regimental commander was tried and executed.[16]

On the following day an even more notorious massacre of a similar number of pris-oners, from the 2nd Royal Warwicks, was perpetrated near Wormhoudt. SS troops from Sepp Dietrich's Division shot several prisoners out of hand and the rest were herded into a barn. When a British officer complained that there was no room for the wounded to lie down, hand grenades were thrown in and orders given for any survi-vors to be shot. Once again, a few badly wounded men survived and escaped to publi-cize the incident, but in this case the officer allegedly responsible, Wilhelm Mohnke, has never been brought to trial.[17]

The excuse of the SS units involved was that they were retaliating for British massa-cres of German prisoners during the fighting round Arras on 21 May. No specific charges were made, but Nicholas Harman resurrected the allegations in 1980 in his book *Dunkirk: the Necessary Myth*. Harman was deliberately imprecise so his passing reference to the possibility of British war crimes was too vague to be established or refuted. Indeed elsewhere in the book he provided an alternative explanation; namely that some 400 'missing' German prisoners might have been drowned in a French ship sunk while carrying them to England.[18]

Two Durham Light Infantry soldiers, interviewed in the Imperial War Museum's project, recalled that German prisoners were safely handed over on 21 May, but their accounts are unfortunately inconsistent. George Self (an NCO with 8th Durham Light Infantry) admits that at Warlus his comrades lost their heads and shot about six enemy soldiers after an apparently dead German had shot a British soldier in the back. But, under Captain Walton's orders, Self says he escorted the remaining prisoners back from Warlus and handed them over to the French. The other witness, somewhat confusingly named Howard Sell (at the time transport officer with 6th Durham Light Infantry), affirms that the prisoners were disarmed and taken to a collecting point for the military police. They were given food and water, and he personally saw them put on lorries.[19] While it is clear that some German prisoners, or soldiers intending to surrender, were killed in the heat of battle, it seems most unlikely that any were murdered in cold blood after they had surrendered and been handed over to higher authorities. Nothing has come to light to lend any credence to SS allegations in mitigation of their own terrible actions which were to be repeated on a far more horrific scale in other places throughout the war.

How serious was the breakdown of the British Army's discipline in the march to the coast, the defence of the Dunkirk perimeter and, most especially, during the evacuation from the ports and the beaches? Critical accounts, such as those of Nicholas Harman and, to a lesser extent, Ronald Atkin, play up some of the much-quoted incidents concerning Anglo-French friction and even open hostility, notably over crossing the canal line, where the British took control and insisted that all vehicles be destroyed. There were also certainly some cases where individuals – of various nationalities – lost their nerve or attempted selfishly to jump the queues for the boats. As regards Anglo-French differences, it must be remembered that the Field Force had government authority to embark from 26 May and that the Royal Navy had been preparing for the likely emergency for the previous week. The French forces had no such orders until early June and even then their naval resources were meagre and unprepared. Understandably there was anger on the French side when it emerged at the Supreme War Council meeting on 31 May that 150,000 British troops had been evacuated to date but only 15,000 French. On a wider view, however, the sad reality was that the alliance was breaking up so that the British and French viewed the evacuation from completely different standpoints.

Discipline was mainly dependent on the degree to which units remained coherent bodies receiving clear orders from their own officers and NCOs – though it must be added that on the beaches some brave officers were successful in calming panics and exerting authority over miscellaneous groups of soldiers. Here are some contrasting experiences in the final phase of the campaign.

We have already seen that the 2nd Battalion Coldstream Guards was nearing exhaustion by 23 May. On 28 May the battalion was ordered to march more than 50 miles that night from Roubaix to the coast. The men had covered 32 miles over congested roads and in torrential rain when they were picked up by lorries and taken to the perimeter defences. The next four days were spent in intense fighting to hold a 2,000 yard sector of the Bergues-Furnes canal in which the battalion's strength was reduced to 200 men. An acting Captain in the 2nd Battalion East Lancashire

Regiment, Marcus Ervine-Andrews, won the VC for conspicuous gallantry defending the Canal de Bergues on 31 May. Beating back a dawn attack he killed 17 Germans with his rifle and many more with a Bren gun. Only eight of his 85 men survived. During these days a procession of stragglers streamed through the Coldstreams' lines, but they also witnessed the inspiring sight of two platoons of the Welsh Guards, remarkably clean and well turned-out, marching across in formation. Colonel Carter recalled that 2nd Battalion Sherwood Foresters did not lose a single man in a continuous forced march of 50 miles. The battalion remained united until it boarded *The Fair Maid of Perth* at Dunkirk when it was split up and the men's rifles taken away. This was infuriating. Major Callander's Cameronians retained their weapons, and their cohesion; indeed so impressive were they that on the beaches they were joined by a huge Welsh Guards sergeant who had been separated from his own battalion. Callander was also outraged when, once aboard the ship, the men's weapons were confiscated and they were separated from the officers. On reaching England, Callander recorded sardonically that he realised the situation must be desperate when he heard British civilians cheering their soldiers.[20]

Many witnesses admitted to the fear they experienced on the beaches, but most expressly rebut the allegations of widespread indiscipline. In general their evidence reinforces the impressions derived from contemporary photographs and newsreels of the long serpentine queues patiently waiting their turn for a passage home. Private Rhodda is typical in writing that he saw no panicking but 'only a bit of a scramble for the boats'. When his own signals officer tried to carry excess kit onto the beaches he was overruled by a naval officer. Alfred Baldwin, who had bravely swum out to fetch a dinghy but then failed to get aboard, was one of the many who paid tribute to a young naval officer who stood in the water for hours holding off with a revolver troops who would otherwise have rushed and swamped the boats.[21] Apart from sheer exhaustion, it was surely the prospect of getting home safely which enabled the majority of the soldiers to endure the dangers and disappointments on the beaches, at Dunkirk and the smaller coastal resorts as far as La Panne. Curiously, however, several evacuees did not realise they were homeward bound even when taken aboard. Major Callander, for example, was surprised to discover that his Cameronians had been shipped directly to England rather than to a more westerly French port whence they could rejoin the fight. Private Johnson was another escaper who, waking aboard *HMS Greyhound*, was amazed to see the white cliffs of Dover.[22] These instances serve to underline the point that many of the other ranks had little idea of where they were and what was happening: perhaps this accounts for some of their later attempts to bring order and meaning to their experiences during these hectic days by writing about them.

The Field Force's precipitate retreat and evacuation was clearly not a victory, but the magnitude of the Allied catastrophe and its implications were muffled for the British public by censorship and the promulgation of 'necessary myths'. The ambivalence fostered by the conflict between personal experience and propaganda is reflected in soldiers' recollections. On the criteria of casualties and prisoners, the abandonment of vehicles and all heavy weapons and the disorganization of the higher formations, their commanders and staffs the campaign had clearly ended in disaster. As Major English reflected: there had been a lot of gallantry and steady fighting, 'but we hadn't been very effective as an Army'. On the other hand, the survivors were surprised and heartened by the heroes' welcome most of them received; there was delight at being free in an English summer after the recent nightmare; and a dogged confidence that with better equipment and training they would be more than a match for the Germans. Colonel Carter summed up a widespread reaction when he remarked, 'It was a defeat... there you are. [The] men were angry but not demoralized.'[23] What probably remains puzzling to later generations is the almost universal, but hardly rational, confidence in ultimate victory after this catastrophe following soon after the debacle in Norway.

As this brief survey has suggested, the British Army's experience of war on the Continent in 1939 and 1940 was more varied and interesting than the obsessive attention paid to Dunkirk might suggest. Though kept too much in the dark by politicians and the high command, this was a reasonably well-educated, literate and inquisitive Army composed mostly of civilians in uniform. Individuals in all ranks from private to general recorded their impressions in great detail, or displayed remarkable powers of recall when interviewed many years later.

From the military historian's viewpoint the main conclusion must be that the other ranks and junior officers paid the price for the government's belated acceptance of a Continental role with inadequate equipment and tanks, an almost total lack of close air support, unimaginative training still based essentially on First World War attitudes, and mediocre leadership. The speed and decisiveness of the Allied rout came as a terrible shock to those who understood the situation, resulting in some bitter criticisms of the politicians and generals held responsible. Understandably too, though it now seems rather shameful, much of the blame was transferred to Britain's recent allies, France and more especially Belgium for the latter's sudden announcement of a ceasefire on 28 May. But there was also a sentiment of profound respect for the *Wehrmacht*, and particularly for the *Panzer* divisions and the *Luftwaffe*. The experiences of 1940 exercised a lasting influence on generals such as Alan Brooke and Henry Pownall, making them very reluctant to open a 'second front' in Western Europe even in 1944.

For the general public a combination of rigorous censorship, abetted by voluntary self-censoring, skilful propaganda and Churchill's defiant rhetoric succeeded to a remarkable degree in concealing Britain's precarious position and the unlikelihood of her ever being able to defeat Germany, given the Nazi-Soviet Pact and American isolationism. Nevertheless, King George VI doubtless expressed the irrational optimism of many of his subjects in his often-quoted remark in a letter to his mother: 'Personally, I feel happier now that we have no allies to be polite to and to pamper.'[24] Thus the underlying interpretation of this peculiar 'victory' was that it signified an escape from Continental commitments, and hence of the terrible prospect of repeating the experience of 1914–1918.

This all-too-brief foray into the British Army's experience of war in 1939 and 1940 leaves a strong impression of the great range and interest of personal accounts for this, and later campaigns in the war, which have scarcely been exploited by historians compared with research using comparable sources on the First World War. It is to be hoped that this volume, *Time to Kill*, will stimulate much deeper and more comprehensive research than has been attempted here.

References

1. Alan Bennett, *Forty Years On* (London: 1969), p. 27.
2. Field Marshal Montgomery, *Memoirs* (London : 1961 pbk edn), pp. 49–50.
3. An analysis of the Territorial Army's performance in 1940 was the subject of Birgadier K. J. Drewienkwicz's unpublished thesis at the Royal College of Defence Studies (1992).
4. David Divine, *The Nine Days of Dunkirk* (London: 1959). Richard Collier, *The Sands of Dunkirk* (London, 1961). Gregory Blaxland, *Destination Dunkirk* (London, 1973). Nicholas Harman, *Dunkirk: the Necessary Myth* (London: 1980). Ronald Atkin, *Pillar of Fire: Dunkirk, 1940* (London, 1990).
5. Ewan Butler and J. Selby Bradford, *Keep the Memory Green. The Story of Dunkirk* (London: 1950). Bruce Shand, *Previous Engagements* (Salisbury: 1990). Anthony Rhodes, *Sword of Bone* (London: 1942. pbk edn 1986). Christopher Seton-Watson, *Dunkirk – Alamein – Bologna* (London: 1993).
6. Michael Howard and John Sparrow, *The Coldstream Guards, 1920–1946* (Oxford University Press, 1951), pp. 26–27.
7. All references to Imperial War Museum sources are to the transcripts of Sound Recordings (The Gort Project) unless otherwise indicated. Victor Gilbey, p. 31. H. W. Dennis, p.16. F. P. Barclay, p 93. G. E. Andow, pp. 87–88.
8. Alfred Baldwin, p. 14. H. W. Dennis, pp. 9, 16. D. F. Callander, p. 9. Montgomery's memorandum is cited by R. Atkin (op cit) p. 37.
9. Barclay, p. 69.
10. Captain J. H. Patterson Diary (1WM), entry for 19 May. A. Rhodes, *Sword of Bone*, pp. 155–57.
11. Major I. R. English, p. 30. S. L. Rhodda 'Recollections of the Retreat to Dunkirk in May 1940' (19 typed pages 1.W.M.). Gilbey (p. 45) first saw Germans on the Commines Canal as late as 27 May. He mentions that 12 German prisoners were sent back to his battalion headquarters. Major E. J. Manley(TAIM 21pp. typed memoirs), who was a corporal in 92 Field Regiment Royal Artillery in 1940, displayed considerable literary skill, particularly in describing the hellish scene on the approach to Dunkirk. Callander, p. 21. Patterson diary entries especially for 26, 27 and 28 May.
12. J. E. H. Neville (ed), *The Oxford and Bucks Light Infantry Chronicle. Vol I. September 1939 – June 1940* (Aldershot: 1949). Major Elliot Viney (1WM interview), and personal interview 19 November 1995.
13. A. F. Johnson (1WM typed memoirs) was an RASC driver who arrived in France only on 14 April and was evacuated from La Panne on 28 May. He graphically describes the lack of control during the retreat and on the beaches (pp. 82–90). Gunner Alfred Baldwin's battery had run out of shells by 28 May. He is a severe critic of absence of control by both junior officers and NCOs (pp. 38–45), but also paid tribute to a magnificent show by Guardsmen marching onto the beach immaculately dressed and with rifles at the slope.

14. S. L. Wright, 6th Battalion Green Howards (1WM. Memoirs 9 typed pp). Major J. W.
     G. Cocke served with 51st Heavy Regiment Royal Artillery – see interview p. 73 for the
     acute lack of water. For Stan Smith's unfortunate experience, see R. Atkin op cit p. 159.
15. English, pp. 39, 52. Howard and Sparrow, *The Coldstream Guards*, pp. 45–49.
16. Atkin, pp. 152–53. Blaxland, pp. 286–87. Cyril Jolly, *The Vengeance of Private Pooley*
     (London: 1956). Another medical officer told Captain Patterson he had seen a line
     of eight ambulances full of wounded men shot up by German tanks which were then
     themselves destroyed by British artillery.
17. Atkin, p. 154. Blaxland, p. 298. The most detailed account is Leslie Aitken, *Massacre on the
     Road to Dunkirk* (London: 1988).
18. N. Harman, pp. 98–9, 231.
19. George Self (interview on cassette only) Reel 6 for the shooting of Germans in Duisans
     cemetery and Reel 7 for the handing over of prisoners to the French. Mr Self had
     read Nicholas Harman's accusation against the Durham Light Infantry before being
     interviewed and rebuts his charge angrily. Harold S. Sell (Reel 7) confirms that he was
     the last person (in the (DLI) to see the prisoners put in lorries to be taken to brigade
     headquarters.
20. Howard and Sparrow, pp. 48–58. *Daily Telegraph* obituary of Lt. Col. M. Ervine-Andrews,
     1 April 1995. Callander, pp. 31–38.
21. Baldwin, p. 38, thought discipline on the beaches was good despite the absence of his
     battery officers. A. Rhodes, *Sword of Bone*, p. 227 provides a moving account of a gallant
     naval officer maintaining order.
22. Johnson, pp. 82–88.
23. English, p. 47. Carter, p. 75ff.
24. J. Wheeler-Bennett, *George VI* (London: 1958), p. 460.

9

Hore-Belisha's Generals: Gort and Ironside

Gort and Ironside were really Hore-Belisha's rather than Churchill's generals. The reforming War Minister had appointed Gort Chief of the Imperial General Staff, and brought back Ironside from Gibraltar in May 1939 to become Inspector General of Overseas Forces with the likelihood that he would command any Expeditionary Force that Britain sent abroad in the event of war. These complementary biographical sketches reveal just how inadequately Britain was prepared for war, not just in the run-up to war but also in the catastrophic operations in 1940.

Neither soldier should, of course, be held primarily responsible for the shortcomings of the command structure or strategic decision making, but their brief months in the limelight exemplify the indecision and confusion resulting from 20 years of neglect.

As regards the most senior command appointments it was a matter of square pegs being forced into round holes. Gort was distinguished for his outstanding bravery but was not intellectually suited to be CIGS. Ideally he would have commanded a Corps under a more senior C-in-C. Ironside had held such a command in North Russia in 1918–1919, but he was probably past his best by 1939. General Sir John Dill would have been a better choice for CIGS but Hore-Belisha felt that he was lacking in the necessary drive and dynamism. What may astonish readers of these sketches is that even after the belated commitment of a small Field Force to the Continent in event of war in February 1939, no C-in-C or Chief of Staff was appointed. So sure was Ironside that he would become C-in-C that on the eve of war he sent a staff officer to Aldershot to organise his headquarters. Gort should have stayed at the War Office because he was familiar with the plans, but his relations with Hore-Belisha were so bad that he was allowed to leave to become C-in-C of the Field Force on the declaration of war taking Major-General Pownall with him as his Chief of Staff. Ironside, who had never served at the War Office and hated desk work suddenly found himself the new CIGS – a demanding post for which on his own admission he was unsuited.

As for the higher strategic direction of the war, the Chiefs of Staff Committee was already in being and a War Cabinet was created in September 1939 following the precedent of 1916–1918. But, as these studies reveal, Chamberlain's profound lack of interest in waging war was a fatal weakness. Churchill's advent to the Premiership in May 1940 brought an immediate transformation. He dominated the War Cabinet and the Chiefs of Staff, in effect making himself Minister of Defence. Churchill's aggressive attitude and ceaseless prodding of his ministers and service chiefs did not prevent numerous operational disasters but henceforth there was no lack of grip in the day to day waging of war.

Gort's career prospects suffered a sharp decline after the expulsion of the British forces from France, and although Churchill continued to admire his fighting qualities, he was never again offered a field command. However, as Governor of Malta in 1942–1944 he was outstandingly successful in rallying the island's defences. Ironside might also have enjoyed a belated 'finest hour' had there been a German invasion after Dunkirk, but he was removed from the command of Home Forces in July 1940 and retired with the rank of Field Marshal.

Sir John Colville's biography of Gort, *Man of Valour* (1972), is a sympathetic study which is unlikely to be superseded; but Ironside's career is badly in need of a scholarly appraisal.

Field Marshal Lord Gort

The late Sir John Colville aptly called his biography of Gort *Man Of Valour*, for whatever his subject's limitations of mind and personality, few ever questioned his outstanding courage. When the French Prime Minister Reynaud dared to do so at the height of Anglo-French friction during the Dunkirk evacuation he received a furious rebuke from Sir Edward Spears. Spears himself reflected:

> It had never occurred to me nor, I fancy, to any of his contemporaries to describe Gort as intelligent above the average. But, as far as that goes, Foch was not intelligent either... But he was an undoubtedly great man nevertheless, for he had other qualities, steadfastness, resolution, courage, and so had Gort, who in addition possessed the great virtue of loyalty.[1]

Gort attained the heights of his profession as CIGS and Commander-in-Chief of the Field Force (between 1937 and 1940) at a comparatively young age, but then suffered the common fate of British commanders at the start of a war, being made the scapegoat for peacetime neglect of the army and relegated to the sidelines.

John Standish Surtees Prendergast Vereker was born in 1886 and succeeded his father as sixth Viscount Gort in the Irish peerage in 1902. He was educated at Harrow and Sandhurst and commissioned into the Grenadier Guards in 1905. In the First World War he performed excellently as a staff officer, particularly in the Operations Branch at GHQ where he played an important part in planning the operations in 1917. But it was as a battalion and brigade commander that he achieved the truly outstanding reputation for bravery which ensured him a distinguished career in the post-war Army. In 1917 he was awarded the DSO and Bar when commanding the 4th battalion Grenadier Guards and was twice badly wounded. In March 1918 he displayed conspicuous bravery at Arras in helping to check the German offensive and was awarded a second Bar. But his greatest exploit was on 27 September 1918 when, again badly wounded, he was awarded the Victoria Cross as temporary commander of the 3rd Guards Brigade in the storming of the Canal du Nord and the Hindenburg Line. He also won the Military Cross and was eight times mentioned in despatches. As Gort's entry in the *Dictionary of National Biography* sums up, he acquired 'a reputation for the rarest gallantry, complete disregard of personal danger and power to keep alive in his troops a spirit of endeavour untamed by loss and strain'.[2]

After the war Gort made steady, if not spectacular, progress. He was an instructor at the Staff College in 1921, was promoted Colonel in 1925, Commander of the Grenadier Guards in 1930, Director of Military Training in India 1932, and in 1936 returned to the Staff College as Commandant. In 1937 Gort's career prospects were transformed when Hore-Belisha appointed him first Military Secretary at the War Office and, shortly afterwards, the youngest ever CIGS. He skipped the rank of lieutenant-general to become a full general and in so doing passed above many officers senior to him on the Army List including Dill, Brooke and Wavell.

In early life Gort had acquired the ridiculous and inappropriate nickname of 'Fat Boy', but was later known familiarly as 'Jack'. In what would now be termed his 'lifestyle' he was austere and self-denying, indeed he seemed to delight in privations and expected others to do the same. On his appointment to the Staff College in 1936 one colonel remarked: 'He will have all the beds made of concrete and hosed down with cold water nightly.' His suggestion that officers might use their leisure hours at Camberley learning to fly rather than following the Drag hunt was not widely appreciated. He also had a schoolboy sense of fun which he never entirely grew out of. In his days as an instructor at the Staff College in the early 1920s he had been a ring leader in various rags, such as squirting hoses under the bedroom doors of those who retired too early on mess nights, and – as will be seen later – he was not above treating the War Minister to similar horseplay in 1939. Gort married his cousin Corinna Vereker in 1911 but this did not prove a successful partnership and was dissolved in 1925. While it seems clear that Lady Gort actually broke up the marriage, Gort himself may have contributed. As his commander in the Shanghai Relief Force in 1927, General John Duncan, revealingly wrote to his own wife:

> He is a bit too intense for peacetime soldiering. He is a very fine soldier and extremely able, but he is in a class by himself and works himself to death. It may be the result of his domestic troubles, but if he was like this before I can quite imagine his wife leaving him.[3]

When Gort was rather surprisingly appointed CIGS in December 1937 his biographer assessed his qualities as follows:

> there was no more honest man than Gort and if none would have called him brilliant, his integrity, experience, shrewd common sense and that most worthy of all qualities, true simplicity... were a combination that was certain to attract loyalty and might reasonably be expected to achieve success.

In the opinion of his contemporaries, however, he was regarded as an ideal man to command a division.[4]

In promoting Gort to the highest appointment in the Army Hore-Belisha hoped he would supply the drive for pushing through overdue reforms while his character would appeal to the troops and enhance the Service's reputation with the public. Sir Ronald Adam as his Deputy would supply the brains and adroitness necessary in the Chiefs of Staff Committee and the Committee of Imperial Defence. Sir John Kennedy's opinion, that 'In the War Office this fine fighting soldier was like a fish out of water',[5] may be too severe, but it soon became apparent that Gort was not ideally suited to be CIGS. As will be illustrated later in this essay, one of Gort's salient characteristics throughout his life was an obsession with detail, sometimes to the exclusion or neglect of the broader picture.

Nevertheless, Gort became CIGS at a time when the energetic and ambitious Hore-Belisha – greatly aided by international events – was bringing Army reform to the forefront of British politics, and he played an important part in the great improvements that were accomplished before the outbreak of war. This is not the place for a detailed account of Hore-Belisha's reforms,[6] but Gort's most important achievement, helped by his able Director of Military Operations Major-General Henry Pownall, was to get the Army's continental commitment recognised by the Government (finally achieved in February 1939), with the resultant rush to get its equipment, weapons and transport modernised – and part of the Territorial Army earmarked for development as its eventual Reserve. Though he remained ignorant of the French Army's weaknesses, Gort was convinced that Germany was Britain's most likely enemy, that the Field Force must be made ready for despatch to France and that the pre-1939 plan to send only two divisions was a completely inadequate contribution to an alliance.[7]

Quite apart from the blighting of individual careers, it was a tragedy for the British Army that Gort and Hore-Belisha proved unable to work amicably together. Pownall, a prejudiced, partisan admirer of Gort thought the two men could never get on: 'a great gentleman and an obscure, shallow-brained charlatan, political Jewboy'. By the summer of 1939 Pownall believed Hore-Belisha was trying to manoeuvre Gort into resignation but he should refuse to budge; the War Minister's Cabinet colleagues were allegedly sick of him (i.e. Hore-Belisha) and would surely oust him from office after the general election – due in 1940. Gort and Pownall disliked and resented many things about Hore-Belisha, but chief among them were his flamboyant personality, his unorthodox style in conducting Army business – particularly appointments – and his reliance for advice on Captain B. H. Liddell Hart, *The Times'* defence correspondent. For his part, it seems unlikely that Hore-Belisha reciprocated Gort's animosity, but the CIGS's distrust and dislike of himself clearly penetrated even Hore-Belisha's thick skin. The unfortunate result was that for several months before the outbreak of war Hore-Belisha and his chief military adviser were barely on speaking terms and saw as little of each other as possible. Hore-Belisha dealt increasingly with Gort's deputy Adam and with junior staff officers such as Kennedy. Thus civil-military relations in 20th century Britain in peacetime reached their nadir in 1939. To judge by the Pownall and Ironside diaries, all the fault was on one side, but Gort's biographer corrects this impression, pointing out that the CIGS offered his political chief no affection or understanding and little credit for his many admirable reforms. A less formal CIGS, capable of overlooking or even laughing at the War Minister's irritating mannerisms and methods, might have gained the latter's confidence and achieved a working relationship. 'Gort stood firmly by his principles and it cannot be denied that he sometimes confused principle and prejudice.'[8]

Clearly the Army's deficiencies on the outbreak of war resulted from years of inadequate funding and political neglect, and Gort as CIGS could only to a very small extent be held responsible for them. Nevertheless he had failed to press the cause of mechanisation and the formation of armoured divisions; the handful of tank experts had been dispersed and not given the key appointments either at the War Office or in commands. Perhaps even more deplorable Gort, though a keen supporter of inter-service co-operation, had failed to win any substantial increase of air co-operation squadrons, much less to gain direct authority for the future Commander of the Field Force over the bombers of the Advanced Air Striking Force.

The Government's omission to appoint a Commander-in-Chief of the Field Force before the declaration of war on 3 September 1939, and the resultant confusion among the three possible choices (Dill, Ironside and – least likely – Gort) have already been outlined in the essay on Ironside and need not be repeated here. Whether or not Gort pressed for the appointment of Commander-in-Chief is uncertain, but he was evidently delighted to escape from Hore-Belisha and the War Office. Gort, like Alexander, made no secret of the fact that he enjoyed the excitement of war. 'Here we go again, marching to war' was his first remark on reaching the Staff College to form his headquarters, and he added, 'I can't expect everybody to be as thrilled as I am'. Middle-aged and with daunting responsibilities, his demeanour struck observers as schoolboyish. Gort took Pownall as his chief of general staff thus, as in 1914, depriving the War Office of the experience of the two officers most fully acquainted with the war plans and arrangements for co-operation with allies.[9]

Gort revered the memory of Marshal Foch for his offensive spirit and his skill in leading the Anglo-French armies in the victorious advance in 1918; he also respected General Georges, commander of the French forces on the Franco-German frontier in 1939. But Gort's command of the French language was poor, and in his determina-tion to be a loyal ally, conscious as he was of Britain's belated and meagre contribution of troops, he tended to be too deferential towards the professorial General Gamelin, Commander-in-Chief of the French Forces. Indeed Gort was so eager to please and do as he was told that the French tended to regard him as 'a sort of friendly and jovial battalion commander'. Spears felt that the British Government should have insisted that Gort be given a place on the Supreme War Council.[10]

As it was, his position in the Allied command structure was a curious one. Gort's headquarters had liaison with Gamelin's (GQG), but he was not under Gamelin's orders. The British Field Force was included in the First Army Group under General Billotte but – initially at any rate – Gort was to receive his orders from Georges. Like his predecessor Sir John French in 1914, Gort was granted the right to appeal to his own Government should he consider that French orders (or, as it turned out, lack of them) might endanger his troops. To make matters even more confused, Gamelin and Georges were on very bad terms throughout the months of the Phoney War and there were frequent rumours that Gamelin would bypass Georges and issue orders direct to Gort.[11]

Gort established his headquarters at the Chateau of Habarcq west of Arras. As he wrote to his daughter Jacqueline: 'I am off to a chateau with no water, no light and no loo.' His staff appeared grossly inflated because Gort had allowed for an eventual expansion to 20 divisions. It was also dispersed over some 50 square miles as a precau-tion against air attack. As a consequence communications within the Field Force were extremely cumbersome: Montgomery described it as 'an amazing layout'.[12]

The two original Corps Commanders, Dill and Brooke, expressed criticisms of the Field Force's equipment, tactics and training, feeling that Gort was too complacent and too obsessed with detail. In their turn Gort and Pownall suspected the Corps Commanders of 'bellyaching' and defeatism. Too much of Gort's time was taken up with ceremonial visits to the French and in entertaining a stream of distinguished visitors at GHQ, but in any case he believed in delegating a large measure of responsibility for training to his subordinates. Montgomery made some sharp criticisms of Gort's leadership in his *Memoirs*, but allowed that he had an impossible task in running a great headquarters as well as exercising direct command over the fighting and administrative forces. The plan was for Gort to appoint two Army commanders under him when four corps were assembled, but only three were in place by May 1940.

Montgomery was justly critical of the deplorable signal communications which rendered the complicated command structure even less effective. As a result of the French obsession with security wireless communications within the Field Force was never efficient; and outside it scarcely existed. During the battle harassed commanders were heavily dependent on the civil telephone service which was frequently out of order and always insecure. Montgomery also charged that Gort's failure to hold field exercises or even indoor war games on the sand table resulted in a total lack of any common policy or tactical doctrine.[13]

Numerous sources show that one of Gort's lifelong traits was an obsession with detail which often struck observers as comical. Thus Sir John Kennedy was taken aback when, at a senior officers' conference with Hore-Belisha present, the first issue Gort raised was whether a tin hat, when it was not on a man's head, should be worn on the left shoulder or the right. Brooke found him tirelessly occupied with tactical questions such as the proper use of hand-grenades and the number a patrol should carry. After a visit to the Maginot Line Brooke tried to discuss the flaws in the French outpost system of defence, but Gort replied 'Oh, I have not had time to think of it but, look, what we must go into is the proper distribution of sandbags.' Colville noted the officers' puzzlement that a Commander-in-Chief should concern himself with such details as tear-off igniting paper on rockets, anti-freeze mixture and night-flying pigeons.[14]

On a much more substantial operational issue, Gort was unhappy about Gamelin's proposal to abandon the frontier defences and advance into Belgium to the line of the river Dyle ('Plan D') in event of a German attack. Gort, Pownall and Ironside were all present at Vincennes on 9 November when Gamelin explained his plans and the safeguards against being surprised in the open and none of them objected. Gort suppressed his reservations in the interests of allied unity: he was under French orders and would advance when told to without reference to his Government. In retrospect this acquiescence in an extremely risky plan was to be widely criticised as a dereliction of duty.[15]

The final rift with Hore-Belisha resulted directly from the minister's visit to the Field Force in mid-November. Sir John Kennedy has left a hilarious but also slightly distasteful account of Gort's schoolboy-like ragging of the fastidious Hore-Belisha, who was trying out a pair of fur-lined but, alas, not waterproof boots with a zip fastener up the back. In foul weather Gort insisted that Hore-Belisha climb a very muddy bank and stand shivering in a howling gale while the former explained a First World War battle, and Pownall did the same a little later. When they at last reached shelter in a chateau Gort opened a window letting in a piercing draught and shouted jovially, 'Isn't it a grand day!' On the way back Hore-Belisha was given bully beef sandwiches and when the minister was eventually offered a decent meal Gort hung around outside making jocular remarks. Even Pownall felt the joke had gone on long enough and was embarrassed. Hore-Belisha endured this ordeal remarkably well and as he was leaving said to Kennedy 'I think Gort realised that I am out to help him.'[16]

Alas, Gort did nothing of the kind. On his visit Hore-Belisha had asked to see the troops rather than the defences and so did not gather a true picture of the work completed and in progress. He made no criticisms to Gort, but on his return to London complained at the slow rate of construction of pill-boxes both in the War Cabinet and the Army Council. Gort was displeased to hear of this but what infuriated him, a stickler for correct procedure, was that Hore-Belisha conveyed verbal criticisms to Gort via the latter's Chief Engineer at GHQ, General Pakenham-Walsh. By the end of November GHQ was buzzing with Hore-Belisha's 'crimes' against Gort; Pownall listed these 'crimes' in his diary and determined that the War Minister must be removed. On 29 November Pownall confided to his diary:

> It's all a disgusting business. A knife in the back of the man who would be free, above all others, to think of beating Germans. We are now here all facing West, to meet the more dangerous enemy there. I have written in full to Grigg, who will know what to do with my letter. We must now await CIGS's visit and the result. Then, assuming a favourable outcome, we must counter-attack on Hore-Belisha. The thing has come to a head and war cannot be carried out thus.[17]

Since this essay concerns Gort rather than Hore-Belisha, there is no need to describe in detail the very effective campaign which speedily convinced the CIGS, the King and the Prime Minister that the War Minister was a liability and resulted in his resignation early in January 1940. It seems unlikely that Gort himself intrigued against the War Minister, but he had a trusted 'hatchet' man in Pownall and must have been broadly aware of his clandestine efforts. Hore-Belisha wrote Gort a conciliatory letter on 4 December, and after a visit from the Prime Minister in which he praised the construction of defences, the storm seemed to be abating. On 27 December Gort wrote to reassure Chamberlain that resentment of Hore-Belisha's misplaced criticisms was now over, though he did hint that confidence and trust in the minister might fail at a critical moment if criticism of armies in the field was not couched in sympathetic language. But, in contrast to Pownall who rejoiced, Gort was surprised at Hore-Belisha's resignation and seemed upset that he might be suspected of causing it.[18]

Major-General A. J. Trythall concludes an extremely interesting article on Hore-Belisha with the speculation that Gort and Pownall pushed what should have been a soluble misunderstanding over the pill-box construction to a showdown because they feared that the War Minister intended to dismiss them. Both generals certainly conveyed this impression at the time but it is not certain that this is what chiefly motivated them. If it did, then they were surely mistaken. Hore-Belisha had been monumentally tactless but repeatedly protested that he was really trying to help Gort and the Field Force. Moreover, when Chamberlain gave him an opportunity to remove Gort in mid-December, Hore-Belisha assured the Prime Minister that he had complete confidence in him.[19] The final irony of the Pill-Box affair is that the frontier defences were irrelevant since Gamelin's 'Plan D' for an advance into Belgium had been approved by the Supreme War Council three days before Hore-Belisha's visit.

In the early months of 1940 Gort and Pownall were angry and alarmed at the Government's apparent determination to become involved in operations in Scandinavia and its corresponding neglect of the Western Front. Senior officers from the War Office and even the Prime Minister left the impression that they regarded the Western Front as secure and thought no action was likely there in the foreseeable future. A brigade was withdrawn from 5th Division for operations in Norway; the despatch of III Corps to France was delayed and the supply of ammunition virtually ceased. Ironside failed lamentably to keep Gort informed of Government decisions, and the Chiefs of Staff even interfered with the Field Force's leave arrangements without consulting Gort.[20] However, critics such as Dill and Brooke felt that Gort accepted these intolerable slights too equably and did not sufficiently stress the likelihood of a German attack. 'His outlook was essentially that of a regimental officer and a Guardsman at that. He found it repugnant to question an order, express disagreement or complain.' The problem which most urgently affected Gort in April and early May, however, was his precise place in the Allied chain of command. Would Gamelin allow Georges to exercise untrammelled command and would the latter delegate responsibility for the co-ordination of the British and Belgian armies to Billotte? Uncertainties remained until the Germans invaded Belgium in the early hours of 10 May and the allies responded to the plea for assistance by implementing 'Plan D'.[21]

Given Gort's temperament and thirst for action his choice between the roles of a commander-in-chief at headquarters and a field commander actually fighting the battle from forward positions, was a foregone conclusion. Taking Pownall and other senior staff officers with him, Gort immediately left GHQ for a Command Post at Wahagnies near Lille. The separation of the Commander-in-Chief from his GHQ for the critical phase of the campaign proved to be an administrative disaster because communications between the shifting Command Post and GHQ broke down almost completely. All reports of German movements, for example, were sent to the Operations section remaining at GHQ but it was often impossible to pass the information to the Command Post. Even Gort's faithful lieutenant Pownall complained in his diary on 14 May that his Commander had been away for eight hours that day – 'too long at difficult times' – but he accepted that the Command Post had to be as close to the fighting as possible. On 16 May Gort added to the communications problems by taking the head of his Intelligence Staff, Major-General Mason-MacFarlane, and *his* senior staff officer (Gerald Templer) and putting the former in command of 'Macforce' to protect the right rear of the Field Force. Montgomery later reflected that the distribution of staff duties between GHQ and the Command Post was 'amateur and lacked the professional touch'. The verdict of the Official Historian was equally severe.[22]

On 12 May General Billotte was appointed to co-ordinate the movements of the First Group of Armies (including the British and Belgian forces), but in the succeeding critical days he conspicuously failed to do so as the allies first advanced to the Dyle line and then retreated to the Franco-Belgian frontier while the *Panzer* columns drove westward behind them to the Channel coast. By 17 May Billotte could not communicate directly with Georges, and Gort had no land telephone lines to either the Belgian or French 1st Army headquarters on either side of him. Gort was obliged to send senior officers to Billotte to discover his plans for the Allied retreat. On 17 May the British liaison officer with 1st French Army accidentally overheard that, due to indiscipline in the withdrawal, a serious gap had occurred in the French line and there were no reserves to fill it. Gort and Pownall were reluctant to believe reports that the French senior commanders' morale was cracking but by 18 May the evidence was overwhelming. Gort visited Billotte that day in a vain effort to cheer him up only to discover that his nominal commander had no plan, no reserves and little hope. He could only point to the map, count up to '*huit panzers*' and say pathetically, '*Et contra ces panzers je ne peux rien faire*'.[23] It was thus not surprising that Gort and Pownall began to lose faith in the French high command and to think about the necessity of saving the Field Force from the impending debacle.

Such anxieties were strengthened on 19 May when the *Panzer* advance severed the Field Force's line of communications with its bases in the Biscay ports. Pownall twice telephoned an uncomprehending War Office to warn that a retreat to the Channel ports might be unavoidable. Unfortunately for Gort, Churchill and the War Cabinet were seriously out of touch with fast-moving events and the following day (20 May) Ironside arrived at GHQ bringing orders that Gort was to march south-west towards Amiens to re-establish contact with the main French armies south of the narrow *Panzer* corridor. The CIGS was quickly persuaded that such a move was impossible. Indeed by now Gort was having to detach further improvised groups (Petreforce, Polforce and others) to try to hold his southern perimeter from Arras along the canal line westward to the coast.[24]

On 21 May Gort ordered a small-scale counter-attack south of Arras to hold up the German advance.[25] French participation in this operation was minimal but for a few hours it made encouraging progress, even against SS units and Rommel's 7th *Panzer* Division. Here was a tantalising glimpse of what might have been had Gamelin retained a central reserve. Two days later Gort was obliged to withdraw the Arras garrison to prevent it from being cut off, but the French generals, notably Blanchard, interpreted this as an attempt to sabotage the counter-offensive which Gamelin – and now his successor Weygand – were planning to cut the *Panzer* corridor by a combined drive from north and south. Despite his waning faith in the French high command, Gort was still prepared to make two British divisions (5th and 50th) available for the northern counter-attack, but in view of the increasing pressure on his (and even more the Belgians') eastward-facing front he felt more and more convinced that the main effort must come from south of the corridor. In view of contemporary and subsequent French criticisms that Gort never seriously contemplated joining in a counter-attack, it is worth noting that Brooke was dismayed at Gort's slowness to recognise the threat to his eastern flank where a Belgian collapse was imminent.[26]

On the evening of 25 May Gort did heed Brooke's warning, moved the two available divisions to the threatened sector and, without consulting the French and in defiance of a War Cabinet order, unilaterally cancelled his part in the projected counter-offensive. This was Gort's most critical decision during the campaign – perhaps in his whole career – and it was desperately uncongenial to him, the loyal ally and combative general *par excellence*. Pownall has sympathetically recorded Gort's growing sense of anxiety, exasperation and impotence during the retreat, and his biographer justly notes that, though his physical stamina was unimpaired, 'his ability to exercise cool judgement in large matters was not matched by a capacity to rise above the smaller worries'.[27]

Nevertheless Gort had made the right decision. Blanchard, Billotte's successor as co-ordinator of the First Group of Armies, accepted it the following day, while the War Office gave him permission to withdraw towards the Channel ports. Had the French forces from south of the corridor been advancing, as was repeatedly claimed, Gort would have been charged with ruining the only hope of thwarting a German victory.

> The Weygand Plan had in fact already been dead for several days before – in French eyes – Gort 'killed' it by his independent decision. Perhaps if any criticism can be levelled at Gort on this score it is that he was doggedly loyal to the ineffectual Blanchard and the French High Command for too long. He might have decided even earlier to make for the Channel ports as Weygand and Reynaud alleged that he had. By delaying this unpleasant decision to the last possible moment he risked the encirclement of the BEF. Thanks to Allied valour in defence – but also to the wrangles and contradictory orders of the German High Command – the great majority of British troops were successfully evacuated.[28]

To the end of the campaign Gort retained his capacity to inject new zest into despairing French generals. One of his liaison officers describes a remarkable interview in which Blanchard talked at length about French plans, after which Gort responded by tapping Cambrai on the map with a pencil and saying slowly and emphatically, '*Oui mon General, il faut tuer les Bosches et il faut les tuer ici*'. Later Blanchard was heard to remark to his chief of staff, '*Tiens, il a bien raison*, Lord Gort'. Pownall admirably summed up Gort's performance in the campaign on 28 May:

With all his faults and fussinesses, he is a great gentleman and a first-class soldier... The most trivial things have always preyed on his mind and now he has a load that he can never shake off all the days of his life. The Commander of the BEF that was driven into the sea in three weeks! So undeserved a fate.[29]

Gort had made up his mind to stay with his troops to face death or capture but Churchill, after consulting Pownall, ordered him to return to England and he did so on 1 June. He never entirely forgave this order, believing that he was being widely criticised for deserting his post for which the Prime Minister was to blame. This suspicion that he was being made a scapegoat was accentuated by an enforced delay in publishing his Despatches. He probably was justified in feeling that Dill and Brooke were cool, if not actually hostile, towards him since they left him to fret on the sidelines with the largely honorary appointment of Inspector General of Training.[30]

In April 1941 Gort was made Governor of Gibraltar, usually a terminal appointment for senior officers and one that irked him. Here, at least, his passion for detail could be legitimately indulged, for example in getting the Rock's cavernous defences deepened and the air strip extended. In fact Churchill had not forgotten him or written him off. In November 1941 the Prime Minister toyed with the amazing idea of re-installing him as CIGS in place of the exhausted Dill who was being posted to Washington; and in March 1942 he flirted with the notion – until dissuaded by Brooke – of appointing Gort to succeed Auchinleck in the Middle East Command.[31]

The change when it came (in May 1942 after exactly one year) was less exalted but still important, namely Governor of beleaguered Malta. The island was under relentless air attacks which had pounded the docks to rubble and blocked the harbour with sunken ships. An amphibious attack from nearby Sicily seemed imminent. Yet, with Rommel's final offensive about to begin, it was vital that Malta hold out as the base for attacks on Axis convoys. Shortly after his arrival Gort helped to secure the safe arrival of a consignment of 60 Spitfires; then, by concentrating all available firepower, Gort saved the supply ship *Welshman* by bringing down all the *Stukas* which attacked it. Not least impressive, Gort supervised the distribution of scarce food and water supplies so successfully that at the height of the crisis two hundred thousand people were receiving rations each day. But Gort's outstanding achievement was to impress on the islanders his own indomitable fortitude and cheerfulness in adversity. He became immensely popular. Indeed his entry in the *Dictionary of National Biography* rates the defence of Malta as his outstanding achievement. His reward was a belated promotion to Field Marshal.[32]

In 1944–45 Gort was briefly High Commissioner and Commander-in-Chief in Palestine. When informed that his predecessor had been fired upon he characteristically remarked that it looked like being fun; but in reality he was terminally ill and had only just begun to gain the respect of both Arabs and Jews, and to reduce terrorist activities, when he was forced to come home. Apart from his daughter's happy marriage to a fellow Grenadier and winner of the VC, William Sidney (later Lord De Lisle and Dudley), Gort's private life had been rather unhappy; his only son had committed suicide in 1941 and at the end of his life he had no home of his own. Just before his death in March 1946 he was awarded an English Viscountcy but this was a doubtful asset since he had no heir and was too ill to take his seat in the House of Lords.[33]

This essay has attempted to bring out Gort's qualities and limitations as a general, but as a portrait of the man it is necessarily incomplete. Several witnesses, for example, attest to his charm and magnetism but these traits are not evident in his photographs and, as little survives in the way of personal papers, have to be taken on trust by those who did not know him. Though he has his supporters, who have praised his performance both as CIGS and C-in-C, this essay inclines to agree with his critics, such as Montgomery and Brooke, that he was promoted above his mental ceiling. Nevertheless he strove to do his best and it is not self-evident that alternative candidates in either post would have done much better. The fairest conclusion may be that had he commanded a division or corps in 1940, he would have done well in command of an Army later in the war. This was the view of a soldier who did enjoy this delayed ascent to the highest military command, Field Marshal Earl Alexander.[34]

Gort's early death and the absence of substantial private papers entailed that – like Dill's – his reputation suffered an eclipse during the post-war 'battle of the memoirs' in which his severe critic, Montgomery, was so prominent. But Gort's positive qualities emerged strongly with the publication of the diaries of his staunch admirer, Pownall, (*Chief of Staff* Vol I, 1972), and in the same year he was the subject of Colville's admirable – and on the whole admiring – biography (*Man of Valour*). This essay opened with Spears' rebuke of a French Prime Minister for presuming to query Gort's outstanding virtues of courage and loyalty, so it may fittingly conclude with his acceptance of Weygand's apology on the same score. 'We have a saying in England, Spears told the General, "a good man to go tiger shooting with" and Lord Gort is *par excellence* such a one.'[35]

Chronology: John Gort

1886, July 10	John Standish Surtees Prendergast Vereker born in London
1899–1904	Harrow School (succeeded as 6th Viscount Gort in Peerage of Ireland, 1902)
1904–5	Royal Military College, Sandhurst; commissioned Grenadier Guards
1911	Married his second cousin, Corinna Vereker (divorced 1925; one s, two d)
1914, August 5	Promoted Captain; to France as ADC to C-in-C I Corps, Douglas Haig
1914–1918	Served continuously in France and Belgium (despatches eight times, MC, DSO, and two bars, VC)
1915	GSO3, I Corps
1916	Promoted brevet Major
1917, April	To command, 4th Battalion Grenadier Guards
1918, March	Commanding 1st Battalion Grenadier Guards
1918, September 27	Won Victoria Cross while in temporary command of 3 Guards Brigade at storming of Hindenburg Line
1919–20	Staff College, Camberley
1921	Brevet Lieutenant-Colonel
1921–3	Directing Staff, Staff College
1925	Colonel
1926	Chief Instructor, Senior Officers' School, Sheerness
1927, January–August	GSOI, Shanghai Defence Force
1927–30	GSOI, 4th Division
1930–32	Commanding 4 Guards Brigade
1932–6	Director of Military Training, India; Major-General, 1935
1936–7	Commandant, Staff College, Camberley
1937, September–December	Military Secretary
1937, December 3–1939, September 3	Chief of the Imperial General Staff; General; KCB
1939, September 3–1940, May 31	Commander-in-Chief, BEF
1940–1	Inspector-General of the Forces; GCB, 1940
1941, May 7–1942, May 7	Governor of Gibraltar
1942, May–1944, July	Governor of Malta; Field Marshal, January 1943
1944, October–1945, November	High Commissioner and C-in-C, Palestine
1946, March 31	Died in London

Field Marshal Lord Ironside

In a diary entry written in June 1940, shortly before his retirement, Ironside reflected that his dazzling career prospects had been diminished in the decade 1926–1936 under the discouraging regimes of Milne and Montgomery Massingberd. The Army was in the doldrums and Ironside felt unwanted; he became irritated at his inability to influence training and organization and lost confidence in his future. Thus, when his belated opportunity came in 1939 Ironside was probably past his best, and moreover he was given an appointment – Chief of the Imperial General Staff – for which he knew himself to be unsuited both by temperament and experience.[36]

Edmund Ironside was born in 1880, the son of a surgeon-major of the Royal Horse Artillery who died when he was still an infant. His mother eked out her pension by regular Continental travel and Edmund showed an early aptitude in foreign languages, in seven of which he became an interpreter. He was commissioned from Woolwich in time to serve in the South African War with the Royal Field Artillery, and shortly afterwards, disguised as a Boer transport driver, he accompanied the German military expedition to South-West Africa where he did useful work for British Intelligence, demonstrating his great resourcefulness and linguistic skill.[37] Six foot four inches tall and correspondingly broad he was inevitably nicknamed 'Tiny'. He was the original of John Buchan's soldier-hero Richard Hannay of *The Thirty Nine Steps, Greenmantle* and *Mr Standfast*. Not least among his distinctions Ironside represented Scotland at rugby.

In temperament Ironside was not so much the archetypal 'gentle giant' as a supremely self-confident, forceful and opinionated commander. He was more typical of his generation in being an open-air soldier who intensely disliked the confines of desk work, particularly at the abominated War Office. In general he held a low, if not contemptuous view of politicians and, in the case of Hore-Belisha, was later to admit in his diary that the War Minster's Jewish origins had increased his antipathy.

Nevertheless after the First World War he was generally regarded as an able and progressive officer. He was closely associated with the radical advocate of mechanization and armoured warfare, 'Boney' Fuller, and conducted a regular and remarkably frank correspondence on professional matters with Basil Liddell Hart. This correspondence reveals a lively mind ranging widely over the trends in modern warfare and ideas for improving the Army.[38] As Ironside's career developed, however, Liddell Hart was adversely impressed by his 'trade union' attitude to promotions, evidenced by his keeping (and openly discussing) a large ledger containing the names of all officers above him on the Army List with his and other people's views of their performance, health and prospects. Also, despite his facility with languages, contemporaries such as his fellow gunner Henry Pownall, noted his intellectual limitations. Pownall rejoiced prematurely at his impending retirement in June 1938, noting in his diary, 'It's a mercy his soldiering days are over... There's always been more bluff and brawn than brain.' This harsh judgement would be more widely endorsed after Ironside's term as CIGS between September 1939 and May 1940.

Ironside passed through the Staff College at Camberley on the eve of the First World War and served throughout on the Western Front. He distinguished himself in successive staff and command appointments, culminating in command of 99 Brigade in the 2nd Division in the Spring of 1918. In September 1918 he was appointed Brigadier General Staff to the Allied expedition to Archangel but took over the command shortly after its arrival, becoming General Officer Commanding in North Russia in 1919 with the substantive rank of major-general. This placed him among the three or four youngest major-generals in the Army. From 1922 to 1926 he was an inspiring Commandant at the Staff College with 'Boney' Fuller as his Chief Instructor, and then commander of the 2nd Division at Aldershot. Thereafter, like other precocious contemporaries who had received rapid promotion, he had to mark time – including a disheartening period on half-pay – until his seniors such as Milne, Massingberd, Harington and Deverell eventually retired.

When Ironside was appointed to Eastern Command in 1936 he had more experience of senior command in war than almost any other serving officer and, but for his age, still seemed a strong contender for command of the Field Force in event of war. He found the Army at home in a dire state of unpreparedness. 'We are in no state to go to war', a typical diary entry reads. 'There are no men and there is no money for their equipment and there is no will amongst the Cabinet Ministers to want an Army.' 'We have nothing with which to fight – literally nothing – and will not have anything for two years.' He concluded that the absence of an Expeditionary Force was a godsend: nobody would dream of sending such a derisory force to the Continent. As late as May 1938 he could write: 'Never again shall we even contemplate a Force for a foreign country. Our contribution is to be the Navy and the RAF.'[39]

It is necessary to devote some space to promotions because an important contention in this essay (as also in that on Gort) is that both officers were given unsuitable appointments – square pegs forced into round holes. This was an unintended consequence of Hore-Belisha's shake-up of the high command in 1937 in the attempt to break up the prevailing system of Buggins' turn and bring forward dynamic, progressive, unorthodox leaders. It is also worth noting, in view of his later criticisms, that Ironside welcomed Hore-Belisha's arrival at the War Office in May 1937: 'We are at our lowest ebb in the Army and the Jew may resuscitate us.' 'He is ambitious and will not be lazy as some of the others were. He starts in when things are at their worst and will have to show results.' He also greeted Lord Gort's appointment as Military Secretary as 'the best piece of news I had heard for many years'.[40]

Towards the end of 1937 Hore-Belisha determined to remove Deverell as CIGS and faced the critical question of who should succeed him. Ironside was in the running but spoilt his chances by an unimpressive performance as a Commander in the major exercise of 1937. For this he was severely (and Liddell Hart thought unfairly) criticized in public by Deverell from a draft prepared by Alan Brooke – no admirer of Tiny's. It is interesting, however, that even Liddell Hart – Ironside's strong supporter and Hore-Belisha's adviser at this period – thought that he was better suited to be Commander-in-Chief in India with Wavell as CIGS. Unfortunately the taciturn Wavell had made a very poor impression on the War Minister and the appointment eventually went to Gort. Ironically Gort would have preferred to hold a revived appointment as Inspector General of the Forces so as to extend his active career. Hore-Belisha's idea was that Gort would be the dynamic 'front man' in pushing through radical reforms while Sir Ronald Adam as his deputy would supply the brains in the sphere of strategy – a dubious arrangement since it was Gort and not Adam who had to present the Army's case in the Chiefs of Staff committee.[41] Ironside told Hore-Belisha he had chosen the right man and had never really pictured himself as CIGS, for which the War Minister was greatly relieved. Yet within a few months Ironside was privately recording his opinion that Gort was completely out of his depth as CIGS.

Early in 1938 Ironside accepted the appointment of Governor of Gibraltar and assumed it would end his military career. However, Gort and Hore-Belisha both held out the prospect of command in the Middle East in event of war, and since Tiny was convinced that Egypt was the hub of the Empire and the place where Britain's main military effort must be made, this was an added attraction. Hore-Belisha also made the 'preposterous' suggestion that the British Army might well be employed in Spain and he (Tiny) would be on the spot to take command.[42]

In December 1938 Hore-Belisha consulted Liddell Hart about recalling Ironside from his exile on The Rock to be Inspector General of Overseas Forces. Liddell Hart was doubtful because he thought there would be confusion of responsibilities between this post and that of CIGS. Sir John French had been Inspector General of Overseas Forces before 1914 and Commander-in-Chief designate. The danger would be that Ironside would regard himself as the virtual Commander-in-Chief and Gort would be relegated to administrative duties. This was all the more likely given Tiny's dominant character and considerable seniority over Gort. Nevertheless Hore-Belisha went ahead, giving Ironside the appointment in May 1939 and making Walter Kirke Inspector General of Home Forces. As regards demarcation of duties he ruled that both Inspectors would be 'outside the War Office' but able to come inside as and when they needed.[43]

Even if Ironside was not officially informed that he was C-in-C designate, it was a reasonable assumption to make and he behaved accordingly. He continued to believe to the very eve of war that the Middle East was the most likely destination of Britain's small and under-equipped Field Force. Friction with Gort over their respective responsibilities soon occurred and was gleefully recorded by Major-General Henry Pownall, Director of Military Operations and Intelligence at the War Office. On Tiny's appointment Pownall expressed the opinion that he was quite unsuited to be a C-in-C on a modern battlefield. 'He would do alright bush-whacking or knocking the Middle East about but he is *not* intelligent, not enough so to deal with a first-class enemy.' Pownall may have been prejudiced but Sir John Slessor, who had known Tiny at various points in his career, recorded an almost identical view.[44] The only incident in Ironside's brief tenure of the Inspector-Generalship that deserves mention here is his visit to Poland in July 1939 to assess the Poles' military capabilities and intentions. He reported prophetically that no Eastern Front really existed, that France would not attack the Siegfried Line and that Poland would be quickly overrun. He urged that an agreement with Russia was essential, but this advice was anathema to the Prime Minister.[45]

When war with Germany seemed certain at the end of August, Ironside was so confident of being appointed C-in-C that he sent his assistant, Colonel Macleod, to Aldershot to assemble his headquarters staff. After an agonizing wait the bomb-shell exploded on 3 September: Hore-Belisha appointed Gort commander of the Field Force for France and made Ironside CIGS. The details of this dramatic incident need not be described again here,[46] but the circumstances and momentous consequences deserve some discussion. Gort and Hore-Belisha had been on extremely strained terms and both were delighted at the chance for Gort to leave the War Office and take a command, for which he was more suited. Tiny's chance of the command of the Field Force may have been harmed by French hints that he would not be acceptable – but their preference was for Dill rather than Gort. Hore-Belisha was now stuck with Tiny for, as Sir John Kennedy put it, he had 'raised a regular Frankenstein's monster in bringing Ironside back from the dead'.[47] Ironside had a commanding presence and a popular reputation, and he was strongly supported by Churchill, now recalled to the Admiralty and a member of the War Cabinet. Churchill overcame opposition – from Kingsley Wood and others – and Ironside was made CIGS. This was a bad mistake for, as Ironside honestly admitted, 'I am not suited in temperament to such a job as CIGS, nor have I prepared myself to be such.' Indeed he had never before held a staff appointment at the War Office. Furthermore, one must ask, since he had been passed over as unsuitable in 1937, why (at the age of 60) was he deemed suitable in 1939? Ironside soldiered on in increasingly irksome conditions but the error in appointing him must be borne in mind when we consider his shortcomings as CIGS.

Eyewitnesses differ on Ironside's performance in the early months of the war and particularly on his relations with Hore-Belisha. Sir John Kennedy paints a gener-ally attractive and positive picture of a rumbustious bull-in-a-china-shop, courageous, self-confident and intolerant of nonsense – political or military. Kennedy retails Tiny's version of his haranguing the War Cabinet but he also records that, far from impressing ministers, Ironside had annoyed them very much. 'His manner with politicians was much too brusque; on the other hand it was a joy to hear him give a straightforward military survey in a military environment.' Francis de Guingand, by contrast, thought that so far from 'nearly reducing H-B to tears', Ironside was very respectful towards the minister and would not have dared to pound the table or harangue him.[48]

Ironside's view of strategic priorities at the outset of war may be summarized briefly. Britain's first task in the West was to build up the French order of battle with the Field Force eventually expanded to some 20 divisions. The initial aim must be to withstand a German offensive which Ironside (correctly) thought Hitler might be willing to risk in the autumn of 1939. He continued to envisage the Middle East as the main theatre in which Britain would ultimately launch an offensive when she had assembled 12 divisions. Ironside described Turkey as 'our front line and our bastion'. 'A door might open in Rumania or Italy; or we might have to send in small forces to put Poland and Czecho-Slovakia back on their feet.' From the outset he was understandably unhappy about the lack of overall direction and the inefficient organization of strategy and policy. After three weeks at war he complained: 'The old gentlemen sitting here in London have no idea of the seriousness of the position… How can we get a unified command of operations? How are we to stop those stupid conferences of the Chiefs of Staff and War Cabinets, discussing the little details of the nothings that have happened?'[49] Things would have to get worse in the months before Churchill became Prime Minister, and Ironside scarcely survived long enough to experience the benefits which ensued.

Ironside's lack of balance and gravitas are evident in the remarks about Poland and Czechoslovakia quoted above. He also displayed instability on two important issues in the autumn of 1939. In September Gamelin raised the possibility of an Allied advance from the defences being prepared on the Franco-Belgian frontier to the line of the Escaut (or Scheldt). Ironside wrote to Gort and spoke out in Cabinet against this projected move: there was a danger of being caught in the open by low bombing attacks, and the Escaut line, unreconnoitred and unprepared, would be linear and ineffective. Yet when Gamelin set out his reasons for the projected advance on 26 September Ironside acquiesced. No firm decision was taken and in the following weeks the General Staff prepared a paper stressing the folly of the advance unless the Allies could be sure of occupying defensive positions before the Germans attacked. Dill and Brooke (the Corps commanders) were unhappy about the project, as were some of the French field commanders. No new arguments were advanced by Gamelin, but on 9 November Ironside and Newall (the CAS) accepted his plan, to the dismay of the General Staff. Ironside explained to the War Cabinet that Gort had been placed under the French command and given the right of appeal to the Government, but since he had not done so they would be ill-advised to intervene.[50] This was a curious line to be taken by the Cabinet's senior adviser on military strategy, particularly as he knew that Gort was determined to play the part of a loyal ally.

The other issue concerned the main role of the RAF's bomber force in the event of a German attack in the West; should it, in short, be concentrated on close-support attacks on the enemy's communications or should it be directed towards 'strategic bombing' of the Ruhr? Ironside was acutely aware of the derisory provision for close Army–Air support and was fighting for the Army to have control of its own aircraft. Yet in discussions with the Air Staff and Churchill, and later with the French war leaders, Ironside vehemently favoured bombing the Ruhr, declaring repeatedly that it would be 'decisive', apparently because he believed the German generals were rigid and inflexible and would be unable to readjust to this chaos in their rear. Slessor remarked that Ironside's assessment went far beyond the Air Staff's claims for the immediate effects of industrial bombing, while Gort was indignant that his CIGS had sold the pass on so contentious an inter-Service dispute.[51]

Ironside was increasingly depressed by the Cabinet's policy of 'wait and see' and the endless, futile discussions. Even Chamberlain, for whom he expressed considerable admiration, was described as 'just a weary, tired old man, dominating at times all the other mediocrities who bear the responsibility with him'. His diary entries on Hore-Belisha become more frequent and more scathing.[52] For his part, the War Minister told Liddell Hart that he wished he had chosen Ironside in the first place rather than Gort. Despite his limitations he had much more drive than any other soldier. He could always get a reasoned opinion from Tiny. On 14 December, with the axe of dismissal poised over his head, Hore-Belisha failed to take Chamberlain's hint that he could have Gort and Ironside replaced if he lacked confidence in them.[53]

Ironside played only a subsidiary role in the notorious 'Pill box affair' which provided the pretext for Hore-Belisha's dismissal from the War Office early in January 1940, so the matter can be covered more fully in the essay on Gort. At the first hint of trouble between the War Minister and the Commander-in-Chief on 19 November, Ironside warned the former to be careful how he dealt with Gort. 'He was put in by the King and must not be monkeyed about.' It seems clear from Tiny's own account that on 28 November he volunteered to go and examine the Field Force's defences for himself. The notion that he had been sent out by the War Cabinet or Hore-Belisha only served to exacerbate the paranoiac atmosphere at GHQ. Whether Ironside went out to France with an open mind may be doubted: he certainly returned a staunch supporter of the GHQ line that Gort had been insulted and that, 'H-B must go'. On 3 December Ironside saw the King, who was angry about the dispute. A fortnight later Tiny noted that in many ways it would be a pity if H-B had to go, but he found him impossible personally. When he heard of H-B's resignation on 6 January he seemed genuinely surprised but felt a sense of intense relief.[54]

Ironside's role in advocating operations in Scandinavia between the end of December 1939 and mid-March 1940 does not enhance his reputation as a sound strategist; indeed it does much to justify Pownall's linking his name with Churchill's as 'the crazy Gang'. The opportunity for British operations in Scandinavia was of course provided by Finland's gallant resistance against the Russian invasion, but from the outset Ironside saw assistance to Finland as no more than a pretext: the real objectives were the occupation of the Swedish iron ore fields around Gällivare and the distraction of German forces away from western Europe. Pownall was right to link the CIGS's name with Churchill's because both men fretted at Britain's inactivity and longed to seize the initiative. But whereas Churchill favoured the lesser plan of mining the Norwegian leads to force German transport vessels into open waters and perhaps provoke a full-scale reaction, Ironside favoured the major scheme of a military expedition through Narvik along the electric railway into Sweden. Tiny believed that if Finnish resistance could be prolonged it would prevent a German advance in the Balkans. If Germany could be provoked into armed intervention in Scandinavia the Middle East would be kept quiet. An offensive through Narvik to Lulea (the Swedish port on the Gulf of Bothnia from which iron ore was shipped to Germany in the ice-free summer months) would offer the Allies a big return for little expenditure. It presented a chance to seize the initiative and throw confusion into German councils. On 26 December Churchill told Ironside that his own scheme – of mining the leads – would soon receive Cabinet approval. He did not think the Germans would be able to take action against Norway and Sweden before May and only then might Britain have to send a force through Narvik to Lulea.

Ironside thought they had stumbled upon 'the one great stroke which is open to us to turn the tables upon the Russians and Germans'. He saw that Norwegian and Swedish co-operation was vital but assumed that it could be obtained. He accepted that once an operation was started in Scandinavia it was likely to grow into a major campaign, but in that event it must be carried through 'despite all other demands made upon our troops and material'. A few days later, however, he and the other Chiefs of Staff warned the Cabinet against implementing Churchill's plan until their own forces were prepared. 'It is like putting a stick inside a hornets' nest without having provided yourself with a proper veil,' he wrote prophetically. Throughout January 1940 he continued to advocate the larger scheme, making the assumptions that 'if we pushed in a brigade to Gällivare' the Germans would be unable to react before May, and also that the enemy was incapable of mounting more than one operation at a time.[55]

At the meeting of the Supreme War Council on 5 February Ironside found Daladier 'genial' and the French delegation delighted at Britain's willingness to shoulder the main burden of the Scandinavian enterprise. Assuming Norwegian and Swedish acquiescence, the essence of the plan was to push a strong force through Narvik and Trondheim:

> We are supplying two divisions and two strong brigades, while the French supply a brigade of Chasseurs Alpins, two battalions of the Legion and four battalions of Poles. This will all pass across the Narvik–Lulea line and we shall sit down in strength upon our L. of C., making sure of Gällivare and Boden. I can see a whole host of objections from the Scandinavians, but what I most fear is a passive resistance – a strike amongst the officials of the railway.
>
> If we bring this off we shall have carried out a great coup, which will upset the even tenor of the German preparations. It may bring in Norway and Sweden. I don't doubt that it will have an electrifying effect upon the Germans. They will have to come out in the open and declare themselves for or against the Russians.[56]

Ironside showed awareness of the risks of the plan, but deemed them worthwhile if the German supply of iron ore could be stopped. He took it for granted that France was secure and could only benefit from the German diversion. This hair-raising scenario did not delight GHQ in France. Pownall penned a most devastating critique against 'those master strategists Winston and Ironside': communications and logistics would be a nightmare even if all went well; there was a real risk of antagonizing Russia; the Germans could *easily* mount an attack on the Western Front as well as in Scandinavia or the Balkans; and why should the Norwegians and Swedes allow us to make their countries a battlefield – if they were so pro-ally and anti-German, why did they not stop the ore supply themselves or let us buy it at an enhanced price?[57]

Ironside continued to support the scheme up to the last minute, despite the opposition of other senior army officers involved in the planning such as Kennedy and Ismay, and Newall (the CAS) who described it as 'hare-brained'. Chamberlain, too, was 'horrified' at the political risks involved, but the expedition was set to go ahead on 12 March when Finland's timely collapse caused its postponement.[58]

Making due allowance for Pownall's hostility to Ironside, his anger at the CIGS's failure to keep GHQ informed about the Scandinavian project and its repercussions on the Field Force in France were justified. As Pownall noted on 12 March, part of 5th Division had actually been withdrawn from France with a view to despatching it to Norway, III Corps had been held up in England, and the supply of ammunition to France had totally ceased in February because it was needed elsewhere. Pownall found consolation in the rumour that Ironside would shortly be appointed Commander-in-Chief in India.[59]

When Anglo-French operations in Norway eventually began in early April the circumstances were entirely different to what Ironside had envisaged: in a brilliant combined operation the Germans seized Bergen, Trondheim and Narvik and soon achieved air dominance over the battle zone. Ironside supported the expedition to take Narvik, but he was almost alone among the decision-makers in realizing it would not be a 'walk-over'. On 14 April Churchill, who from the outset had dominated the British response, insisted, against the CIGS's violent protests, that the rear half of the convoy carrying troops to Narvik be diverted to Trondheim. This predictably caused chaos and got the operation to seize Trondheim through a pincer movement from landings at Namsos and Andalsnes off to the worst possible start.

Ironside, whose previous relations with Churchill had been very good, now became exasperated at the First Lord's attempt to supervise all military operations as if he were a company commander. He also found Churchill's see-saw changes of mood hard to cope with. The CIGS justifiably felt that his proper responsibility for military advice could not be exercised due to the frequent rambling discussions of the Chiefs of Staff, the ill-named Co-ordination Committee and the War Cabinet. As he noted on 19 April: 'Strategy is directed by old people who collect odd bits of information. This is discussed quite casually by everyone.' Two days later he questioned the sanity of trying to run operations by committee with every morning's Cabinet meeting taken up with descriptions in detail of every little incident in the fighting. It was like a lot of children playing a game of chances.[60]

Perhaps Ironside's most important achievement in the Norwegian campaign was to insist on the speedy evacuation of the Central Front (Namsos and Andalsnes) on 26 April. British ministers were relieved, but the CIGS was unhappy that he had felt obliged to force through this decision without consulting the French. On 7 May he fairly summed up the campaign as a muddle in every way. 'Always too late. Changing plans and nobody directing. To bed very upset at the thought of our incompetence.' He was obliged to admit that, contrary to his stereotyped view, the Germans had displayed a remarkable ability to improvise. An even greater shock was impending.[61]

Ironside, like Gamelin, had at times hoped that the Germans would attack on the Western Front in the winter months of 1939–40, and he deluded himself, despite ominous signs, that French morale was sound. As late as 31 March he expressed a poor opinion of German generalship and staff work: an attack on the Western Front would be a terrible gamble for them. In October 1939 he had mentioned the Ardennes as a possible approach route for the Germans, but at that time their main thrust (in planning) was directed at central Belgium and the Netherlands.[62] It seems probable that in May 1940 the CIGS was as surprised as the other Allied war leaders by the bold execution of the Manstein Plan.

Ironside's role in the battle of France was not of great significance. He knew his days as CIGS were numbered when Dill was brought back from France in late April as VCIGS. Gort and Pownall at GHQ had completely lost confidence in him. Lastly, even before he became Prime Minister on 10 May, Churchill was now presiding over both the Chiefs of Staff and the Co-ordination committees as a virtual Minister of Defence. On 19 May, however, Ironside was instructed by the War Cabinet to go over to France and order Gort to retreat south-west so as to link up with the main French armies supposedly assembling for a counter-attack to smash through the *Panzer* corridor now stretching tenuously to the Channel coast. Gort and Pownall quickly convinced him that the War Cabinet was hopelessly out of touch with events and that a retreat northward to the Channel ports offered the only – faint – hope of escape. Ironside also witnessed the French commanders' moral collapse and was sufficiently exasperated to shake General Billotte by his tunic buttons. He believed that only a minute portion of the BEF could escape.[63]

On 27 May Dill replaced Ironside as CIGS. He welcomed the change to a job more to his liking – Commander-in-Chief Home Forces – further sweetened by Churchill's promise of a field-marshal's baton in due course. The War Cabinet rightly believed he would infuse more drive and purpose into defence preparations and, as seemed all too likely, would be the best commander to lead the ill-trained, ill-equipped and totally inadequate forces remaining in the United Kingdom against an invading army.

Ironside understandably, though wrongly, assumed that Hitler would have ordered thorough planning for the invasion, but he was more realistic than the Chiefs of Staff in appreciating that the Germans would be unlikely to attempt an invasion before achieving command of the air. When Ironside took up his command the most vulnerable area of the coastline seemed to lie between the Wash and Folkestone, but after the fall of France the whole of the southern coast was threatened. The number of troops available was superficially impressive but there was a dearth of guns and tanks, training was defective and the means of mobility lacking. Initially therefore Ironside had no alternative to organizing a largely static 'crust' of beach defences, with blocks and stop-lines further inland and a small mobile reserve north and west of London to counter-attack landings in East Anglia or on the south coast. In the first half of June Ironside's difficulties were exacerbated by the removal of some of his best units for the ill-fated second BEF.

Ironside presented his complete plans to the Chiefs of Staff Committee on 25 June. They comprised five main elements. First, an extended 'crust' along the probable invasion beaches whose defenders would fight where they stood to gain time and break up all penetrations. Second, there would be blocks manned by Local Defence Volunteers (later renamed the Home Guard) equipped with 'Molotov cocktails' and other devices to use against tanks. Thirdly, small, local mobile reserves would be mounted in armoured fighting vehicles such as 'Ironsides'. Fourthly, there was to be a strong static defence line constructed to stop any breakthrough from reaching London or the industrial Midlands. Lastly, there was the GHQ Reserve consisting initially of one armoured and the equivalent of three infantry divisions.[64]

On the following day Ironside's scheme was severely criticized by Lord Hankey (Chancellor of the Duchy of Lancaster) and the Vice Chiefs of Staff. They were alarmed at the implication that 'the main resistance might only be offered after the enemy had overrun nearly half the country, and obtained possession of aerodromes and other vital facilities'. They also deplored the plan's lack of attention to the south coast. This scheme they described as 'completely unsound' and 'nothing short of suicidal'.[65]

The Chiefs of Staff were more sympathetic to Ironside's problems and confirmed that his plan of defence was 'generally sound', but they required him to revise his paper clarifying his determination to resist the enemy on the beaches and his intentions regarding the location and use of reserves[66] Ironside and his chief of staff, General Sir Bernard Paget, were exasperated by repeatedly being summoned to explain their plans; and although Churchill nominally supported the Commander-in-Chief, his memorandum of 28 June caused further confusion. In this paper, in curious contrast to his recent and famous 'We shall fight them on the beaches' speech, he wrote that 'The battle will be won or lost, not on the beaches, but by the mobile brigades and the main reserves.'[67] By the end of June Ironside believed that the Chiefs of Staff were confused about what the priorities for home defence should be or what could reasonably be expected given the limited forces available. He was also aware of criticism from some of the senior commanders, including Montgomery, Auchinleck and, above all, Brooke who took up Southern Command on 26 June. Brooke felt strongly that more effort should be put into creating a strong reserve for mobile operations; he also believed that the Germans' main thrust would come not across the North Sea but across the Channel against the south coast.[68] On 17 July Brooke seized his opportunity when showing Churchill the south coast defences to convince the Prime Minister that a change of Home Forces Commander was needed and that he was the man for the job.[69] Two days later Ironside's supercession by Brooke was announced. Ironside took his sudden replacement philosophically. Though sometimes irritated by Churchill, he had greatly admired his courageous leadership during the prolonged crisis since he had become Prime Minister. Churchill in turn appreciated Ironside's performance as Commander-in-Chief Home Forces and the soldierly dignity with which he accepted his supercession. He was promptly promoted field-marshal and in 1941 received a peerage.

Reviewing the *Ironside Diaries* in 1962, A. J. P. Taylor concluded: 'Few men have been less successful as CIGS, and none has been more conscious of it.'[70] Ironside was certainly aware of his shortcomings and he had recognized from the outset that he was far from ideally suited for the post. In conclusion, however, three points may be advanced in mitigation of Taylor's severe judgement. In contrast to the other two services, the Army was largely inactive during Ironside's period in office. Secondly, with the notable exception of Churchill, Chamberlain's War Cabinet took a predominantly passive and Micawberish view of grand strategy that was alien to Ironside's restless temperament. Finally, he had to function in a loose structure of decision-making through a plethora of committees with ill-defined responsibilities which were lacking in co-ordination and direction from the top. One may question whether any other CIGS between, say, 1922 and 1945 would have done better in these circumstances.[71]

Chronology: Edmund Ironside

1880, May 6	Born in Edinburgh
1883–7	Tonbridge School
1887–9	Royal Military Academy, Woolwich; commissioned Royal Artillery
1899–1902	South African War (despatches, Queen's Medal with 3 clasps, King's Medal with 2 clasps)
1908	Captain
1909–12	Brigade Major
1913–14	Staff College, Camberley
1914, October	GS03, 6th Division
1915	GS02; married Mariot Ysobel Cheyne (one s, one d); awarded DSO
1916–17	GSO1, 4th Canadian Division; brevet Lieutenant-Colonel
1918	Commanded 99 Infantry Brigade, 2nd Division; awarded CMG; promoted brevet Colonel
1918, October–1919, October	C-in-C Allied Troops Archangel; promoted major-general; knighted (KCB) 1918 (his account, *Archangel 1918–1919*, published 1953)
1920	Commanded Ismid Force
1921	Commanded North Persian Force
1923–6	Commandant, Staff College, Camberley
1926–8	Commanded 2nd Division, Aldershot
1928–31	GOC Meerut District, India
1931–3	Half-pay, Lieutenant, Tower of London
1932–6	Quartermaster-General, India; promoted General, 1935
1936–8	GOC Eastern District
1938–9	Governor and C-in-C, Gibraltar
1939, May–September	Inspector-General of Overseas Forces
1939, September 3–1940, May 27	Chief of the Imperial General Staff
1940, May 27–July 19	C-in-C Home Forces; promoted Field Marshal
1941	Created Baron Ironside of Archangel
1959, September 22	Died in London

References

1. Sir Edward Spears, *Assignment to Catastrophe* (One volume edition, 1956), pp. 168, 322.
2. Cyril Falls' entry in D.N.B. Supplement 1941–1950.
3. J. R. Colville, *Man of Valour: Field-Marshal Lord Gort VC* (1972), pp. 45–69 (henceforth referred to as 'Gort').
4. Gort, p. 77. C. N. Barclay, *On Their Shoulders: British Generalship in the Lean Years 1939–1942* (1964), p. 36 (Henceforth referred to as 'Barclay').
5. Sir John Kennedy, *The Business of War* (1957), p. 5.
6. See R. J. Minney, *The Private Papers of Hore-Belisha* (1960) and Brian Bond, 'Leslie Hore-Belisha at the War Office, 1937–1940' in J. Gooch, I. F. W. Beckett (eds), *Politicians and Defence* (1981).
7. Gort, pp. 88–92, 120–21.
8. Brian Bond (ed), *Chief of Staff* Vol I (1972), pp. 203, 210–11 (Henceforth referred to as 'Pownall'). Gort, pp. 136–38. Kennedy, pp. 13–14.
9. Spears, pp. 43–44, 56. Barclay, p. 37. Brian Bond, *France and Belgium 1939–1940* (1975), pp. 38–40.
10. Spears, pp. 43–44, 56.
11. John C. Cairns, 'Great Britain and the Fall of France' in *Journal of Modern History* 1955, pp. 365–409.
12. Gort, p. 149. Viscount Montgomery, *Memoirs* (1958), p. 52.
13. Montgomery, pp. 52–56. Gort, p. 156.
14. Kennedy, p. 36. Gort, p. 156. Sir A. Bryant, *The Turn of the Tide* (1957), pp. 75–80 (henceforth referred to as 'Brooke').
15. Bond, *France and Belgium*, pp. 53–55. Spears, p. 60. Gort, pp. 153–54.
16. Kennedy, pp. 36–37.
17. Pownall, p. 259ff and especially pp. 262–65.
18. Gort, p. 166. Pownall, p. 279. A. J. Trythall, 'The Downfall of Leslie Hore-Belisha' in *Journal of Contemporary History* (1981), pp. 391–411.
19. Trythall, pp. 405–08. Kennedy, p. 43.
20. Brooke, pp. 75–80. Gort, pp. 172–73.
21. Bond, *France and Belgium*, pp. 103–04. Barclay, pp. 41–42. Montgomery, pp. 52–54.
22. Gort, pp 190–191. Pownall, pp. 315–16. Montgomery, pp. 57–58. Brooke, p. 94n.
23. Miles Reid, *Last on the List* (1974), pp. 31–32. Bond, *France and Belgium*, pp. 110–11.
24. Gort, pp. 199, 206–07. Barclay, p. 46. Pownall, pp. 323–24.
25. Brian Bond, 'Arras, 21st May 1940' in C. Barnett and others, *Old Battles and New Defences* (1986).
26. Brooke, pp. 122–23.
27. Gort, pp. 214–15.
28. Bond, *France and Belgium*, pp. 136–37.
29. Reid, pp. 43–44. Pownall, p. 352.
30. Reid, p. 58. Pownall, pp. 357–58. Gort, pp. 224, 233, 235–37. Kennedy, pp. 64–65.
31. Brooke, p. 339. Martin Gilbert, *Winston S. Churchill: Finest Hour* (1983), p. 1234.
32. Gort, pp. 247–54.
33. Gort, pp. 261, 267.
34. Gort, pp. 244–45.
35. Spears, p. 188
36. R. Macleod & D. Kelly (eds), *The Ironside Diaries 1937–1940* (1962), p. 365 (Henceforth referred to as 'Macleod').

37. Geoffrey Powell, 'John Buchan's Richard Hannay', *History Today*, August 1987.
38. B. H. Liddell Hart, *Memoirs* Vol I (1965), p. 81. All other references are to Volume II. See also the Liddell Hart–Ironside correspondence in the Liddell Hart Centre for Military Archives at King's College, London.
39. Macleod, pp. 24–25, 57–58.
40. Macleod, pp. 24, 26.
41. Liddell Hart, *Memoirs* Vol II, pp. 21–23. R. J. Minney, *The Private Papers of Hore-Belisha* (1960), pp. 68–70 (Henceforth referred to as 'Minney').
42. Macleod, pp. 38–39, 52–53, 59–60, 64.
43. Liddell Hart, *Memoirs* II, pp. 74, 239. Minney, p. 210.
44. Brian Bond (Ed), *Chief of Staff* (1972), Vol I, pp. 203, 206, 215–216 (Henceforth referred to as 'Pownall'). Pownall specualted that Hore-Belisha had deliberately appointed Ironside in order to provoke Gort into resigning. For Sir John Slessor's unflattering opinion of Ironside see *The Central Blue* (1956), p. 242.
45. Macleod, pp. 75, 18–82, 85.
46. See Pownall, pp. 222–23 and Macleod, pp. 93–94.
47. Sir J. Kennedy, *The Business of War* (1957), pp. 18–20.
48. Kennedy, pp. 18–25. F. de Guingand, *Operation Victory* (Paperback Edition, 1960), pp. 35–38. Minney, p. 234.
49. Kennedy, pp. 25–26. Macleod, pp. 103–10 passim.
50. Kennedy, pp. 27–31, J. R. Colville, *Man of Valour, Field-Marshal Lord Gort VC* (1972), p153 (Henceforth referred to as 'Gort'). Macleod, pp. 113, 136, 394. Slessor, p. 251.
51. Macleod, pp. 141–42. Slessor, pp. 246–47, 252. Gort, p. 175.
52. Macleod, pp. 125, 136, 158. Kennedy, pp. 40–41.
53. Liddell Hart, *Memoirs* II, pp. 264, 269. Minney, pp. 266–67.
54. Macleod, pp. 164–67, 194–96.
55. Macleod, pp. 188–92. Pownall, pp. 280–88.
56. Macleod, pp. 215–16. See also R. A. C. Parker, 'Britain, France and Scandinavia, 1939–40' in *History*, October 1976, pp. 369–87.
57. Pownall, pp. 280–83.
58. Kennedy, pp. 48–49. Macleod, p. 228.
59. Pownall, pp. 288–93.
60. Macleod, pp. 257–59, 265, 268, 273.
61. Macleod, pp. 284–85, 296.
62. Liddell Hart, *Memoirs* II, p. 265. Macleod, pp. 125, 204, 241.
63. Gort, pp. 172–73. Pownall, pp. 323–25. Macleod, pp. 277, 290–91.
64. Cab 79/5 COS (40) 193rd Meeting 25 June 1940. B. Collier, *The Defence of the United Kingdom* (HMSO, 1957), pp.129–30.
65. Cab 80/13 COS (40) 490. Letter from Lord Hankey to the COS Committee, 25 June 1940. Cab 79/5 COS (40) 195 26 June 1940.
66. Cab 79/5 COS (40) 197 27 June 1940. Cab 80/13 COS (40) 495 Memorandum by the COS 27 June 1940.
67. Cab 80/13 COS (40) 498. Note by the Prime Minister to the COS Committee, 28 June 1940.
68. Sir A. Bryant, *The Turn of the Tide* (the Alanbrooke Diaries, 1957), pp. 189–90 Field-Marshal Viscount Montgomery, *Memoirs* (1958), pp. 68–70. J. Connell, *Auchinleck* (1959), pp. 156–57.
69. Bryant, *The Turn of the Tide*, pp. 194–95. W.S. Churchill, *The Second World War* Vol II (1949), pp. 233–34.
70. *The Sunday Observer*, 11 November 1962.

71. Many authorities suggest that Dill would have been preferable to Gort as CIGS in 1937 or to Ironside in 1939, but note Sir Alexander Cadogan's diary entry for 29 April 1941, 'Dill is the most unimpressive – if charming – personality I have ever come across. Almost I am persuaded to believe in Ironside!' D. Dilks (Ed), The *Diaries of Sir Alexander Cadogan 1938-1945* (1971), p. 374.

10

Arras, May 1940: a Case Study in the Counter-Stroke

This research paper resulted from a small History Group, commissioned by the Director-General of Army Training, which held several meetings in the old War Office building in the early 1980s. The objective was to discover if lessons could be learnt from historical counter-attacks, or counter-strokes which might be useful to NATO forces in event of a Soviet offensive in Western Europe.

The collected essays were at first confined to confidential distribution and study in military institutions, but in 1986 were published by Brassey's Defence Publishers under the title *Old Battles and New Defences. Can We Learn from Military History?* As I made clear in my conclusion I was far from certain that military historians could derive 'lessons' from past conflicts that could be directly applicable to contemporary strategic problems, but they could provide case studies which might be beneficial.

In this instance our information and tentative conclusions were mercifully not put to the test because the Soviet incursion never happened. However, the Arras operations on 21 May 1940 have subsequently been explored on numerous Staff Rides and continue to interest historians because of their supposed influence on the outcome of the campaign and, in particular, on Britain's survival after Dunkirk.

On re-reading this essay after so many years I am struck by the great amount of detail required to establish what happened, and also by the difficulties of drawing clear lessons from these extremely confused events.

Though a small-scale action, the battle of Arras on 21 May 1940 is famous for two reasons: it was the only real British offensive during the melancholy withdrawal to Dunkirk; and it exerted a shock on the German high command out of all proportion to its strength. Arras, in fact, is a tragic might-have-been for it suggests that the deep-thrusting *panzer* columns were indeed extremely vulnerable to counter-attack. If only the British and French had possessed strong armoured reserves capable of a pincer movement to cut off the German *panzer* divisions from their slow-moving infantry and other supporting units, then the outcome of the campaign might have been very different.

The task of the historian is to describe as accurately as possible what actually happened even at the cost of deflating comfortable myths. But in the case of Arras the hasty improvisation, errors and confusion which characterized so much of British planning and execution may provide useful lessons to the contemporary strategist concerned with the possibility of a counter-stroke by I British Corps in the 1980s.

Operational Background 10–20 May

On 13 May the first German troops crossed the Meuse and by the following morning large numbers of tanks were over: the drive towards Abbeville and the Channel coast began. The advance was led by three armoured corps, namely; XLI (Reinhardt), XXXIX (Schmidt) in the northern sector and, to the south of them crossing at Sedan, XIX (Guderian). Moving at a speed hitherto scarcely imaginable, on 19 May XXXIX Corps approached Arras from the direction of Cambrai with Major-General Rommel's 7th *Panzer* Division leading. This thrust threatened to sever the British Expeditionary Force's line of communications with its bases in the Bay of Biscay and, more immediately, exposed its vulnerable rear areas containing the bulk of the British Expeditionary Force's ammunition and supplies. Moreover, Arras had to be held if there was any hope of the Allies in the 1st Army Group linking up with the main French forces south of the *panzer* corridor.

By the evening of 19 May all three German corps had advance units on the line of the Canal du Nord (see map 1). To the north lay the French First and Seventh Armies and the British Expeditionary Force – relatively unscathed as yet but in some confusion as they retreated from Belgium and Holland. South of the Somme unco-ordinated French units were trying to form a defensive line. To the west, however, armoured corps commanders, Guderian, Reinhardt and Schmidt were all supremely confident and eager to maintain their breakneck rate of advance. The senior commanders, particularly Kleist (*Panzer* Group) and Rundstedt (Army Group A), grew increasingly anxious however as the gap between the *panzer* spearheads and the mass of the following infantry increased. They understandably expected a powerful French counter-attack from north and south to chop off the heads of their dangerously isolated mechanized spearheads which were bound to experience fuel shortages and breakdowns. A pause was ordered on 17 May to enable the infantry to close up and the *panzer* leaders, notably Guderian and Rommel, had to shrug off further restraints from their superiors. From the outset Hitler was worried about the exposed southern flank and interfered with OKH. Halder (Army Chief-of-Staff) talked Hitler round and the advance continued. On 19 May, however, Jodl's diary referred to the *Führer's* great anxiety about French and British armoured attacks from the north, though Halder was content and even welcomed them. As a result, Jodl lamented, OKH and OKW were passing on contradictory orders.[1]

By 20 May Rommel and his leading troops, the 25th *Panzer* Regiment, were approaching Arras. Even he considered he had overstretched himself and went back to chivvy on his infantry regiments. All that day his reconnaissance groups were meeting with stiff resistance from Arras and the villages on its southern outskirts. Meanwhile SS *Totenkopf* Motorized Division, following in the wake of 8th *Panzer* Division which had raced ahead to Acq, was beginning to arrive on Rommel's left. On his right flank 5th *Panzer* Division was moving up a day's march behind. Rommel had excellent ground and air intelligence of the British strength in Arras and along the line of the river Scarpe. His leading units were tired and somewhat disorganized. Most commanders would have opted for a pause to allow for rest and consolidation: Rommel characteristically decided to attack round the south-west of Arras on the next day – 21 May.

On 10 May the bulk of the British Expeditionary Force began an advance of some 70 miles to its allotted sector on the river Dyle. It had scarcely taken up its positions when news was received of the German breakthrough on the Meuse. The British Expeditionary Force withdrew in stages to the Dendre and the Scheldt (or Escaut) reaching the latter by 20 May. General Lord Gort, Commander-in-Chief, British Expeditionary Force, woefully ignorant of the rapidly worsening situation to the south of the British Expeditionary Force, detached a scratch collection of units known as 'Macforce' (under Major-General Mason-MacFarlane) to protect his right rear, and a more coherent body, 'Petreforce', (under Major-General R. L. Petre) to hold Arras and the canal line to the south-east. Arras itself was rapidly converted into a formidable defence zone, but along the canal line two brigades of the 23rd Division would be no match for Reinhardt's *Panzers* supported by artillery and dive bombers.

On the evening of 19 May Gort ordered the 5th and 50th (Northumbrian) Divisions supported by the 1st Army Tank Brigade to move south to Arras to deliver a counter-attack. This sounds quite a formidable force, but when allowance is made for detachments and reserves, the actual units available comprised only the 151st Infantry Brigade (of 50th Division) and two regiments of the Tank Brigade. The infantry had been marching almost constantly (and with little sleep) for 10 days in extremely hot weather and needed much more than the few hours rest they were granted on 20 May. The tank situation was even worse by 20 May. The 1st Armoured Division had not yet arrived in France so the only armour of substance was Douglas Pratt's 1st Army Tank Brigade (4th and 7th Battalions Royal Tank Regiment). Despite the warnings of Gort's newly-appointed Adviser on Armoured Fighting Vehicles, Brigadier Vyvyan Pope, the tanks had been sent up to the Dyle, ordered to and fro, and then pulled back – all on their own tracks because no transporters were available. They

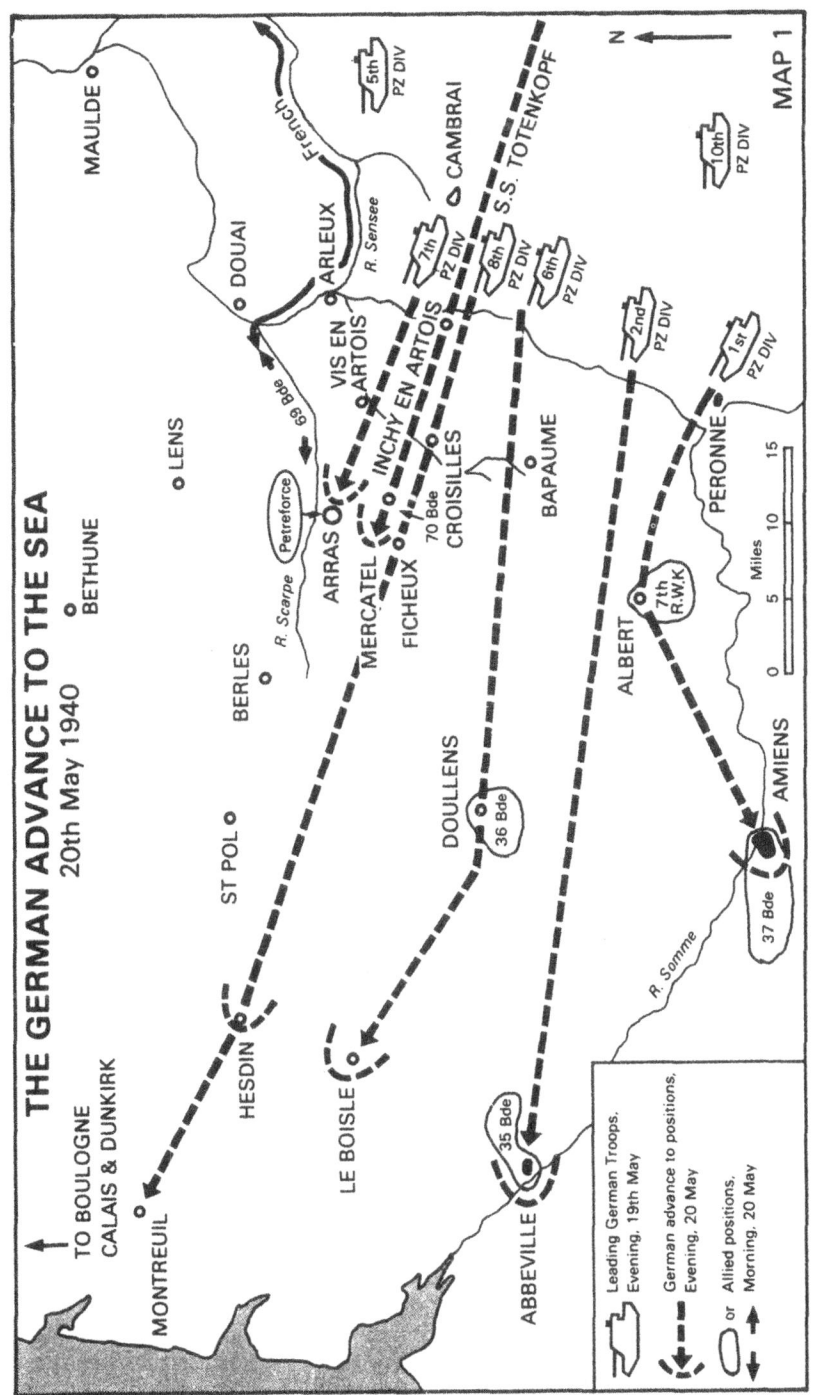

Map 1

had covered at least 120 miles in five days, in the process losing about 25 percent of their strength through worn out tracks. This useless shuttling to-and-fro of the Tank Brigade was an avoidable error.[2] As for the infantry component of the counter-attack, the 6th and 8th Battalions Durham Light Infantry were to prove themselves courageous fighters but they were not ideally suited for this demanding role. They were Territorial battalions with very limited pre-war training. Their only regular personnel comprised two officers (Adjutant and Quartermaster) and six warrant officers. More seriously, although by now well-trained as infantry, they had had no practice whatever in co-operation with other arms. Most of the troops had never even seen a tank let alone practiced field manoeuvres with them.[3]

The Origins of the Order for a Counter-Stroke

For the Allied High Commands 20 May was a critical and confusing day. Gamelin had been replaced by Weygand as Commander-in-Chief of the French Armed Forces but the latter was still in the process of taking over. German forces reached the Channel coast thus cutting off the British Expeditionary Force's line of communications and, in effect, forcing Gort either to retreat to the Channel ports or try to fight his way out to the south-west. Early on the morning of 20 May the Chief of Imperial General Staff, Ironside, arrived at Gort's headquarters with an unequivocal order from the War Cabinet to adopt the latter alternative. Gort quickly convinced him that this was impracticable because seven of his nine divisions were in contact with the enemy. The main effort to plug the gap, Gort insisted, must be made by French forces from south of the Somme, but he would play his part by employing his two unengaged divisions (i.e. 5th and 50th) at Arras the following day. Subsequently, after Ironside and Pownall (Gort's Chief-of-Staff) had persuaded the French to launch a simultaneous attack (on 21 May) with two divisions towards Cambrai, it looks as though Gort's Command Post began to regard Franklyn's limited operation as part of the projected Allied counter-attack to close the gap. Yet, according to both the Official History and Franklyn himself no fresh orders were issued, nor was Franklyn told of the French role. In the event the French were obliged to postpone their attack towards Cambrai and only the remnants (about 70 tanks) of Prioux's Light Armoured Division co-operated by protecting Franklyn's right flank.[4]

    According to Franklyn who was Commander of the 5th Infantry Division and of 'Frankforce', he received the following orders from Gort:

1. To move to Arras, dealing with any enemy which we might or might not meet en route.
2. To relieve French armoured troops, holding the line of the River Scarpe, east of Arras, also any British troops which I might find there.
3. To make Arras secure, gaining as much 'elbow room' as possible south of the town. To the best of my memory he used the term 'mopping up'. I certainly got the impression that I was only likely to encounter weak German detachments.[5]

The terms of these orders – essentially a mopping up operation in support of the garrison at Arras – explain why the bulk of two divisions was used to reinforce the town and the line of the Scarpe to the east and only a small part employed on what is known to history as the 'Arras counter-attack'.

What remains truly astonishing is that good intelligence of German strength in the Arras area, known at GHQ on 20 May and to Franklyn on 21 May, was not passed on to subordinate commanders. For example, on the morning of 21 May it was reported that an enemy tank column had attacked Arras the previous day; the 70th Brigade had been overwhelmed south-west of Arras; enemy tanks had been seen between the Arras–Doullens road and the Arras–St Pol road (i.e. between British troops and their start line); and strong columns of infantry and tanks had been seen on the evening of 20 May leaving Cambrai by the road to Arras. Despite these details and similar ominous intelligence the orders to Major-General Martel, the force commander under Franklyn, merely said that enemy infantry and tanks were known to be operating south and south-west of Arras but 'in numbers not believed to be great'. Thus, despite the excellent work of the 12th Lancers, it was apparently not realized that strong enemy forces were well beyond the Arras–Doullens road. Consequently, though the right column of the 'counter-attack' fought its way forward for several miles, its infantry never reached the 'start line'. As a Durham Light Infantry officer who took part in the battle later reflected:

> If this information had been received and properly assessed, it is difficult to believe the operation would have taken place in the form it did. As it was information received about the enemy by the two (infantry) battalions was virtually NIL.[6]

Franklyn's orders were given to Martel and his subordinates at 6:00 a.m. on 21 May:

> The 151st Infantry Brigade and divisional troops, was to attack with the 1st Army Tank Brigade under its command. The attack was to be launched round the south of Arras and to clear the area of the enemy as far round as the River Sensée. It was to be carried out in two phases. The first as far as the River Cojeul and the second to the Sensée.
>
> During the second phase the 13th Infantry Brigade of 5th Division was to co-operate by advancing over the River Scarpe. The 3rd Durham Light Infantry were to move out on the right flank of the attack. They had very little left except the 70 tanks, but if these moved out on this flank they would be ready to deal with any tank attack which the enemy might launch against this exposed flank...
>
> The operation resolved itself into clearing an area about 10 miles deep and four miles wide and I stated that I proposed to carry this out by advancing through the area with two mobile columns.

The area was, of course, much too large to be dealt with by an advance with troops extended over this front when only such a comparatively small force was available. It was a case for attacking in two columns each on a narrow front.[7]

Franklyn had ordered both columns to cross the start line at 2:00 p.m. but as the troops had an approach march of eight miles Martel requested a postponement until 3:00 p.m.

Though few accounts mention him, Brigadier Pope was again active at this conference, urging Martel and Pratt to keep to the timetable.

Assembly of the British Force

The 1st Tank Brigade reached Vimy on the night of 20–21 May, the last tank coming in at about 5:00 a.m. They had had a hazardous journey from Orchies via Carvin and Lens moving at an average speed of 3 mph on roads crammed with refugees who were frequently attacked from the air. After this long trek only 16 Mark IIs and 58 Mark Is remained serviceable. The latter accommodated a crew of only two: a driver and a commander in the turret who manned the single machine gun (mostly .303 Vickers) and operated the wireless set. The Mark Is therefore had no armour-piercing capacity but at least their thick armour was proof against the German 3.7 mm anti-tank gun. By contrast the Mark II (or Matilda) was the most heavily armoured tank then in operation anywhere, equipped with a 2-pdr gun as well as a machine gun and manned by a crew of four. To rectify the imbalance in the two tank battalions, seven Mark IIs from the 7th Royal Tank Regiment were loaned to the 4th.

As we have seen, the infantry battalions reached the forming up areas at Vimy desperately in need of rest. Just north of Duisans on the approach march next morning the 8th Durham Light Infantry came upon the wreckage of a German artillery column ambushed earlier by British or French tanks assisted by the 12th Lancers. This had a most cheering effect on the men.[8]

The speed with which the action was improvised resulted in serious shortcomings. Air support was requested from London but in the event not one aircraft appeared. The British Expeditionary Force's Air Component was in the process of withdrawal to bases in Kent, so Franklyn had no air formation in France which he could call upon for close support. In fact the Air Ministry ordered 57 Blenheims to attack targets between Arras and the sea on 21 May but they had no effect on the battle. It is hard to believe that reconnaissance sorties were flown over the Arras area on the morning of 21 May for none of the six German armoured divisions were reported – only infantry moving across the Arras–Cambrai road in open order!

There was no time for a proper reconnaissance and very few adequate maps were available. Radios had been checked and 'netted' a few days earlier but thereafter radio silence was maintained to conceal movement. As a consequence when the battle began few of the tanks could communicate with each other. There was no time for officers in the different arms to get to know each other. Major (later Brigadier) Jeffreys, soon to find himself commanding the 8th Durham Light Infantry in the battle, recalled 'There was no equipment for communication between infantry and armour. I wonder if it had ever been considered?'[9] Perhaps most serious of all, the precipitate haste of the planning entailed that no tank officer was present at the final Order Group. The infantry battalion commanders were placed in control of each column but this was not made clear to the Royal Tank Regiment commanders, thus paving the way for confusion and acrimony.[10]

The two columns (composed as follows) left Vimy at 11:00 a.m. on 21 May:

Right–Hand Column
7th Royal Tank Regiment
8th Durham Light Infantry
365th Battery, 92nd Field Regiment Royal Artillery
260th Battery, 65th Anti-Tank Regiment Royal Artillery
One Platoon, 151st Brigade Anti-Tank Company
'Z' Company, 4th Royal Northumberland Fusiliers
Scout Platoon, 4th Royal Northumberland Fusiliers

Left–Hand Column
4th Royal Tank Regiment
6th Durham Light Infantry
368th Field Battery Royal Artillery
206th Battery, 52nd Anti-Tank Regiment Royal Artillery
One Platoon 151st Brigade Anti-Tank Company
'Y' Company, 4th Royal Northumberland Fusiliers
Scout Platoon, 4th Royal Northumberland Fusiliers

The right-hand column on the outer periphery had the longer and more difficult route to follow. It was meant to wheel west of Arras through Maroeuil, Warlus and Vailly, while the left or inner column travelled by way of Ecurie, Achicourt, Beaurains to Henin.

Expert opinion at the time (except in the 7th Royal Tank Regiment) reckoned that the 4th Royal Tank Regiment was better trained and more efficiently led. Both columns were supposed to cross the start line of the Arras–Doullens road at 2:00 p.m.[11]

The German Advance Results in an Encounter Battle

Franklyn's composite force might have been adequate for 'mopping up' weak enemy advance parties but in reality it was being thrust into what the British commander called 'a hornets' nest' – that is a formidable armoured force led by the redoubtable Rommel and itself poised for an advance around the west of Arras. This advance involved the 7th *Panzer* and SS *Totenkopf* Divisions in a swing aimed north towards

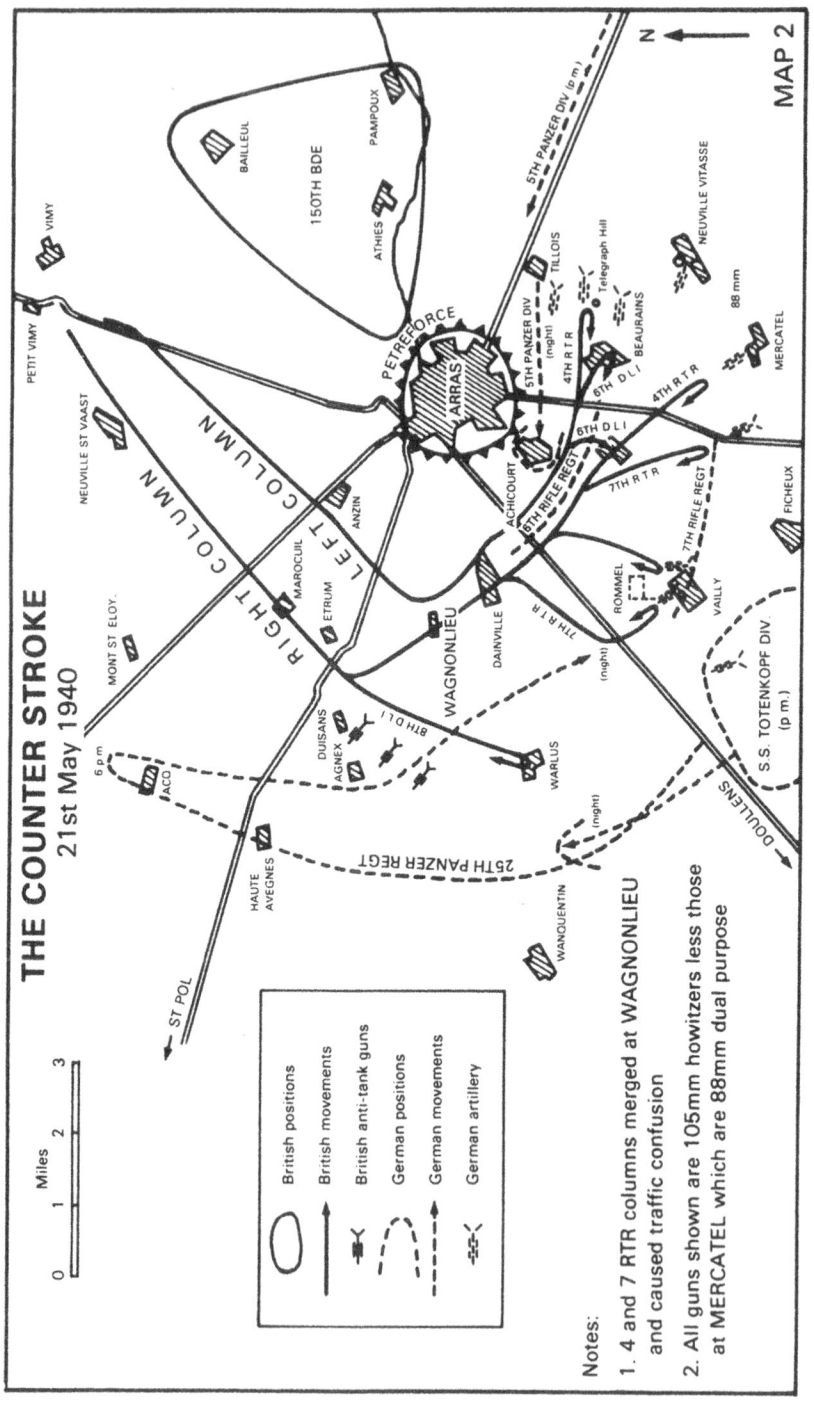

Map 2

Lille which would cut across the route taken by 8th *Panzer* Division the previous day in its thrust to Acq. Rommel did not expect much opposition in the early stages of his new advance and, by coincidence, set the time of the start at precisely that at which the British were due to cross the Arras–Doullens road. Rommel's route would take the bulk of his divisions just to the west of the right-hand British column, but his 6th Rifle Regiment was slap in the path of the left-hand British column. Meanwhile 3rd and 5th *Panzer* Divisions were not yet ready to advance east of Arras so Rommel's right flank was left completely exposed. Rommel had intended to lead the advance in person but his infantry regiments were so slow in closing up that he went back to chase them up.[12]

The Battle

The left-hand British column had the shorter distance to cover and its tanks were better organized, for example a few of its radio sets were working. Nevertheless by the time the leading tanks reached the start line it was clear that only the motor-cyclists of the 4th Royal Northumberland Fusiliers could keep up. The tired infantry of the 6th Durham Light Infantry being well behind, the column commander, Lieutenant-Colonel Miller, agreed that the tanks should go on without them. But a mile before reaching the start line at Dainville the tanks encountered the leading elements of Rommel's 6th Rifle Regiment. A company of 4th Royal Northumberland Fusiliers and a troop of Mark I tanks were detached to clear the village.

The 4th Royal Tank Regiment went on unsupported and enjoyed a brief 'happy time' against the surprised German column. As Lieutenant (later Brigadier) Peter Vaux, who commanded a light tank relates:

> To our great surprise we found we had come straight into the flank of a German mechanised column which was moving across our front. They were just as surprised as us and we were right in amongst them (because, you see, they were in the trees) – and for some quarter of an hour or so, there was a glorious 'free for all'. We knocked out quite a lot of their lorries: the Germans running all over the place.[13]

Between 3:00 and 5:00 p.m. the British tanks advanced through the enclosed country between Achicourt, Agny and Beaurains, overrunning Rommel's defensive screen because his 37mm anti-tank guns were incapable of penetrating their armour. In some cases a dozen or more shells simply bounced off. The German gunners fled or were shot down, while their infantry took cover in the surrounding villages. It was an inspiring period for the British tank crews who at last, albeit briefly, held the upper hand as they advanced to Beaurains, knocking out enemy infantry, lorries and anti-tank guns. Meanwhile the 6th Durham Light Infantry cleared the villages of Agny and Achicourt taking many prisoners, but were ordered not to proceed beyond Beaurains because the right-hand column was not making good progress and there were enemy tanks ahead. Lieutenant Vaux and the leading British tanks reached Telegraph Hill beyond Beaurains where about 20 of them were knocked out by German 105 mm field guns firing over open sights. These enemy guns should have been engaged by counter-battery action by the 50th Division's artillery but in fact the divisional artillery took no part in the battle. It would have required Forward Observation Officers forward with the British tanks but this had not yet become standard practice.[14] Lieutenant-Colonel Miller's supporting battery did arrive in time but again there was a failure of communications between forward observer and the guns: the latter were obliged to shoot off the map, without observation, at a secondary target.

In the early evening British tanks and infantry in Beaurains and Achicourt were subjected to a prolonged artillery and dive-bombing attack, the latter directed by an unmolested spotter plane above the battle. Moreover, 5th *Panzer* Division was now approaching Beaurains. At 8:15 p.m. the column commander decided to concentrate in Achicourt; the column had clearly shot its bolt and there were no fresh troops to exploit its success or even to hold the ground occupied. Once again Brigadier Pope had been active – by car and on foot – close to the battlefront urging forward and re-directing battalion commanders. He reported critically that:

> in this action the commanders generally were too far back. In an armoured action it is essential that commanders should be well up to take immediate advantage of fleeting opportunities and to deal with sudden changes in the situation.[15]

The right column started on time but thereafter just about everything went wrong. As an 8th Durham Light Infantry officer recalls:

> The CO (of the 8th Durham Light Infantry) met the CO of the tanks, but liaison did not extend further down. A scout car with a tank liaison officer who was in communication with his CO was to move with 8th Durham Light Infantry headquarters. Soon after reaching the assembly area at Maroeuil contact was lost with the 7th Royal Tank Regiment because the scout car radio ceased to function… that was the last we saw of 7th Royal Tank Regiment.[16]

In fact the right column's scout cars raced ahead while the motor cycles stayed behind and went into reserve. Worse was soon to follow for enemy troops, survivors of an attack on the rear echelons of the 8th *Panzer* Division the previous day, were found to be occupying Duisans well on the 'home side' of the start line which was supposed to be clear of the enemy. Duisans was cleared by British and French tanks and a company of the 8th Durham Light Infantry, but as Kenneth Macksey comments:

> the foundations of an early breakdown in this sector had been laid, because if an attack is to start amongst uncertainty and confusion its sequel can hardly be less than utter chaos.[17]

The tanks were already well ahead of the infantry but, to make matters far worse, the tank commander took the wrong road out of Duisans, turning east and making for Dainville rather than taking the cross country route south via Warlus to Vailly. It is not clear whether the column commander had been given ambiguous directions or whether it was a simple map-reading error. The disastrous consequences were quickly apparent for the 7th Royal Tank Regiment shortly found themselves entangled with the rear of the 4th Royal Tank Regiment in the final stages of their skirmish in Dainville. About this time a few individuals in the 7th Royal Tank Regiment saw the daunting sight of the 25th *Panzer* Regiment (with about 150 Mark III and IV tanks) moving north-west on the skyline about four miles to the south-west. Had the 7th Royal Tank Regiment followed their correct route via Warlus to Vailly they would surely have come into contact. In the event the 25th *Panzer* continued almost unchallenged to Acq, annihilating en route a scout car platoon of the 4th Royal Northumberland Fusiliers. These German tanks would later counter-attack from west to east.

Not to mince words, the system of command in the right-column had completely broken down. None of the radio sets was working and the 7th Royal Tank Regiment commander and his adjutant were both killed. Thanks in part to Pope's intervention the tanks were re-directed towards Vailly but there was no co-ordination. The confusion was epitomized by a party of French tanks attacking some British anti-tank guns which responded vigorously. However, as a Durham Light Infantry officer recalled, the right column received more support from French tanks than British. One Matilda, commanded by Tom Craig, approached Vailly and found it packed with German infantry. Unbeknown he was only a thousand yards from Rommel who had rushed back to take personal command. His (Rommel's) own account gives some idea of the shock effect of this rather disorganized British attack:

> Running along behind the battery lines, we arrived in Vailly and then called up the vehicles. The enemy tank fire had created chaos and confusion among our troops in the village and they were jamming up the roads and yards with their vehicles instead of going into action with every available weapon to fight off the oncoming attack. We tried to create order. After notifying Divisional staff of the critical situation in and around Vailly, we drove off to a hill, west of the village. Here we found a light anti-aircraft troop and several anti-tank guns located in some hollows in a small wood, mostly totally under cover. Over by the road the leading enemy tanks were across the road and had shot up one of our Mark IIIs. At the same time other tanks were coming down the road from Bac du Nord and across the railway. It was an extremely tight spot, for there were also several tanks close to Vailly on the north side. The crew of a nearby howitzer battery now left their guns and, swept along by the retreating infantry, ran.[18]

The right column's advance ground to a halt before the line of German guns in and around Vailly. Near Mercatel at the furthest point of the British advance the enemy used 88 mm anti-aircraft guns for the first time in their devastating anti-tank role. The battery designated to support the right column was held up by congested roads and played no part at all in the fighting at Duisans and Warlus. One anti-tank battery came into action near Duisans but the other never reached Warlus.

The infantry of the 8th Durham Light Infantry did not take part in the fighting around Vailly but two companies (the other two being left in Duisans) made a tremendous effort to reach Warlus. That village was also cleared and more prisoners taken. Just beyond Warlus, and still short of the Doullens road, which was strongly defended, the 8th Durham Light Infantry were stopped by intense small arms and mortar fire. At about 5:30 p.m. they were attacked by German tanks from their front and right flank and experienced their first *Stuka* dive-bombing attack. The *Stukas* arrived just when the inexperienced British infantry were tiring and losing momentum. They had a shattering effect on the troops' morale though they only caused about 10 casualties. As the regimental history bluntly states:

> Many of the troops were in a dazed condition and it was only with the very greatest difficulty that they were persuaded to get to their feet and to move on again.[19]

After a few similar experiences British troops realised that the *Junkers* 87 dive-bomber had much more bark than bite.

When darkness came the surviving tanks of the 7th Royal Tank Regiment and the 'A' and 'D' companies of the 8th Durham Light Infantry were attacked by a strong force of German tanks and infantry and surrounded in Warlus. To their surprise the British were also attacked by tanks coming from the north and west: this was the 25th *Panzer* Regiment which had reached Acq, only to be immediately ordered by Rommel to turn about and rescue their comrades who had been in a critical state for several hours. By the time the 25th *Panzer* Regiment returned to the battlefield however the British had set up an anti-tank screen of 2-pdr guns of the 260th Battery Royal Artillery which accounted for about 20 of Rommel's tanks. This was by far his greatest loss so far in the campaign. His 6th Rifle Regiment had also suffered heavy casualties.

The British troops under Lieutenant-Colonel Beart surrounded in Warlus seemed to have no hope of escape as darkness fell and their ammunition was nearly exhausted. Then, as the Durham's regimental history describes:

> Six French tanks with two armoured troop-carriers smashed their way through the German cordon and rumbled into the village. The tanks had arrived just in time and a plan was quickly drawn up for a break-out. At 0330 hours every Bren carrier and truck which had not been hit during the battle was used to evacuate the survivors of the small force which had held Warlus so gallantly. With the French tanks covering them the vehicles ran the gauntlet of German

fire and raced out of the burning village. This unexpected and daring move took the enemy by surprise and, although some of the trucks and carriers were hit, the sortie was successful and the overloaded vehicles rejoined the rest of the 8th Durham Light Infantry at Petit Vimy.[20]

The left-hand column was also fiercely attacked on the ground and from the air as it withdrew from Achicourt. The 5th *Panzer* Division despite being fired on by the 150th Brigade, which made a raid across the Scarpe on 21 May, joined in the pursuit from the direction of Tillois. Many vehicles were lost in the retreat and some platoons of the 6th Durham Light Infantry fought on until killed or taken prisoner. By this time men were falling asleep as they marched and had to be kicked awake by officers and NCOs.

Brigade headquarters was nowhere to be found so the withdrawal continued until the early hours of 22 May, when the survivors reached Ecurie due north of Arras.

The Effects of the Battle on the Enemy

As we should expect, the immediate shock of the British attack was most evident in the German divisions involved. Rommel, not a commander prone to exaggerate the opposition, did so on this occasion. His divisional battle report reads:

> Between 15:30 and 19:00 hours heavy fighting took place against hundreds of enemy tanks and following infantry. Our anti-tank gun (PAK) is not effective against the heavy British tanks, even at close range. The enemy broke through the defensive line formed by our PAK, the guns were put out of action or overrun and most of their crews killed.

The report lists seven officers, 17 NCOs and 65 men killed, 116 (all ranks) wounded and 173 missing.[21]The total estimated as missing was probably an underestimate because the British took about 400 prisoners. About 30 German tanks had also been destroyed. However the immediate effects of the British counter-attack must not be exaggerated. True, elements of the 7th *Panzer*, SS *Totenkopf* and the 5th *Panzer* had been thrown into confusion – even panic – for a few hours and forced to take up defensive positions. It was an unusual sight to see *Panzer* and SS troops running away! But, as, we have seen, Rommel quickly rallied his forces and adopted the textbook solution to the crisis. The British attack had been checked by a formidable line of guns (including 88mm); fresh units were called up to seal the flanks; and a counter-attack launched with tanks and infantry closely supported by *Stuka* dive-bombers. By late evening on 21 May the situation was more or less restored.[22]

We must now examine the wider repercussions of the battle on supporting units and the higher German command. Although II Army Corps, then south of Cambrai, was not directly involved, there was a 'slight panic' *('eine leichte Panikstimmung')* among its staff because the Arras attack reminded them of the French 'miracle of the Marne' in the autumn of 1914. Reinforcements, specifically 12th Infantry Division, were hurried to the Arras area, first to seal off the enemy attack and then counter-attack on the flanks. The 12th Infantry Division's diary noted that this was the first order to adopt a defensive position it had received so far in the campaign.[23]

General von Kluge, commanding the 4th Army, had been one of the senior generals who had displayed anxiety about the vulnerable flanks resulting from the *Panzer* divisions' headlong rush towards the Channel. His Army's war diary for 21 May reveals his reaction to the crisis:

> The enemy break-through at Arras is blocked. The northern part of Mormal Forest is cleared... Nothing new from the southern front. The bridgeheads are being held, apparently there has been no contact with the enemy. The OB (von Kluge) has withheld the command to take up position on the line Arras – St. Pol – Hesdin – Etaple to ensure first a build-up of a *Panzer* wedge according to orders and the clearing of the situation at Arras... *Today was the first day on which the enemy had achieved some success.* (added emphasis)[24]

At OKH General Halder, the Army Chief-of-Staff, was not perturbed by the setback at Arras. At 5:00 p.m. on 21 May he commented that the high ground at Arras would be decisive and ordered 4th Army to bring up its infantry divisions as quickly as possible. By 5:00 p.m. on 22 May OKH was quite satisfied with the position at Arras and ordered a general northward advance round the west of that city.[25]

At 1:30 on 22 May Army Group A war diary noted:

> The *Führer* wants to be briefed about the situation at Arras. Strong enemy forces there have tried to break out towards the south... In the evening of 21 May they succeeded in pressing back the 7th *Panzer* Division at a few places, after which the push was blocked. A weaker attempt by the opponent to break through between Douai and Arras was foiled.
>
> The *Führer* demands that all available mobile (*schnellen*) troops in the area on both sides of Arras and to its west up to the coast, and the Infantry Divisions to the east of Arras (i.e. of the 2nd, 12th and 16th Armies), be deployed in order to clear up the situation between Maubeuge and Valenciennes.[26]

On 23 May Halder confirmed that all was going well in the advance directed towards Calais. On this day General Kleist (the *Panzer* Group Commander) was reluctant to press forward until the crisis at Arras was totally settled, and he was also apprehensive about an attack from the south of the Somme. On 24 May Halder admitted that the infantry were slow in moving up to Arras but there was no danger from the south of the Somme so it was all right for Kleist to push on.[27]

Thus in the operational sphere it is evident that although the British action caused shock waves at least up the *Panzer* Group and the 4th Army commanders, Rommel on the spot and Corps commanders involved quickly stabilized the position by applying the textbook solution. Their ability to summon up overwhelming *Luftwaffe* support at short notice was clearly of crucial importance. On the negative side, the failure of the French to launch a supportive attack from south of the Somme quickly confirmed Halder in his confident belief that it was safe to press on.

Nevertheless the British action *did* have wider repercussions. A leading German authority on these events has written:

> The news that a critical situation had arisen at Arras undoubtedly had a certain psychological effect on the Germans.[28]

At the *Führer's* headquarters in particular, General Warlimont noted that Hitler was somewhat uneasy on the evening of 21 May because his infantry divisions were not pressing forward fast enough. He stayed in the map room until 1:30 a.m. The following day Hitler interfered hourly in operations; Keitel, Jodl and Göring siding with him in his anxiety against Halder and Brauchitsch who remained calm and confident that all was going well.[29] How closely this anxiety influenced the famous 'halt order' on 24 May we shall examine shortly.

Aftermath for the British at Arras

First, however, we should stick to chronology by concluding our account of the British forces in and around Arras. During 21 May Petreforce, holding Arras, and the brigades extended towards the east along the Scarpe, were reinforced with a view to participating in Gort's major attack to the south. Regiments were fed into the line as they arrived resulting in an 'organizational patchwork' which would have handi-capped the chances of an offensive – had it taken place.[30]

On 22 May the Germans planned to resume the advance held up on the previous day. The 5th *Panzer* Division would swing wide to the west of Arras – roughly following the line of the British withdrawal – with the 20th Motorized Division on its inner flank. East of Arras the 12th Infantry Division would drive northward across the Scarpe. These two thrusts would converge near Vimy thereby isolating the Arras garrison. In fact German progress west of Arras was slow on 22 May – largely due to the confusion caused by hasty improvization to meet the British counter-attack – while on the eastern side of the city there was a stalemate along the Scarpe. By the evening of 23 May, however, Arras was virtually surrounded and at 7:00 p.m. Gort ordered Frankforce to hold out to the last. At midnight Gort rescinded the order. It now seemed doubtful whether the French offensive from the south would ever take place (in fact it did not) so Gort was prepared to suffer French accusations of betrayal by saving as many of his troops as possible. The bulk of the garrison fought its way out under cover of darkness abetted by a dense ground mist, just avoiding the German pincers which closed on Vimy Ridge.

Wider Effects of the Arras Counter-Offensive

The highest claims made for the influence of the Arras action on the German 'halt order', and hence indirectly for the escape of the British Expeditionary Force, were made by Captain (later Sir Basil) Liddell Hart. After describing the effect of Kluge's and Kleist's cautionary advice on Rundstedt, Liddell Hart concludes:

> It may well be asked whether two battalions have ever had such a tremendous effect on history as the 4th and 7th Royal Tank Regiment achieved by their action at Arras.[31]

i.e. to save the British Army from being cut off from its escape route. There is much truth in the retarding effect of Kluge's and Kleist's reports to Rundstedt, as we shall see, but Liddell Hart's key witness was Rundstedt himself. In an interview with Liddell Hart on 26 October 1945 the Field-Marshal reportedly said:

> A critical moment in the drive came just as my forces had reached the Channel. It was caused by a British counterstroke southward from Arras on May 21. For a short time it was feared that the *Panzer* divisions would be cut off before the infantry divisions could come up to support them. None of the French counter-attacks carried any serious threat such as this one did.[32]

But in the interview Rundstedt had not linked the Arras action with the halt order; on the contrary in 1945 he blamed Hitler for intervening to stop the *Panzers* against the advice of Kleist and himself. This, he said, cost them victory.

The 'halt order' given by Rundstedt on 24 May and in effect extended until 27 May has fascinated students of the campaign because *in retrospect* it seemed to be the miracle or *deus ex machina* which made possible the escape of the British Expeditionary Force. At the time however there appeared to be strong operational reasons for a *pause* (as distinct from a three-day halt of the armour). Rundstedt, like all his senior colleagues, assumed that the British Expeditionary Force and the other forces in the pocket were trapped; nor did he know that the second phase of the conquest of France would prove to be as easy as it did.

Thus the origins of the halt order can be found in operational considerations in which the temporary setback at Arras played a significant but not dominating part. Let us briefly trace the chain of events. On 23 May Kleist informed the Commander of 4th Army by telephone that his armoured forces had suffered heavy losses in equipment:

> His forces were expected to safeguard the Somme front and establish strong bridgeheads; in addition, he was to take Boulogne and Calais and secure the territory in between; finally, he was to turn eastward and deploy on a 35 mile front for a vigorous attack in the Ypres–Dunkirk direction. Kleist pointed out

that in the 14 days of the campaign his divisions has suffered such losses in equipment that up to 50 percent of his tanks had been put out of action. His group was therefore not in a position to attack a strong enemy unless reinforced.

Later that afternoon Kluge telephoned Rundstedt to pass on this information and summed up the situation as follows:

> A decision was necessary by the next day, May 24, as to whether they should go north or east of Arras. In his view the men, too, would welcome it if they could close up a little more. Therefore he proposed that the situation on the Arras sector should be finally cleared up, that the mechanised units on the left wing should be allowed to close up, and that, if possible, the 2nd Mechanized Infantry Division on the Somme should be relieved.

Rundstedt endorsed these views and, much to the disgust of the two *Panzer* Corps commanders, Guderian and Reinhardt, ordered that the armoured forces should halt on 24 May to allow the remainder of the 4th Army to close up.[33] The British official historian underlines the reasonableness of Rundstedt's decision. His prior concern was to consolidate his position in case of further French and British counter-strokes. Moreover his armoured divisions were widely dispersed – the 9th near the Somme, the 2nd and 10th at Boulogne and Calais, the 1st facing Gravelines, the 6th and 8th opposite Aire and the 3rd, 4th, 5th and 7th near Arras. They were beginning to suffer heavily from breakdowns and battle losses and would soon be needed to spearhead the southern offensive. When Hitler visited Rundstedt on 24 May he endorsed the halt order but overturned a directive from Brauchitsch subordinating Army Group A to Army Group B for the final phase of Dunkirk. On 25 and 26 May Hitler left the decision as to whether or not to unleash the German tanks across the Canal line to Rundstedt and he declined to move. On 26 May Hitler intervened to insist that the armoured thrust towards Dunkirk be renewed but it was too late for a start to be made that day. Rundstedt may have exaggerated the likelihood of further counter-strokes from north and south (the Allies had abandoned hope of launching them by 25 May), but he was surely correct in judging that the marshy terrain around Dunkirk was unsuitable for tanks. Despite their protests at the halt, neither Guderian nor Kleist favoured the use of tanks to attack Dunkirk after viewing the position at close quarters.

As the official historian sums up, the German high command's problems at the time of the halt order derived from delays and setbacks imposed on their armies in the preceding few days – the counter-stroke from, and defence of Arras notable among them. In short, neither the orders of Hitler nor those of anyone else 'allowed' the British Expeditionary Force to escape.

> The plain truth is that the German Army and Air Force did their utmost to prevent it but failed.[34]

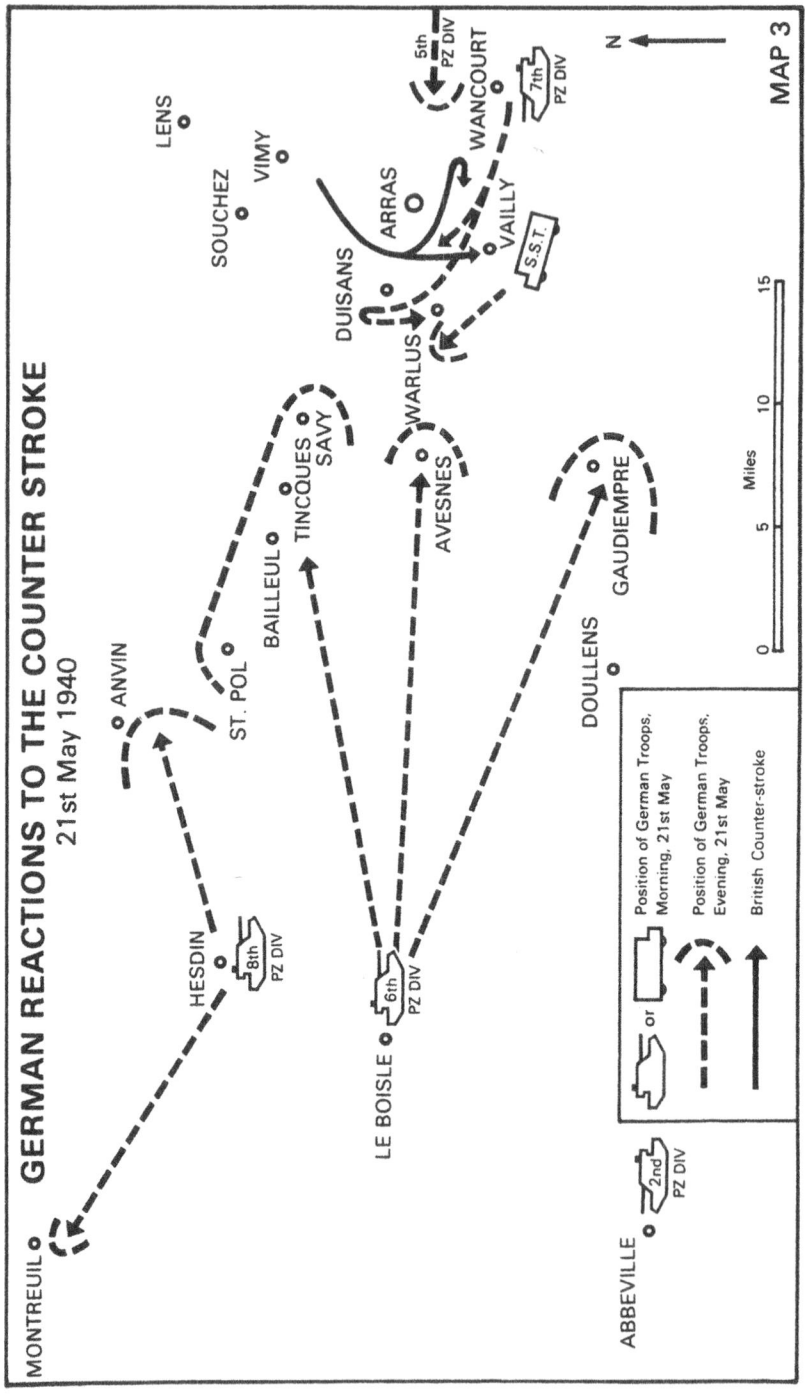

MAP 3

GERMAN REACTIONS TO THE COUNTER STROKE
21st May 1940

N

5th PZ DIV

WANCOURT

7th PZ DIV

LENS

VIMY

SOUCHEZ

ARRAS

DUISANS

VAILLY

S.S.T.

WARLUS

TINCQUES

SAVY

BAILLEUL

AVESNES

ST. POL

ANVIN

GAUDIEMPRE

DOULLENS

HESDIN

8th PZ DIV

LE BOISLE

6th PZ DIV

MONTREUIL

ABBEVILLE

2nd PZ DIV

Position of German Troops, Morning, 21st May

or

Position of German Troops, Evening, 21st May

British Counter-stroke

Miles

0   5   10   15

Map 3

The appreciation which best places the Arras battle in context in accounting for the 'miracle' of Dunkirk is that of Kenneth Macksey. He shows how the counter-stroke at Arras caused such reverberations of alarm that it obliged the leading German divisions to turn back on May 21–22 to guard their flank and rear leaving only a thin screen on the Channel coast. Moreover commanders such as Kleist became increasingly worried by the vulnerability of the long and thinly-guarded flanks of the corridor. For a brief but vital period more attention was paid to security than to further exploitation. The pause imposed on 2nd *Panzer* Division, for example, enabled Boulogne to be reinforced and defended gallantly until 25 May. Similarly Calais was only weakly defended on 22 May but reinforcements were rushed there and held 6th and 10th *Panzer* Divisions at bay until the port was overrun on 26 May. These divisions might have pushed on and taken Dunkirk virtually unopposed, but by 27 May the British and French forces had created a strong defensive position. Thus Macksey argues convincingly that in terms of divisions delayed and diverted, the defence of Arras helped to make possible the evacuation from Dunkirk. He also speculates that the counter-stroke at Arras had an unsettling effect on the German command causing head-on attacks against prepared positions, the bunching of divisions and many other signs of uncertainty. All this may seem a lot to claim for such a small-scale operation but two considerations have to be borne in mind: first, the Germans exaggerated the size of the attack and were unaware of the muddles and shortcomings on the British side; second, they had been expecting Allied counter-attacks ever since the break-out from the Meuse bridgehead, and Arras seemed a forerunner of greater Allied efforts to break through their extremely vulnerable corridor.[35]

Summing Up and Historical Lessons

1. The counter-attack was hastily improvised and on far too small a scale. The jibe about using tanks in 'penny packets' was in this case justified. Had the counter-attack consisted of two complete divisions and an armoured division it might well have disrupted the German advance. This is the tantalizing 'might have been' to which advocates of armoured warfare such as Liddell Hart legitimately refer. As regards lack of time for preparation, one cannot say that Gort would have done better to wait until 22 May. By then his troops would have rested and re-organized and more French support might have been available; but on the other hand Rommel and the divisions on his flanks would probably have driven past Arras.
2. Lack of time seriously weakened the power of the counter-stroke, even allowing for the small size of the force available. There was no time for reconnaissance on the ground or for checking that radios were working and on net. The infantry, already far from fresh, were hard put to reach the start line and most of the guns completely failed to do so due to congested roads.
3. Good intelligence about the formidable strength of enemy forces already close to Arras, or approaching from the direction of Cambrai, was available to Gort and Franklyn on 20 May but was not passed on to the column and battalion

commanders. Instead they were led to believe that this was a 'mopping up' operation against small infantry detachments. It is surprising that neither Franklyn nor Martel seems to have asked for clarification on this vital point.

4.   The nature and objective of the operation was not made clear to Franklyn, nor the amount of French support he would receive. Franklyn was given very limited objectives – though ones that proved well beyond the capacity of his tiny force – but he realised from his contacts with the French that a genuine counter-stroke was under consideration and that they understood his sortie to be part of it. Once again one might have expected him to seek clarification.

5.   Air support was totally lacking on the British side while it was absolutely essential – probably the single most important factor – in the German recovery and counter-offensive after their early reverses. True, this battle occurred at the most awkward moment when the Air Component was in the process of withdrawal to Kent, but the fact remains that there was no air formation in France on which General Franklyn could call for close support at short notice. Royal Air Force reconnaissance sorties over the Arras area on the morning before the battle had amazingly failed to report any German armoured forces.

6.   To the layman the British command structure seems too complex and fragmented in relation to the size of the force. Franklyn was in overall command but delegated the actual field command to an officer of similar rank – Martel. The commanding officers of 6th and 8th battalions Durham Light Infantry were given control of their respective columns, but some vestigial authority remained with the commanders of 4th and 7th Royal Tank Regiment under their brigadier – Douglas Pratt. Finally, Brigadier Pope exercised an ill-defined but nonetheless important role as a general galvaniser and whipper-in on the battlefield. Who actually commanded during the battle, say, between 3:00 p.m. and 8:00 p.m. remains something of a mystery. Pope's criticism – that the column commanders were too far back – seems fully justified.

7.   The counter-stroke was only a combined action in the most superficial sense. The infantry battalions had too far to march to the start line (about eight miles on a very hot day) without the extra handicap of discovering the enemy well on the 'home side' of it. Consequently the tanks got about three miles ahead and were out of radio communication. The infantry caught up in the left column only when the tanks had shot their bolt and began to fall back. In the right column all semblance of a combined action were lost when the tanks took the wrong road and became entangled with the left column. Thereafter the tanks fanned out in the general direction of Vailly and fought a series of heroic, small group or individual actions. Only in the later stages when the survivors were penned in around Warlus and Duisans was there some semblance to a combined action. The artillery batteries detailed to support the columns played a minor part in the left hand column's battle and none in the right column's. This was mainly due to unavoidable delays on the approach roads, but there also proved to be inadequate means of communication between Forward Observation Officers and guns. As

for the anti-tank batteries, they provided valuable support to the right column in the early stages near Duisans and in the later stages by forming a screen against 25 *Panzer* Regiment's drive from the north-west (from Acq towards Vailly). They seem to have played a smaller part in the left column's battle.

Co-operation with the French tanks operating on the British right flank was erratic. Eye witnesses in both columns report exchanges of fire with the French and also of French crews hiding under their tanks until pulled out by the British. On the positive side the French tanks provided more support to the 8th Durham Light Infantry in the right column than did 7th Royal Tank Regiment, and played a vital part late in the evening in extricating the garrison from Warlus. As in so much of the campaign of 1940, Anglo-French co-operation was a hit-or-miss affair depending largely on the goodwill and gallantry of individual officers.

8. Considering the inexperience of most of the troops and junior officers the performance of infantry, tank crews and anti-tank gunners was superb. Officers testify that the infantry were tired and 'browned off' at the start but the initial successes – particularly the sight of wrecked German vehicles and troops running away – acted as a tonic. The intense *Stuka* dive-bombing attacks between about 5:30 p.m. and 6:00 p.m. had a devastating effect on morale, but the troops rallied and continued to fight until late in the night. This performance was all the more praiseworthy in that several commanding officers, including those of the 4th and 7th Royal Tank Regiment were killed.

9. Obviously the timing of a counter-stroke is of crucial importance. In this case it was brilliant – better in fact than Gort and GHQ could possibly know. It achieved surprise and hit the more vulnerable sections of a *Panzer* division on the move and on an unprotected flank. For an hour or two it enjoyed remarkable success due mainly to the Mark II's firepower and thick armour rather than to superior mobility. The shock effect was all the greater because the German high command had been expecting a counter-stroke of this kind for the past few days and tended to exaggerate its strength. Unfortunately the British Expeditionary Force had nothing to spare to exploit this temporary advantage while the anticipated French attack from the south never occurred. Consequently Halder, who remained calm and confident throughout, was quickly able to restore the situation round Arras by the classical method of rushing up infantry divisions to block the thrust, and counter-attacking with armour on the flanks.

10. Nevertheless this German recovery was bought at a high price. Rommel's and other divisions driving westward were effectively halted on 21 and 22 May while those already to the west of Arras were turned north-eastward to guard against further counter-strokes. Thus, while it is an exaggeration to claim that the action at Arras 'saved the British Expeditionary Force', it did play a significant part in disrupting the German advance and causing delays from which the British Expeditionary Force profited.

Relevance of these 'Lessons' to the 1980s

The military historian is not well-qualified to extract contemporary lessons from case studies and his chief hope must be that the evidence he produces will 'speak for itself' when examined by serving officers. The lessons from the battle of Arras in 1940 must therefore be both tentative and rather general.

1.   Arras shows that even a small and hastily improvised force (well within the scope of I British Corps today) can deal a powerful counter-offensive stroke against an enemy who has advanced very rapidly and left vulnerable flanks or rear echelons.
2.   Good timing is essential, and with the means of surveillance and communication now available that should be easier to judge than in 1940. It is easy to imagine how an ill-timed stroke against a more powerful enemy could result in complete disaster – as did the mismanaged French efforts in May 1940.
3.   Unlike Arras, a modern counter-stroke clearly demands a genuinely combined, all-arms effort from the ground forces with close air support available directly to the force commander. In this respect it is the close German land–air co-operation in 1940 that requires study rather than its absence on the Allied side.
4.   Experienced, well-trained and fully equipped professional troops are essential for such an operation, well though the Territorial infantry fought in 1940. But even modern professionals would be at a disadvantage if they had marched in hot weather and gone short of sleep for 10 days before carrying out their attack. It is hard to imagine such a long build-up in Europe in the 1980s, though of course other hazards (such as the use of gas or fear of radiation) might have a comparable effect in exhausting the defenders before the chance came to counter-attack.
5.   In the Arras operation the British had only one ally to worry about – the French. But that operation demonstrates the misunderstandings and muddles that can occur when allied units are hastily 'roped in' at a late stage. It is clearly not much use the British developing a highly effective counter-stroke if their allies on either side are not fully involved in the planning and clear about their roles.
6.   Finally, there is the most difficult problem of all. Supposing the counterstroke is brilliantly successful in the short-run, causing severe dislocation and confusion to the enemy advance. What is meant to happen after that? Can the counter-stroke be exploited and converted into a full-scale counter-offensive designed to send the enemy reeling back – as happened repeatedly in the North African campaigns of 1940–1942? Or is it merely intended to gain time so as to delay escalation and permit diplomatic exchanges to take place? Such strategic and political problems take us well beyond our brief: it would have taken a much more powerful counter-stroke than the Allies were able to mount by 21 May 1940 to have *defeated* the *panzer* divisions which had already scythed through the French armies and reached the Channel coast. Now, as then, the small British force must presumably aim at *dislocation* rather than outright victory?

References

1. K. Macksey, *The Shadow of Vimy Ridge*, (Kimber 1965), pp. 197–98. B. H. Liddell Hart, *The Tanks*, Vol. 2, (Cassell, 1959), pp. 8–11. W. Warlimont, *Inside Hitler's Headquarters*, (Weidenfeld & Nicolson, 1964), p. 96.
2. R. Lewin, *Man of Armour: a Study of Lt. Gen. Vyvyan Pope*, (Leo Cooper, 1976), p. 96.
3. Letters to the author from Brigadier P. Jeffreys, 4 December 1983, and Major I. English, 25 November 1983.
4. B. Bond, *France and Belgium 1939–1940*, (Davis-Poynter, 1975), pp. 114–17 and L. F. Ellis, *The War in France and Flanders 1939–1940*, (HMSO, 1953), pp. 87–88.
5. General Sir Harold Franklyn, *The Story of One Green Howard in the Dunkirk Campaign*, (Richmond, Yorkshire: 1966), p. 14.
6. Ellis, pp. 88–90. Macksey, p 209. Major English's letter.
7. G. Le Q. Martel, *Our Armoured Forces*, (Faber & Faber, 1945), p. 64. Lewin, p. 116.
8. English's letter. Martel, p. 62.
9. Ellis, p. 97. Jeffreys' letter.
10. Macksey, pp. 207–08.
11. I have followed Macksey's account, pp. 208–09; Martel (pp. 64–65) differs on some details.
12. Macksey, p.210. H. A. Jacobsen (ed), *Decisive Battles of World War II: The German View*, (Deutsch, 1965), p. 50. B. H. Liddell Hart (ed), *The Rommel Papers*, (Collins, 1953), pp. 29–30.
13. Quoted by Macksey, p. 211.
14. Jeffreys' letter.
15. Lewin, p. 117.
16. English's letter.
17. Macksey, p. 217.
18. English's letter. Macksey, pp. 221–22.
19. Quoted by Macksey, p. 223. Also in Jeffreys' letter and video recording of Staff Tour to Arras (1982).
20. Quoted by Macksey, p. 227.
21. *Die 7 Panzer Division im Zweiten Weltkrieg*, Hg Traditions verband, Krefeld, p. 78.
22. Jacobsen and Rohwer, *op. cit.*, p. 50. Ellis, p. 97.
23. H. Tesky, *Bewegungskrieg. Führungsprobleme einer Infanterie Division im Wesrfeldzug 1940*, (Heidelberg: 1955), pp. 44–45.
24. H. A. Jacobsen, *Diinkirchen*, (Kurt Voinckel Verlag, 1958), p. 59.
25. H. A. Jacobsen (ed.), *Dokumente zum Westfeldzug 1940.* (Hg Gottinger, 1960), pp. 58–59, 63.
26. *Ibid.* p. 65.
27. *Ibid*, pp. 68, 70, 73–74.
28. Jacobsen and Rohwer, *op. cit.*, p. 51.
29. Warlimont, p. 97.
30. Macksey, p. 228.
31. Liddell Hart, *The Tanks*, Vol. 2, (Cassell, 1959), pp. 18–19, and *The Rommel Papers* pp. 33–34.
32. Liddell Hart Papers, Centre for Military Archives, King's College, London. 9/24/132 Talk with F. M. von Rundstedt, 26 October 1945. This note does not include the final sentence quoted in *The Tanks* and *The Rommel Papers*, i.e. 'None of the French counter-attacks carried any serious threat such as this one did.'
33. Jacobsen and Rohwer, p. 54. Warlimont, pp. 97–98. Warlimont believed that Rundstedt's temporary halt for operational reasons was justified. He added that when Hitler gave Göring the task of finishing off the British Expeditionary Force the German tanks had to be kept out of danger from the *Luftwaffe*.
34. Ellis, pp. 347–52.
35. Macksey, pp. 235–40.

11

Alanbrooke and the Mediterranean Strategy, 1942–1944

This study of Alanbrooke as a strategist seemed particularly appropriate for a *festschrift* in honour of Sir Michael Howard since the latter had wrestled with all these issues in his official history of *Grand Strategy* (vol IV). It seemed to me that Sir Arthur Bryant had grossly exaggerated and distorted Alanbrooke's achievement in determining Allied strategy and in doing so had understated his crucial role in resisting Churchill's wilder schemes and curbing the Americans' enthusiasm for a cross-Channel invasion in 1943 or early 1944.

Though still little known to the general public because his only field command was that of a Corps in 1940, a strong case can be made that Alanbrooke was Britain's most important soldier in the Second World War, and even perhaps the greatest of all the Service leaders. Since my study appeared (in 1992) Alanbrooke's *War Diaries 1939–1945* have been admirably edited by Alex Danchev and Dan Todman (Weidenfeld and Nicolson, 2001).

Alanbrooke's reputation as one of Britain's outstanding military leaders of the Second World War is not in question. General Sir Alan Brooke was promoted Field Marshal on 1 January 1944 and in September 1945 became Lord Alanbrooke of Brookeborough. General Ismay, whose personal experience went back to the Earl of Cavan in the early 1920s, rated Alanbrooke as 'certainly the best Chief of the Imperial General Staff under whom I served at close quarters'; while Montgomery, though admittedly countering American criticism, stated publicly in 1959 that he regarded Alanbrooke as 'the best soldier produced by any nation during Hitler's war'.[1] Sir David Fraser's impressive biography *Alanbrooke* (1982) provides conclusive evidence to support these high opinions. What is at issue is how far as CIGS (from December 1941) and chairman of the Chiefs of Staff Committee (from March 1942) Brooke consciously pursued a preconceived strategic plan, and to what extent it was his strategy that won the Allied victory in Europe. Twenty years ago, in *The Mediterranean Strategy In The Second World War*, Michael Howard demolished the notion of a specific 'British Way in Warfare' in the Mediterranean cunningly designed to preserve British imperial power while at the same time excluding the Soviet Union from the Balkans and Central Europe. Churchill's policies, however, rather than Alanbrooke's lay at the centre of this analysis.

The theme of this essay is that the extravagant claims made by Sir Arthur Bryant in editing *The Turn Of The Tide* (1957) and *Triumph In The West* (1959) misrepresented Alanbrooke's invaluable contribution as a foil to Churchill by stressing his role as a 'maker of modern strategy'. David Fraser's biography is more judicious and persuasive, but unfortunately the overall impression of his study is marred by the addition of an Epilogue in which Bryant repeats in even more emphatic terms his own opinions about Alanbrooke's pre-eminence as a strategist which caused so much controversy when the two volumes of edited diaries and autobiographical notes were first published.

That Bryant imported his own preconceptions is suggested by his excited letter to Alanbrooke on first reading the latter's diaries :

> For the rest, the book would give me the chance to do what I had hoped to do in the unfinished official shorter War History Of Sea Power 1939–45, on which I worked in my spare time for seven years for the Admiralty and Air Ministry: to present, free from all the cluttering mass of detail of the full official War Histories, the broad strategic perspective of the War which you, and you alone, I think always saw clearly. In one of my chapters in *The Age of Elegance*, I called Wellington 'Neptune's General' and the title might apply as aptly to you. Had Hitler seen the strategic truth as you saw it, I don't see how we could have held and turned the tide in that year of decision, 1942.[2]

Bryant also enclosed the copy of a lecture he had given which, he said, 'shows the war inevitably took the course you foresaw and planned'. In another letter Bryant claimed that one chapter, to be entitled 'A Momentous Journey', 'will prove your genius – not merely state it'.[3]

Alanbrooke shunned publicity and had not hitherto contemplated publishing his diaries – not surprisingly since not only were they scathing about most of the people he had worked with, but also were so cryptic and intermittent (being conceived as substitutes for letters to his wife), as to be scarcely publishable without the editor's elaborate running commentary and his own post-war notes. However, Bryant's skilful presentation exceeded Alanbrooke's expectations: 'You have seen so clearly what my strategy was, and looked at the war through the self-same spectacles as I did.' On 23 October 1956 Alanbrooke expressed to Bryant 'feelings of the most deep gratitude for having understood what I aimed at during the war and my reasons for doing so. It has always been a source of some sadness to me that so far very few have realised this. I do feel that your book will assist others to understand what my strategy was and why I stuck to it so fast'.[4]

Alanbrooke's 'sadness' about the public's ignorance of his personal contribution to the Allied victory was doubtless in part a reference to Churchill's virtual monopoly of credit on the British side through his prompt publication of a six-volume *History* skilfully emphasizing his own prominent role. Indeed, Lord Moran recalled Churchill 'rather aggressively' affirming that he himself had been responsible for all the strategic decisions that mattered. Moran records the feeling of dismay when the *Diaries* were published:

> Nobody… wanted to argue about Winston's skill or lack of skill in planning the strategy of the war, though that is the crucial issue raised by the *Diaries*. Nobody was prepared to see him treated dispassionately as an historical figure.[5]

Reviewers less sympathetic to Alanbrooke than Moran derived the picture of a 'dedicated, all-seeing field marshal doing his best to win the war almost single-handed at the conference table while constantly being hampered and harassed by the childish petulance of Winston Churchill and the strategic ignorance of his American colleagues, Marshall and Eisenhower'.[6]

When it became clear to Alanbrooke that Churchill had been deeply hurt by the publication of *The Turn Of The Tide*, he became very unhappy and sent Churchill a copy of the book with a fulsome inscription.[7] This, however, did not prevent Bryant reviving the controversy two years later when he repeated his claims on Alanbrooke's behalf as the chief architect of the Allied victory.[8] Finally, in sharp contrast to David Fraser's careful and perceptive summing up in his biography, Bryant re-asserted in his Epilogue that it had been:

> the strategic perception and genius of this unassuming and reticent soldier at Churchill's side which, *more than any other single factor* [emphasis added], had turned the tide of triumphant Axis victory in 1942… And that, thereafter,… his strategic genius had been largely instrumental in bringing about the defeat of Nazi Germany's bid for world dominion.[9]

It is necessary, at the onset, to say a few words about Alanbrooke's character and approach to strategy. This reserved and rather prim Ulsterman concealed a sensitive and somewhat pessimistic temperament behind a curt and often abrasive manner. His professional outlook contained a curious mixture of almost arrogant self-confidence and gloomy forebodings in times of crisis. Although a first class staff officer with a special expertise in gunnery, he had not been a progressive on the crucial issues of mechanisation and armoured warfare in the 1930s. His approach to strategic problems was that of an orthodox professional soldier neither rooted in theory nor concerned with politics. Moran described him as 'incurably matter of fact. Indeed. it sometimes seemed that he had put his mind into a strait-jacket'.[10]

Fraser has noted that, unlike his predecessor as CIGS, Sir John Dill, Alanbrooke was not particularly imaginative:

> he did not on the whole originate ideas. He was above all, as a strategist, cautious and realistic: rocklike and uncompromising on what was professionally right, never losing sight of essentials and always keeping matters exactly in balance.[11]

If one consideration can be said to have dominated Alanbrooke's thinking as CIGS it was a profound respect for the efficiency and power of German ground and air forces as he had experienced them in 1940; first as a Corps Commander on the retreat that terminated at Dunkirk and, secondly, as the reluctant Commander of the Second BEF which was unceremoniously bundled out of Normandy and Brittany in mid-June. Alanbrooke, like most senior officers who had shared these searing experiences, had no illusions about the difficulties of a cross-Channel attack or about the even greater problems of developing a successful landing. His frequent allusions to this issue in his diaries might be summarised as: 'don't risk a cross-Channel attack until the German forces have been so weakened (or the country has collapsed internally) that victory is certain', and with the implication 'and not even then if avoidable'. Churchill and the Chiefs of Staff had embodied this assumption in their strategy of 'closing the ring' since 1940, but it was a viewpoint which the Americans always found hard to understand.[12]

It is of course a drastic simplification of Alanbrooke's position in a complex decision-making structure to refer to 'his strategy'. He was *primus inter pares* as chairman of the Chiefs of Staff Committee, but his colleagues exerted considerable influence, particularly where naval and air aspects were involved, and indeed Portal sometimes spoke out at inter-Allied conferences on general strategic issues. Furthermore the COS was itself served by a host of specialist advisers and tri-service sub committees such as the Joint Planning Staff and the Joint Intelligence Committee. It would, in short, be implausible to attribute to a general staff officer in Alanbrooke's situation a personal strategic vision which could be sustained unmodified through all the pressure of internal expert advice and discussion – quite apart from the need to accommodate allies and the unpredictable actions of the enemy.

In fact, as the Official Historian of Grand Strategy, John Ehrman, has pointed out, the COS never managed to separate the discussion of strategic policy from the press of daily business and therefore were rarely free to discuss strategy as such. This deficiency, if such it was, was offset by the continuous, dynamic, multifarious stimulus provided by Churchill as Minister of Defence. All accounts bear witness to Churchill's intimate participation and central role in strategic discussions throughout the period 1940–1945.

> The War Cabinet and Defence Committee were in the background, the Prime Minister and the Chiefs of Staff conducted the war from day to day, and the Prime Minister dominated that combination.[13]

Alanbrooke certainly wished Bryant to stress that he had followed a clearly defined and consistent strategy. He drew the latter's attention to his diary entry on 3 December 1941, three days after becoming CIGS. In this he had written:

> I am positive that our policy for the conduct of the war should be to direct both military and political efforts towards the early conquest of North Africa. From there we shall be able to reopen the Mediterranean and to stage offensive operations against Italy.[14]

Although this marked the emergence of a 'Mediterranean policy', other contemporary references show that the Chiefs of Staff were still thinking defensively in terms of containment. Indeed at this time Alanbrooke suggested that the Western Mediterranean, including any operations against Sicily or Sardinia, should become an exclusively American responsibility. It seems that Alanbrooke's main purpose was to reopen the Mediterranean as a traffic route to the Far East. Churchill had already perceived the possibilities of further offensive operations in the Mediterranean after the clearance of North Africa, though he was apt to press for several operations simultaneously.[15]

The greatest objection, however, to Alanbrooke's later claim to have pursued a consistent Mediterranean strategy is that throughout the spring and summer of 1942 he went along with the Anglo–American agreement to give priority to a cross-Channel offensive. Thus on 14 April he recorded:

> A momentous meeting at which we accepted their (i.e., American) proposals for offensive action in Europe in 1942 perhaps, and in 1943 for certain. They have not begun to realise all the implications of this plan and all the difficulties that lie ahead of us.[16]

As late as 20 June 1942 in Washington Alanbrooke could note:

> We fear the worst and are certain that North Africa and North Norway plans for 1942 will loom large in their (i.e., Churchill's and Roosevelt's) proposals, whilst we are convinced that they are not possible.[17]

This extract is remarkable in two respects. First, the context makes clear that the 'We' included King and Marshall as well as the COS ('at least as military men we were in agreement as to the policy we should adopt'); and, secondly, it is curious that Alanbrooke should link North Africa, where a great campaign was already in progress, with northern Norway, which remained one of the Prime Minister's least practical obsessions.

Alanbrooke was already making scathing criticisms of Marshall's incompetence as a strategist, but there is no evidence that in the summer of 1942 he tried to persuade the latter of the impracticability of a cross-Channel assault. Nor did Alanbrooke press the merits of a North African invasion (code named GYMNAST and later TORCH) on Marshall. The reason was that with Rommel currently threatening to invade Egypt, and Russia's survival still in the balance, he was uncertain, even pessimistic, about Allied prospects in the Eastern Mediterranean. These doubts were understandable, but as Fraser remarks, they must be remembered in assessing claims that he consistently saw the clearance of North Africa as an *indispensable* preliminary to cross-Channel operations. Moreover GYMNAST had no support among the American chiefs of staff because they suspected it would lead to the postponement of ROUNDUP. They were right. It was of course Roosevelt and Churchill who together insisted that GYMNAST-TORCH must be launched in 1942 as the only feasible operation for American forces in the European theatre. When this decision was conveyed to the COS on 23 July 1942, Alanbrooke noted revealingly:

> Winston anxious that I should not put Marshall off Africa by referring to Middle East dangers in 1943. Told him I must put whole strategic picture in front of Americans. Foresee difficulties ahead of me.[18]

Great though these difficulties were, Alanbrooke had been overly pessimistic in his assessment of the Allied predicament in 1942. As he wrote from the vantage point of 1 January 1943:

> Wherever I looked I could see nothing but trouble. Middle East began to crumble, Egypt was threatened. I felt Russia would never hold, Caucasus was bound to be penetrated and Abadan... would be captured, with the consequent collapse of Middle East, India etc.[19]

Through the winter months of 1942–1943 Alanbrooke fretted at the slow progress of the Allies in completing the clearance of North Africa not appreciating, as

Churchill certainly did, that the delay was to the Allies' long-term advantage since Hitler's large-scale reinforcements, thanks to his refusal to permit withdrawals, would inevitably go into the bag and thereby pave the way for easier operations against Italy. As Liddell Hart noted:

> Brooke's feelings of impatience at the time were very natural… but they all run contrary to Bryant's interpretation of his strategy and his claims for its subtlety.[20]

Between September and December 1942 the COS agreed on a Mediterranean strategy for 1943. Their aims included the release of shipping resources, the acquisition of new bases for the bombing of Germany and measures designed to force the collapse of Italy. The invasion of Sicily was agreed but no plans were made for a land campaign in Italy itself. If Italy collapsed the Germans would have to take over not only the Italian mainland, but also extensive Italian commitments in the Balkans and the Aegean. This enforced dispersal of German forces would reduce pressure on the Russians on the Eastern Front and thereby compensate in part for the failure to open a Second Front in North-West Europe in 1943. Alanbrooke's diary entries in December 1942 dwell on the COS's determination to wean both Churchill and Marshall away from the invasion of France in 1943.[21]

Alanbrooke's performance at the Casablanca conference in January 1943 perhaps constituted his greatest contribution to the making of Allied strategy. Assisted by the failure of the Allied Christmas attack in Tunisia and by signs that the campaign would continue for several months longer, Alanbrooke played a dominant role in gaining agreement for an extension of operations in the Mediterranean, at least for the greater part of 1943. His interventions in the debates of the Combined Chiefs of Staff revealed a mixture of pessimism and optimism for the coming year. At the meeting on 14 January, for example, he stressed that shortage of shipping imposed a stranglehold on all offensive operations: 'We must defeat the U-boat or we might not be able to win the war.' But in the same discussion he suggested the possibility of a sudden German collapse, in which case we might be able to win final victory in Europe by the end of 1943. He argued, with thorough supporting evidence, that Italy and the Balkans offered better prospects for amphibious operations because Germany would therefore be compelled to disperse her resources; our immediate objectives should be to knock-out Italy and try to bring Turkey in on the Allied side. He countered Marshall's advocacy of a cross-Channel attack in 1943 by pointing out that the Anglo–American effort would be small compared with the Russian and would not exert great influence until Germany was weakening. The latter had 44 divisions in France against a maximum 22 Allied divisions (dependent on the immediate transfer of landing craft from the Mediterranean), so the invasion would probably be defeated or hemmed in a bridgehead. In any case the invasion could not be launched before the late summer which would entail that no assistance would be given to the Russians in the meantime.[22]

The CIGS was for once in agreement with the Prime Minister in favouring an amphibious operation against Sicily rather than Sardinia, but he had an exhausting time in persuading his colleagues. The joint Planning Staff favoured Sardinia because they had serious doubts about success against the more strongly defended Sicily. Mountbatten supported them, and both Portal and Ismay were wavering. After 'a three hours hammer and tongs battle', the CIGS flatly refused to go back to the Americans and tell them we did not know our own minds. In any case he strongly disagreed with them. This was Alanbrooke at his decisive best, but there is a certain irony in his insistence on the option which led logically to the invasion of the Italian mainland and subsequently to an attritional campaign, whereas Sardinia would have provided bomber bases and the possibility of amphibious threats without a full-scale invasion.[23] Interestingly, Alanbrooke told the CCS:

> he did not believe we could undertake any further operations in Italy from Sicily in 1943, unless Italy collapsed completely. We should be very careful of accepting any invitation to support anti-Fascist insurrections. To do so might only immobilize a considerable force to no useful purpose.

He also erred on the cautious side on how soon operation HUSKY (against Sicily) could be launched and how long it would take to complete. Finally, it must be noted that, prominent though the CIGS had been in arguing the British viewpoint, it was Dill and Slessor who between them provided a formula which satisfied the American chiefs of staff on the linkage between the European and Pacific theatres of war. Without Dill's wise and emollient background role Alanbrooke's tactless treatment of the Americans on this and other occasions might have been disastrous.[24]

By the time the British delegation arrived in Washington for the Trident Conference in May 1943 Axis resistance in North Africa had been ended and hesitation about the invasion of mainland Italy after Sicily had largely disappeared. The Joint Planning Staff was optimistic that Italian resistance would soon collapse, in which case the country should be occupied as far north as Rome, a bridgehead established on the Dalmatian coast and Turkey pressed even more strongly to enter the war. Alanbrooke and Churchill both set great store on Turkey's entry into the war much to the puzzlement of the Americans. At the CCS meeting on 19 May, Alanbrooke argued more cautiously for the advantage of going into Italy after HUSKY but 'how far needed further discussion'. Alanbrooke thought the Allies could exploit success in Italy without crippling ROUNDUP for which he suggested 1 May or 1 June 1944, by when the Russians would again be active on the Eastern Front after the spring thaw. Marshall said sharply that the British proposals magnified the results to be obtained in Mediterranean operations and minimised the forces that would have to be used and their logistic requirements; on the other hand the British were unduly pessimistic regarding cross-Channel prospects in view of the Allies' vast airpower. The CCS were obliged to resort to 'Off the Record Meetings' in a closed session with only the Chiefs of Staff and a secretary present in order to reach a compromise between the British position and the divergent strategies of General Marshall and Admiral King. Alanbrooke felt the resultant compromise – priority given to preparations against Italy

– was a personal triumph. Nevertheless he recalled later that his temporary inability 'to bring the Americans along with us' filled him with depression, and at times almost with despair.[25]

Given the Americans' earlier opposition to involvement inside the Mediterranean and Alanbrooke's reservations about what to do after Sicily, the decision to invade Italy seems, in retrospect, to have been taken almost casually. Liddell Hart is surely right to suggest that it was 'the logic of events resulting from loss of time, more than the logic of argument' which swung Allied strategy into this channel rather than a hectic attempt to assemble forces and landing craft for a cross-Channel attempt in the late summer of 1943.[26]

HUSKY was successfully launched on 9 July, and a week later Eisenhower and his colleagues accepted that an invasion of the mainland should speedily follow. Joint planning for a landing near Naples in the Gulf of Salerno began, but Alanbrooke characteristically urged caution, fearing that the German speed of build-up against such a hazardous landing would risk disaster. However, on 22 July he accepted that the risk of this operation (AVALANCHE) was worth taking.[27]

When the Quadrant Conference assembled at Quebec in mid-August 1943 it was becoming evident that the lack of landing craft would prevent the Allies from exploiting Mussolini's fall from power by giving Badoglio's Government the confidence to change sides. Nevertheless there was a general expectation, especially among the British delegates, that Hitler would not commit large forces to the defence of southern Italy and that the Allies would quickly advance north of Rome. Alanbrooke argued that the further dispersal of German forces was necessary to give OVERLORD a reasonable chance of success and that operations in Italy would serve this purpose. But how far up the peninsula should the advance be pressed? He thought they should go beyond the narrow Apennine 'waist' to seize the north-western plain for airfields and as a possible gateway into southern France for which French troops could be employed. He calculated it would take 20 Allied divisions to hold the Apennine line which might need three of the seven divisions allocated to OVERLORD. If the Milan–Turin area were taken all seven might be required, but a decision should be deferred. The Americans were not pleased. King suggested that the COS had serious doubts about OVERLORD. Marshall said that if OVERLORD was not given over-riding priority it would be doomed and the whole strategic concept would have to be recast: the American forces in Britain might well be reduced to an Army corps necessary for an opportunist cross-Channel operation. We should in effect be relying on our bombing force alone with the outcome uncertain. Alanbrooke recorded his complete failure to get Marshall to realize the relation between the cross-Channel and Italian operations, but American impatience with the growing British enthusiasm for a major campaign in Italy is easy to understand. Dill as well as Alanbrooke found Marshall 'most unmanageable and irreconcilable. Even threatening to resign if we pressed our point'.[28]

Again it took a closed session to smooth over the worst of inter-Allied friction and again Alanbrooke got most of his demands accepted in principle, aided as he was by the Italian Government's undertaking to surrender as soon as the Allies landed on the mainland. Thus it was agreed that Rome should be captured, air bases established at Foggia and in the Campagna, and the Balkan guerrillas helped with supplies across the Adriatic. In practice, however, the availability of scarce landing craft would determine what could be attempted, and it was agreed that preparations for OVERLORD (target date 1 May 1944) should have priority. When the conference ended Alanbrooke experienced a profound reaction of emptiness, depression, loneliness and dissatisfaction over results, and although he was in a better mood the following day (25 August), these diary entries do reveal the great emotional commitment which he invested in his arguments about strategy.[29]

When Italy capitulated on 8 September the Germans reacted quickly not only by pouring forces into Italy but also by seizing the Italian-held Aegean islands, including Rhodes. Churchill drove his CIGS to distraction by his obsession with the recapture of Rhodes as a prelude to setting the Balkans ablaze and bringing Turkey into the war. On 8 October Alanbrooke recorded that Churchill had worked himself into such a frenzy of excitement over Rhodes that he risked endangering relations with the President and the Americans and the future of the Italian campaign. Roosevelt adamantly refused to come to Tunis to discuss Rhodes and Eisenhower refused to release forces from Italy where the speed and strength of German reaction had confounded hopes of a rapid advance from Salerno.[30] This episode also clearly indicated that the Americans were becoming the senior partner.

Although Alanbrooke always publicly upheld his commitment to OVERLORD, several diary entries in October 1943 suggest that this wavered in the bitter reaction to the frustrated hopes of an easy occupation of southern Italy. In mid-October the COS received a note from the PM 'wishing to swing the strategy back to the Mediterranean at the expense of the Channel'. 'I am in many ways entirely with him,' Alanbrooke noted, 'but God knows where this may lead as regards clashes with the Americans'. On October 25 he noted:

> Our build up in Italy is much slower than that of the Germans and far slower than I expected. We shall have to have an almighty row with the Americans who have put us in this position with their insistence to abandon the Mediterranean operations for the very problematical cross-Channel operations. We are now beginning to see the full beauty of the Marshall strategy! It is quite heartbreaking when we see what we might have done this year if our strategy had not been distorted by the Americans.[31]

Alanbrooke's comments, though understandable as a reaction to the glittering prospects first raised by the Italian capitulation and then dashed, due mainly to the Allies' lack of shipping, were neither accurate nor just. The Americans had by no means abandoned the Mediterranean operations agreed upon at Quebec; indeed they could justly retaliate that it was the British who were trying to transform the subordinate theatre into the major one. More specifically, Alanbrooke's diversionary strategy had succeeded in its main objectives: North Africa and the Mediterranean sea route had been cleared; bombing bases were established in southern Italy; and nearly 50 German divisions had been drawn into Italy and the Balkans. The Americans, in short, were justified in insisting that OVERLORD must be given first priority although they remained committed to an advance in Italy at least as far as Rome. Dill at least grasped this point when writing to Alanbrooke on 16 October:

> I do not believe it was ever possible to make the Americans more Mediterranean-minded than they are today. The American Chiefs of Staff have given way to our views a thousand times more than we have given way to them.[32]

As for Alanbrooke's bitter remarks about setting the Balkans ablaze and winning the war in 1943 had it not been for American myopia, his biographer assesses whether he possessed a visionary Mediterranean strategy which went further than was practicable within the limits of Anglo–American agreement. He concludes that despite frequent references to the value of Turkish intervention and the desirability of support for Balkan guerrillas, the diaries do not present a coherent, alternative Mediterranean strategy. As he admits, Alanbrooke's reasoning in this outburst remains an enigma.[33]

On 11 November 1943 the COS and the Prime Minister agreed on the strategy to be recommended at the forthcoming Cairo Conference. While stressing that they did not recoil from or wish to side-track their commitment to take part in a cross-Channel attack in the late spring or early summer of 1944, they added:

> We must not, however, regard OVERLORD on a fixed date as the pivot of our whole strategy on which all else turns.

German strength in France might make OVERLORD impossible at one extreme or her collapse might make it comparatively easy at the other (RANKIN being the code-word for the easier option). In the meantime the German forces should be stretched to the utmost, including the following operations: the Italian offensive should be pushed to secure the Pisa–Rimini Line; measures should be intensified in support of the Balkan partisans, if necessary by forming a bridgehead on the Dalmatian and Albanian coasts; Turkey should be brought into the war and the Dardanelles opened. If all these efforts entailed a delay in assembling the forces in the United Kingdom necessary for OVERLORD this should be accepted. Alanbrooke realised this would cause 'a pretty serious set-to' with the Americans but complained 'I am tired of seeing our strategy warped by their short-sightedness'. He did indeed have 'the father and mother of a row' with Marshall on 26 November, but once again the Americans proved remarkably accommodating and in a closed session accepted that the agreed date – 1 May 1944 – was not sacrosanct as D-Day for OVERLORD.[34]

At the Teheran Conference immediately after the Cairo meeting with the Americans (and Chinese), Alanbrooke's proposals met with tougher opposition from Voroshilov and Leahy, but he stuck to his guns and once again was remarkably successful in defending the British policy.

At the Military Conference on 29 November, Alanbrooke argued that there were about 27 German divisions now in Italy and our aim should be to drive them north of Rome by an amphibious landing and to destroy 11 or 12 divisions in the process. He opposed going on the defensive in Italy and urged that landing ships be retained in the Mediterranean, even though this would entail putting back OVERLORD to 1 June. Voroshilov suggested that, compared with Marshall, the CIGS was lukewarm about OVERLORD, but the latter insisted he still considered it of vital importance but did not wish to see it fail, as under certain conditions it was bound to fail. He tried to explain to Voroshilov the problems of the Channel crossing and gaining beachheads. Leahy's doubts about the British commitment to OVERLORD were answered in the same terms. The CCS agreed that the Italian advance should be pressed on to the Pisa–Rimini Line and that 68 LSTs must be retained in the Mediterranean until 15 January 1944. An invasion in the south of France in support of OVERLORD (ANVIL and, later, DRAGOON) would be planned to coincide with OVERLORD. Stalin would be informed that these operations would take place 'during May'.[35]

In post-war reflections Alanbrooke wrote that he had been deeply impressed by Stalin's military brain and perceived that his arguments at the Teheran Conference had been prompted not by current strategic considerations but entirely in the light of his future political plans. He felt sure that Stalin wished to keep the Allies out of the Eastern Mediterranean and the Balkans, and would also be content to see the Italian campaign closed down with the Allies still south of Rome. Alanbrooke feared that if the Italian offensive ceased, Roosevelt would insist on transferring six divisions to invade Southern France on 1 May, thus allowing the Germans a month to annihilate them before OVERLORD was launched. Bryant regarded Alanbrooke's performance at this conference as second only in importance to that at Casablanca; he had played a key role in getting the date of OVERLORD deferred to 1 June 1944 so as to permit an advance to the Pisa–Rimini Line, and the date for the invasion of southern France made more flexible so that it would neither risk defeat in isolation nor seriously affect the continued offensive in Italy.[36]

Through the spring and summer of 1944 Alanbrooke, working through Dill in Washington, tried to persuade Marshall that ANVIL was unnecessary; the most effective support for OVERLORD in the Mediterranean being to continue the Italian offensive thereby making it impossible for the Germans to withdraw divisions and send them to France. Dill wrote on 20 March 1944 that he hoped the US Chiefs of Staff would quietly drop ANVIL:

> Their great fear is that the Germans will, within the next month or so, give up Italy to all intents and purposes, leaving merely rearguards... to delay our advance till OVERLORD has been defeated.

He had done his best to persuade Marshall that the Germans could take very little out of Italy to oppose OVERLORD. He calculated that the Germans had 24 divisional identities in Italy but a real strength in numbers of only 18 divisions: the Joint Intelligence Committee estimated that they would need this number (18) to hold the Pisa–Rimini Line even if hard pressed by OVERLORD, provided vigorous Allied offensive pressure was maintained.[37]

Alanbrooke replied a week later that he despaired of getting Marshall to understand the situation in Italy. It had been clear to him (Alanbrooke) that ANVIL could not take place simultaneously with OVERLORD, while to launch it later would entail weakening the Italian front to such an extent that the defending German forces would no longer be held there.[38] On 2 August, by which time Rome had been captured and OVERLORD was clearly succeeding, Alanbrooke admitted to General Maitland Wilson that he had been defeated over ANVIL (it was in fact launched successfully on 15 August), but it could not do much harm at this stage of the war.

> Alex's wild talk about his advance on Vienna killed all our arguments dead! It is a pity because I do not see Alex advancing on Vienna this year unless he does it in the face of crumbling German resistance, and in that case he has ample forces for the task, and greater than he will be able to administer over snow-covered mountain passes.[39]

By this time Alanbrooke's notions of future strategy were being influenced by his political reading of the post-war situation. He and the COS believed that Russia, not Germany, was already the dominating power in Europe 'and cannot fail to become the main threat in 15 years from now. Therefore foster Germany, gradually build her up and bring her into a Federation of Western Europe'. He appreciated that it would be difficult to do this under the cloak of a holy alliance between England, Russia and America, particularly as he was well aware that Britain's influence in Washington was waning.[40]

Alanbrooke's scepticism regarding Alexander's enthusiasm for an advance to Vienna has already been noted, and he has been specifically cited as a critic of both Alexander's and Churchill's advocacy of such an operation. Indeed commenting on Churchill's statement at the Quebec Conference on 13 September 1944 in the 'Notes on My Life' prepared in the 1950s for Bryant's edition of his diaries, Alanbrooke wrote:

> We had no plans for Vienna, nor did I ever look at this operation as becoming possible.[41]

However on 12 September 1944 Alanbrooke's habitual caution had been temporarily undermined by the widespread assumption that German resistance was crumbling. As the minutes of the CCS 172nd meeting record:

He saw… great advantages in a right swing at Trieste and an advance from there to Vienna. However, if German resistance was strong, he did not envisualize the possibility of our forces getting through to Vienna during the winter. Even so the seizure of the Istrian Peninsula would be valuable as a base for the Spring campaign or as a base from which our forces could be introduced into Austria in the event of Germany crumbling. It had not only a military value, but also political value in view of the Russian advances in the Balkans.[42]

The remarkable outcome at Quebec of Alanbrooke's, Portal's and Churchill's advocacy of continuing the Allied advance through to the North Italian plains, accompanied by amphibious operations against Istria was that Marshall, Leahy and King all agreed that no American troops or landing craft (LSTs) would be removed, at least until 15 October.

Bryant was in no doubt that Alanbrooke's obdurate insistence on the continuation of the protracted slog up the Italian peninsula had been essential to the success of OVERLORD by the absorption of enemy divisions which would otherwise have been sent as reinforcements to France. Liddell Hart was among those critics who queried this claim. In a longhand note in his copy of *Triumph In The West*, Liddell Hart wrote:

> The constant keynote (is) that the continuation in 1944 of the Allied offensive in Italy was the most important factor in the success of the Normandy landings by drawing the German reserves to Italy, and that the continuation of the offensive in Italy was mainly due to Alanbrooke's insistence.
>
> Yet, most strangely and surprisingly, it is shown on page 198 (that) German strength in the West rose by six divisions from 53 to 59 between January and June whereas the German forces in Italy remained the same as before.
>
> Such an exaggerated claim shows Bryant's shallowness as a military analyst, but also leaves a puzzle as to why Alanbrooke allowed him to make such claims. The figures show that Tito's partisans in Yugoslavia drew off and pinned down a larger proportion of the German strength than did the Allied armies in Italy.[43]

As Liddell Hart pointed out in his review of *Triumph In The West* referred to earlier, the balance of distraction in Italy was most favourable to the Allies in the autumn of 1943. By October 1943, 18 German divisions had been drawn into Italy to resist 15 Allied divisions, while the German garrison in the Balkans had also increased rapidly to 15 divisions. In the whole Mediterranean theatre each side had 33 divisions but the Allied total included 10 in reserve in Egypt and Palestine.

Thereafter the balance of forces in Italy became less favourable to the Allies due to the Germans' stubborn resistance south of Rome and the acceptance of Alanbrooke's strategy of persisting with the frontal offensive against formidable natural defences. On 6 June 1944 there were 28 German divisions in south-eastern Europe, 28 in Italy (but with a real strength in manpower of only 23), 18 in Norway and Denmark and 59 in France and the Low Countries.[44] Liddell Hart assesses the Allied strength in Italy at this time as the equivalent of 30 divisions (as against the Official History's 25). John Ehrman comments that although the Mediterranean strategy succeeded in containing a rising proportion of German forces, it

> did not succeed in preventing the enemy from re-inforcing North-West Europe. Indeed in the months preceding OVERLORD the number of German divisions rose in France and the Low Countries at times when they did not fall, but rather rose slightly, in Italy and South-East Europe.

He adds significantly that In January 1944 there were 24 *Panzer* divisions facing the Russians, and eight in the rest of Europe, whereas in mid-June the figures were 18 and 15. He concludes that the operations of late 1943 and early 1944 specifically in Italy did not fulfil the requirement laid down at the Cairo Conference for the dispersal of potential enemy reinforcements against OVERLORD. At the end of April 1944, when the enemy's main dispositions seemed to have been made, 'the picture for June looked in some respects forbidding'.[45]

Bryant would have been on firmer ground had he contended that without the distraction of the Italian campaign the German reinforcements to northern France could have been increased considerably and with potentially disastrous results for OVERLORD and its immediate aftermath. The scale of the Allied assault and early build-up was limited by the shortage of landing craft, so it can be argued that their divisions left in Italy were not available and therefore not wasted. The Official History of British Intelligence in the Second World War may also be deemed to support Alanbrooke's strategy in that it demonstrates the immensely detailed knowledge he and his colleagues possessed by 1943–1944 of the German order of battle in Italy and the Balkans, and in particular the acute shortage of weapons and equipment that most divisions were known to suffer.[46]

Liddell Hart also makes the valid point that Hitler's fear of Allied amphibious landings (most of which did not take place) and partisan activity, especially in Yugoslavia, tied down no fewer than 64 German divisions (including 18 in Norway and Denmark). He suggests that Churchill understood the value of such distraction and dispersal of enemy forces better than Alanbrooke. If the primary aim of Allied operations on the Italian mainland was the distraction of enemy forces then it was a dubious choice because the length of the peninsula, its rocky spine and formidable rivers made it ideal terrain for the defenders – as Kesselring's forces so stubbornly demonstrated to the very end of the war in Europe. These conditions might have been turned to the Allies' advantage had they possessed ample assault shipping and for long enough.[47] However, from the outset of the mainland campaign Alanbrooke was well aware that the Americans were insistent that most of the available shipping must soon be moved back to Britain in time for OVERLORD. He was remarkably successful, as we have seen, in gaining successive reprieves for LSTs to provide amphibious assistance to the slow landward advance in Italy, but in the last resort he always had to accept – after successfully preventing a cross-Channel assault in 1942 or 1943 – that OVERLORD must be given priority over the Mediterranean in 1944.

This essay has contended that in exaggerating Alanbrooke's role as an architect of Allied strategy, Sir Arthur Bryant did his hero a disservice in diverting attention away from his truly invaluable, albeit less intellectually creative, contribution. In his admirable concluding summary, David Fraser underlines that, at its best, Churchill's grand strategic vision was superior to that of his professional advisers. Churchill, metaphorically, liked to paint great pictures to which events might be made to conform. Sometimes the vision was flawed or unattainable with the means available, and Churchill was at his worst in refusing to accept unpalatable facts. Nevertheless his visions, based on instinct rather than on rational calculation, were sometimes magnificently vindicated. Thus it was Churchill who first grasped the opportunities offered by a Mediterranean campaign; and his insistence, imprudent though it seemed to his advisers, which made possible the North African campaign and all that flowed from it. Alanbrooke by contrast was a pragmatist rather than a visionary. In Fraser's words:

> He saw the next step clearly, and those beyond as far as they could be inspected and measured. For the rest he liked to wait and see. He was cautious.[48]

As his diaries plainly reveal, he never fully understood, or approved, Churchill's method of conducting argument. It is equally doubtful if he ever fully appreciated Churchill's imaginative vision as a strategist: in failing to make this distinction Bryant's judgement was faulty.

Lord Moran was more perceptive. Because Bryant gave too much credit to Alanbrooke for his share in the shaping of strategy, we should not on that account give him too little. Some of Churchill's projects were not merely risky but positively dangerous and might have led to catastrophe if carried out. One is tempted to say that the more absurd the project, the more tenaciously Churchill clung to it. It was above all Alanbrooke's responsibility to see that these projects were not implemented.

> With his feet firmly planted on the ground, he stood for a sense of proportion, for method, for good sense. If anything had happened to him I do not know any other soldier who would have stood up to the Prime Minister so effectively… In short he kept Winston on the rails in the conduct of the war. That is his epitaph.[49]

References

1. Ismay to Alanbrooke, 14 March 1957, 13/3/1/8. Alanbrooke Papers, Liddell Hart Centre for Military Archives, King's College, London. Montgomery's speech at the Institute of Transport, 3 November 1959, 13/2/91 Alanbrooke Papers.
2. Sir Arthur Bryant's Correspondence. Letter to Alanbrooke n.d. Imperial War Museum. Quoted in David Fraser, *Alanbrooke* (1982), p. 544.
3. Bryant to Alanbrooke, 24 April 1955. Imperial War Museum.
4. Alanbrooke to Bryant, 21 and 23 October 1956.

5. Lord Moran, *Winston Churchill: The Struggle For Survival 1940–1965* (paperback edition, 1968), p. 748.
6. Milton Shulman's review of *Triumph In The West* in the *Evening Standard*, 2 November 1959.
7. Moran, p. 751.
8. Sir Arthur Bryant, *Triumph In The West* (1959), pp. 197, 460. See also B. H. Liddell Hart's review article 'Western War Strategy' in *Royal United Services Institute Journal* February 1960, p3, henceforth referred to as 'Liddell Hart'.
9. Fraser, *Alanbrooke*, p. 541.
10. Moran, p. 755.
11. Fraser, pp. 215, 217.
12. Michael Howard, *Grand Strategy* Vol IV (1970), pp. 197–98.
13. John Ehrman, *Grand Strategy* Vol VI (1956), pp. 327–34.
14. Alanbrooke to Bryant, 2 August 1956. Imperial War Museum. See also Bryant (ed), *The Turn Of The Tide*, p. 278.
15. Michael Howard, *Grand Strategy* Vol IV, pp. 197–98, 216, 228: Liddell Hart, p. 4.
16. Bryant, *The Turn Of The Tide*, pp. 355, 359.
17. Ibid, p. 403.
18. Fraser, pp. 258–59, 268–70. Bryant, *The Turn Of The Tide*, pp. 423–28.
19. Fraser, p. 309.
20. Liddell Hart, p. 5.
21. Michael Howard, *The Mediterranean Strategy In The Second World War* (1968), pp. 35–36. Bryant, *The Turn Of The Tide*, pp. 529–35.
22. Minutes of 55th, 57th and 58th Meetings of the Combined Chiefs of Staff (CCS) Casablanca Conference 6/COS/1 Alanbrooke Papers.
23. Ibid Minutes of 65th Meeting CCS Bryant, *The Turn Of The Tide*, pp. 543, 557–58.
24. Minutes of 58th Meeting CCS. Fraser, pp. 311–12, 320–22. Bryant, *The Turn Of The Tide*, p. 550. On Dill's vital role as Head of the Joint Staff Mission in Washington see Alex Danchev, *Very Special Relationship* (1986).
25. Michael Howard, *The Mediterranean Strategy*, pp. 37–39. Fraser, pp. 342–44, 348. Bryant, *The Turn Of The Tide*, pp. 618–20. Minutes of the Third Meeting Trident Conference 19 May 1943. Minutes of 88th and 89th Meetings CCS Trident Conference. 6/COS/2 Alanbrooke Papers.
26. Liddell Hart, p.6.
27. Fraser, p. 356.
28. Minutes of 108th Meeting CCS at Quadrant Conference, August 1943. 6/COS/3 Alanbrooke Papers. Bryant, *The Turn Of The Tide*, p. 106.
29. Bryant, *The Turn Of The Tide*, pp. 714–18.
30. Bryant, *Triumph In The West*, pp. 50–54.
31. Ibid pp. 55–59.
32. Dill to Alanbrooke 16 October 1943. 14/38 Alanbrooke Papers. Howard, *The Mediterranean Strategy*, pp. 47–49.
33. Fraser, pp. 372–73.
34. Bryant, *Triumph In The West*, pp. 64–67, 83–84.
35. Minutes of Military Conference, Eureka Conference, Teheran 29 November 1943. Minutes of 132nd Meeting CCS 30 November 1943. 6/COS/4 Alanbrooke Papers.
36. Bryant, *Triumph In The West*, pp. 90–93, 97, 107–09. Howard, *The Mediterranean Strategy*, p. 56.
37. Dill to Alanbrooke, 20 March 1944. 14/22 Alanbrooke Papers.
38. Alanbrooke to Dill, 30 March 1944 idem.

39. Alanbrooke to Wilson, 2 August 1944 (typed copy) 14/10 Alanbrooke Papers. Bryant, *Triumph In The West*, p. 256.
40. Bryant, *Triumph In The West*, p. 242.
41. Bryant, *Triumph In The West*, p. 283 note. Sir William Jackson, *The Mediterranean And The Middle East* Vol VI Part III (1988), pp. 354, 368.
42. Minutes of 172nd Meeting CCS Octogon Conference, 12 September 1944. 6/COS/5 Alanbrooke Papers. John Ehrman, *Grand Strategy* Vol V (1956), pp. 510–12.
43. Liddell Hart holograph note in his copy of *Triumph In The West* in the Liddell Hart Centre for Military Archives, King's College, London.
44. Liddell Hart review op cit pp. 9–10. Bryant, *Triumph In The West*, pp. 198–200.
45. Ehrman, *Grand Strategy* Vol V, pp. 279–80.
46. F. H. Hinsley and others, *British Intelligence In The Second World War* Vol 3 Part I (1984), Chapter 34 passim and Appendix 8, and Vol 3 Part 2 (1988) Chapter 50 passim, especially pp. 339–40.
47. Liddell Hart review, p. 10.
48. Fraser, pp. 514–17.
49. Moran, pp. 752–53. Fraser's judgement on the value of Alanbrooke's relationship with Churchill (p. 535) is also worth quoting: 'To be chief adviser to a genius demands a certain genius of its own sort, and Alanbrooke possessed it.'

12

General Sir William Slim and the Fourteenth Army in Burma

In September 2002 I led a British-based party of five scholars to a conference in Tokyo with a similar number of Japanese academics. Our aim was to examine different command levels in the Malaya and Burma campaigns between 1941.and 1945. Although the conference exposed some differences in cultural approaches to discussing the qualities and defects of senior military commanders, it was definitely successful as an exercise designed to develop Anglo–Japanese co-operation in the study of military history. The conference papers were published under the title *British and Japanese Military Leadership in the Far Eastern War, 1941–1945* (Cass, 2004).

It may be considered that I awarded myself an easy subject in writing about a successful and popular commander, Sir William 'Bill' Slim, but I tried to portray his military career and its culmination in Burma 'in the round', including some early setbacks and serious errors of judgement – which he frankly admitted in his memoirs *Defeat into Victory*. I made full use of several existing biographies, notably Ronald Lewin's *Slim: the Standard Bearer*, and although there have been several more since 2002 I remain generally satisfied with my depiction of an outstanding British general.

Slim is now widely regarded as one of Britain's best, if not the best Army commander in the Second World War. Some historians would place Montgomery in the top spot: he held the highest field command for longer that Slim and in three very different theatres – North Africa, Italy and North-West Europe. On the other hand Slim took command after a more clear-cut and humiliating defeat; his area of operations never enjoyed a high political priority; and conditions – in terms of geography, climate and logistics – were terrible almost beyond imagination.

What is not in dispute is that Slim was far more admired as a personality than Montgomery. The latter achieved renown with the British public as 'Monty', but Slim was affectionately and universally known as 'Uncle Bill', the soldiers' general *par excellence*. Slim has been described as a persuasive leader in contrast to Montgomery who was a dominant one.[1] Slim certainly looked every inch the military commander with his stocky figure, strong face and jutting jaw.[2] One has only to compare his appearance with the thin and rabbit-faced Percival,-who surrendered at Singapore, to see what an advantage this was. But in Slim's case physical attributes truly reflected a sterling character. He combined the traits of essential modesty with complete self-confidence. He understood the very varied temperaments and qualities of his motley forces – Indian, British and Colonial – and seems to have been equally popular with all of them.

In terms of Britain's grand strategy in the Second World War Burma can hardly even be rated as a secondary theatre; indeed its low priority along with Malaya goes far to account for the rapidity and severity of defeat in late 1941 and early 1942. Without American support, particularly in air transport, the reconquest of Burma could hardly have been contemplated, yet America's strategic interests were essentially concerned with logistical and military support to Chiang Kai-Shek and not at all with the reconquest of British colonial territory. Consequently, it remained uncertain until late in the war that a north to south offensive through the most formidable terrain would even be attempted.

After the humiliating defeats in 1942 the Burma theatre received very little attention in the British media compared with Dunkirk, the blitz on British cities, the dramatic see-saw of the North African campaigns (in which General Rommel achieved a remarkable popularity) and the culminating advance from Normandy to the Baltic. Consequently, with some justice, British soldiers in India and Burma felt resentfully that they were a 'Forgotten Army' in a neglected theatre. The flamboyant, publicity-seeking Admiral Lord Mountbatten attempted to alter this perception as Supreme Commander in the area from October 1943, but even so the names which established themselves with the British public were his own and that of Major-General Orde Wingate, the eccentric leader of the Chindits killed in an air crash in March 1944. Wingate was the equivalent of T. E. Lawrence in the First World War, his deeds and controversial personality overshadowing Slim's achievement as Lawrence's has done to Allenby's. As Duncan Anderson has pointed out in a perceptive essay, Slim only became one of 'Churchill's generals', that is to say known personally and respected by Britain's war leader, at the very end of the.war.[3] Sir Basil Liddell Hart, for so long the chief authority on British generals' reputations, gives Slim only 10 entries in the index of his *History of the Second World War*[4] against Mongomery's 56, but the discrepancy is in fact much greater because many of the latter's references are to several consecutive pages.

Even after the Second World War Slim's had not become a household name in Britain despite his ascent to the head of the Army (Chief of the Imperial General Staff) in 1948. He had made only a fleeting appearance in the popular film *Burma Victory* and was, in effect, squeezed out of public attention by the more controversial characters and exploits of Mountbatten and Wingate. What changed these perceptions dramatically was the publication of Slim's memoirs of the campaign, *Defeat into Victory*, in 1956.[5] The book was very well-written, explained complicated events lucidly, and reflected the author's modesty and dignity in refraining from inflated claims and vendettas. Rarely in this genre has a commander admitted to making so many mistakes, some potentially disastrous, or been willing to attribute so much of his success to others. In some cultures, the qualities of modesty and understatement are not highly regarded, but in Britain they raised Slim's status to that of military hero. The Official History of the war in Burma subsequently portrayed Slim as mainly responsible for victory while displaying a surprising degree of hostility towards Wingate. Full-length studies by Sir Geoffrey Evans (one of his divisional commanders) in 1969, and Ronald Lewin (an excellent historian) in 1976, both praised him almost unreservedly. In Lewin's judgement he had achieved the lofty status of Sun Tzu's 'Heaven-born captain' or ever-victorious general.[6]

There is a lesson here for all successful generals, and perhaps also for students of military history; namely that reputations may be made and certainly enhanced by well-written and well-timed memoirs. Consider, for example, the influence of those of U. S. Grant, T. E. Lawrence, Montgomery and Guderian. Ronald Lewin revealed that Slim had published widely in the inter-war years under a pen name, and loved writing only a little less than soldiering. Lewin also revealed that Slim (again like Grant) had brilliantly worn the 'mask of command'; that is, so far from being callous or nerveless he was in reality sensitive, self-critical and prone to doubt. As his former chief engineer told Lewin: 'Of all his many attributes I never cease to admire his calmness and courtesy when the strain… for long periods on end must have been well nigh unbearable. His imperturbability did not stem from insensitivity, but rather from a superhuman self-discipline.'[7]

Although Slim's professional career as a commander culminated in a brilliant and deserved victory in 1944–1945, he had served a long and by no means entirely successful apprenticeship. Moreover, like most successful military leaders, he had enjoyed a fair measure of good fortune.

William Slim's origins differed sharply from most British generals of that era. His social background was lower-middle-class, his father being an unsuccessful Birmingham ironmonger. 'Bill' Slim, born in 1891, won a scholarship to attend the local grammar school, but his prospects seemed limited; despite his early interest in military history and soldiering Sandhurst and an officer's career were not available to him for financial and social reasons. He was briefly an elementary schoolteacher in a Birmingham slum district, and then a junior clerk in a metal-tubing firm. Though never a student at the local university, he had been allowed to enlist in the Officer Training Corps (OTC) so that on the outbreak of war in 1914 he was one of the thousands of keen but strictly amateur soldiers who were given temporary commissions. His humble origins and tough work experience proved very useful in his natural rapport with ordinary soldiers.[8]

'Bill' Slim had a 'good war' in 1914–1918 in that he displayed leadership qualities in brief but intense periods of active service (with the Royal Warwicks) in Gallipoli and Mesopotamia. He was severely wounded in. both campaigns and sent to convalesce as a junior officer on the staff in India where he transferred to the Army in India because there he could live on his pay without a private income. He had witnessed the terrible results of incompetent administration and poor staff work, especially at Gallipoli; and would henceforth give these unglamorous aspects of soldiering a high priority. Also in Mesopotamia, he gained valuable insight into the causes of low morale and how they could be overcome.

In the inter-war period (1919–1939) Slim was clearly picked out as a 'high flyer' among Indian Army officers. Selected for the Staff College at Quetta he passed out top to be rewarded by the 'plum' posting as the Indian Army representative on the instructing staff at the (British) Staff College at Camberley. This was followed by an even more prestigious assignment to attend the course at the Imperial Defence College for the most promising officers of the three services along with representatives from the Commonwealth and the Foreign Office. Slim had proved himself a good student and a good teacher with a sharp analytical mind and a firm grasp of military realities. He was not, however, noted as a theorist or an innovator. Regimental service with 6th and 7th Gurkhas provided experience with first-class soldiers and close friendships with several officers who would later become his senior subordinates in Burma.[9]

Even with these credentials few could have predicted Slim's eventual achievements in 1939. He had at last been promoted lieutenant-colonel but had been outdistanced in terms of age by several rivals in the Indian Army. This relatively slow progress was to prove a blessing in disguise. Britain's habitual military unpreparedness in peacetime entails that it is usually disastrous to be a senior commander at the start of war. Many of Slim's peers came to grief in the ferocious onslaughts by German and Japanese forces in 1940 and 1941, whereas he spent the first 30 months of the Second World War in military 'backwaters' fighting the far less formidable Italians and Vichy French.

Slim's first experience of leadership in combat, commanding 10th Indian Brigade against the Italians on the Sudan–Ethiopian border in November 1940 might well have been his last. His task was to re-capture the fort of Gallabat just inside Sudan, followed by the strongly-held nearby fortress of Metemma across the frontier. Gallabat was quickly taken but at high cost. Nine of Slim's 12 tanks were knocked out by mines or boulders and their crews were then shot up by his Garwhali troops who mistook them for Italians. With his own slender air cover destroyed, Italian bombers and fighters pounded Slim's troops inside the fort and the Essex regiment, recently inserted into his brigade under protest, panicked and fled. This was a cause of lasting bitterness on the part of Essex regimental officers towards Slim, whom they accused of poor planning, and helps to account for General Noel Irwin's unsuccessful attempt to get Slim removed from his Corps command in Burma in 1943.[10] After consulting his senior officers Slim decided not to risk an attack on Metemma, but instead withdrew to a ridge which dominated Gallabat and effectively deterred an Italian advance. Slim took full responsibility for this failure which was made to seem even worse when it emerged that the Metemma garrison was about to surrender when he called off the attack. He resolved in the future to be bolder and more aggressive.[11]

That he got another chance was due to a series of accidents resulting in his unexpected promotion to command of 10th Indian Division in Iraq in May 1941. In an operation in which poor communications and horrendous supply problems posed more difficulties than the Vichy French colonial garrison, Slim devised a risky two-pronged assault to capture Dier-ez-zor in eastern Syria. A minor crisis occurred when the column making a wide sweep through the desert ran out of fuel. The time-table went awry but Slim held his nerve and movement was resumed by draining the tanks of vehicles on the line of communications. The attack was completely successful; Slim's self-confidence was strengthened; and he gained further command experience in the ensuing occupation of Persia.[12]

At the beginning of 1942 Slim's future as a senior commander was far from assured, particularly as General Auchinleck regarded him as no more than a 'competent second division player'. Thanks, however, to the lobbying of two of Slim's former colleagues in 6th Gurkhas (Major-Generals Scott and Cowan), in March 1942 Slim was appointed commander of Burma Corps under the newly-arrived Army Commander-in-Chief, General Sir Harold Alexander.

This proved to be Slim's golden opportunity, but initially it looked more likely to signal an ignominious end to his career. With Malaya, Singapore and southern Burma already lost, the rapidly advancing Japanese ground forces, fortified by dominance in the air, looked unstoppable. These operations had already destroyed the career of one officer, General Tom Hutton, an able chief of staff suddenly handed the poisoned chalice of field command in a chaotic retreat, and would soon account for others, including Brigadier John Smyth VC, who was held responsible for the disaster at the Sittang bridge.

The difficulties facing Slim would have overwhelmed a less robust commander. His own retreating forces were defeated and demoralized whereas his formidable opponent held the initiative and his morale was sky-high. Slim's two divisions were poorly trained and ill-co-ordinated; they were road-bound and, as yet, had no answer to Japanese tactics of rapid cross-country movements to set up road blocks in their rear.

At the time Alexander received most of the credit for what was depicted as a heroic retreat in appalling conditions, but the historical verdict on his role is now very critical.[13] Alexander allowed operations to drift and never gave his corps commander clear directives. Was Slim to counter-attack, retain as much territory as possible, including the oil fields in central Burma, or was he to strive to keep Burma Corps intact? Slim's instinct was to attack, but his only realistic hope was to draw his two divisions together. This proved impossible because Alexander repeatedly allowed units to be detached to support the Chinese in eastern Burma. After several offensives had failed or been called off Alexander finally, on 25 April, issued the order for a withdrawal to India.

Although in *Defeat into Victory* Slim would blame himself for several operational errors, and even admit to being indecisive at a critical point when Japanese infiltration seemed to have cut off the retreat across the Chindwin, the withdrawal may still be regarded as a remarkable achievement.[14] At Monywa and Shwegyin, for example, Slim extricated his forces from impending disaster with great skill and he displayed impressive powers of leadership combined with improvisation in narrowly winning the race, against not only the enemy but also the monsoon, in bringing his exhausted, hungry and disease-ridden troops to the comparative safety of Assam. Burma Corps' fighting soldiers retained their discipline and their morale, but these combat units were preceded across the frontier by an indisciplined mob, mostly of Indians from the line of communications. No longer in organized units, and having deserted their officers wrote Slim, 'they banded together in gangs, looting, robbing, and not infrequently murdering the unfortunate villagers on their route.[15]

Slim never lost heart or hope in these darkest days. He remained outwardly calm and confident, using every opportunity to make personal contact with his troops; skilfully varying his approach to achieve the biggest impact on different groups and nationalities. In effect he prevented a military disaster by sustaining morale. In Lewin's elegant summary, 'He did well in manoeuvering his divisions, but he did better in making them the partners of his spirit.'[16] In similar vein, Sir Geoffrey Evans suggests that the officers and troops of Burma Corps knew that Slim had done all that was humanly possible; hence the rousing farewell they gave him when he relinquished his command at Imphal. Evans even goes so far as to suggest that 'this was Slim's greatest test as a commander in the field and that the two months' operation was his finest contribution to eventual victory over the Japanese'.[17]

Slim's first step in turning defeat into victory was a cool analysis of the reasons for failure in 1942. Most of them lay beyond his own responsibility. There was, first, a terrible lack of preparation because no one in higher authority had expected an invasion of Burma. Consequently the ground forces provided to defend the country were utterly inadequate: two hastily assembled and inexperienced divisions, one of them equipped for desert warfare. The total elimination of the weak allied air force was a crippling blow, but Slim believed the eventual key to victory would come from outfighting the enemy, soldier for soldier, on the ground. For Slim, however, the most distressing aspect had been the contrast between allied generalship and the enemy's. The Japanese leadership had been confident, 'Bold to the point of foolhardiness, and so aggressive that never for one day did they lose the initiative'. Poor allied intelligence contributed to Japanese tactical dominance. Wide turning movements or 'hooks' through the jungle to set up road blocks on the allied line of communications succeeded again and again, thereby breeding an inferiority complex.[18]

Slim reserved the severest criticism, though surely too harshly, for himself. He had repeatedly tried and failed to pass to the offensive and regain the initiative. He had not realized how the enemy, so formidable so long as they were allowed to advance, could be thrown into confusion by the unexpected. He resolved to profit from the lessons of a bitter defeat and to act more boldly in future.

Between mid-1942 and the end of 1943, Slim laid the theoretical and practical foundations for eventual victory. His principles and methods, profoundly relevant to the theme of military leadership, can only be briefly discussed here. Among the tactical lessons he inculcated were the following: the individual soldier must learn to move and fight in the jungle; he must conquer the tendency to panic when enemy parties infiltrated behind his lines and believe that it was the Japanese who were 'surrounded'; there should rarely be frontal attacks and never frontal attacks on narrow fronts; tanks could be used in almost any type of country except swamp; and, perhaps most important, 'there are no non-combatants in jungle warfare' – even medical units must be prepared to defend themselves.[19]

He goes on to describe in fascinating detail the steps he took to improve the health of his soldiers, including a more varied diet, better hospital facilities, tough measures to combat jungle diseases (especially malaria) and the air evacuation of serious casualties. He analysed the complex factor of morale into three elements: spiritual, intellectual and material. He had no doubts about the justice of the allied cause; believed firmly that ordinary soldiers and not just officers would respond to reasoned appeals regarding leadership and eventual victory; and understood that soldiers would appreciate most of all that living conditions, equipment and weapons must all be as good as possible. An innovation which did a great deal to boost morale was the publication of a theatre newspaper – *Seac*. Mountbatten rather than Slim probably deserves the chief credit for enlisting the services as editor of a brilliant young journalist, Frank Owen, but the latter gave the venture his full support.[20]

Although other armies have made remarkable recoveries from humiliating defeat, Duncan Anderson is surely right to stress the magnitude of Slim's achievement in 1942 and 1943.[21] The theatre of war could hardly have been more forbidding: several hundred miles of virtually roadless, jungle-clad mountains, swamped for half the year by the monsoon rains. An Army whose role was uncertain and hence whose priority was very low for supplies and manpower. Perhaps most problematic of all was the mixed composition and poor motivation of Slim's forces: British, Indians, Gurkhas, East and West Africans, few of whom can have been deeply committed to the restoration of British control over Burma. Finally, after their experiences in 1941–2, Slim's motley forces were in awe of the supposedly unbeatable Japanese.

Slim's first step in raising morale was to convince his Army that the Japanese were not supermen and could be defeated. He set up a realistic and demanding training schedule in India in which units were sent into the jungle for weeks at a time. The tactical emphasis was placed on attack rather than defence. The second, complementary step, was the great amount of time Slim devoted to travelling long distances to talk to his troops; in putting over his aims and ideals in simple language which all could understand. This was a rare attribute among British generals in either of the World Wars and is perhaps attributable to Slim's relatively humble origins, lack of higher education, and early experience in the Birmingham metal industry. Through this combination of practical reforms, improved training and doctrine and his genius for personal communication, Slim had revitalized Fourteenth Army and given it – something rarely evident at that level – a proud sense of identity. His universal nickname of 'Uncle Bill' encapsulates the magnitude of his achievement.

Although Slim had stamped his personality and ideas on Fourteenth Army he had no say on Allied grand strategy and only a limited influence on operational strategy within the Burma theatre. As an Army commander his chief responsibilities were to maintain relations with allies (notably Stilwell) and senior subordinates (notably Wingate) and, above all, to make a few vital decisions about the location and timing of offensives, responding to enemy initiatives and the summoning of reinforcements.

As Supreme Allied Commander in the theatre, from October 1943, Mountbatten deserves praise for shielding Slim from a good deal of the political interference from London which posed such a problem for field commanders nearer home and in the Middle East.[22] As the senior land forces commander under Mountbatten, General Sir George Giffard also worked well with Slim but difficulties arose when he was replaced, in November 1944, by Sir Oliver Leese, who had taken over from Montgomery as commander of Eighth Army in Italy.

Much can be gathered about Slim's personality and leadership qualities from his relations with the American commander in the China–Burma–India theatre, General 'Vinegar Joe' Stilwell. To describe the latter as 'prickly' would be a weak understatement. He appeared to despise British senior officers – whom he called 'limeys' – and refused point-blank to serve under Giffard. Yet he *was* willing to accept Slim's operational control. Thus was a 'military nonsense' created whereby Slim would by-pass Giffard to report directly to Mountbatten regarding Stilwell's American and Chinese forces. This illogical command set-up worked because Stilwell respected Slim and generally agreed with him on broad objectives. When difficulties arose Slim's sensible solution was to fly to Stilwell's headquarters and discuss matters face to face. Stilwell insisted that this unusual command arrangement was not to be made public, and it did not survive his own removal from the theatre of operations.[23]

Though they differed sharply in other ways, Slim's daily routine as an Army commander closely resembled Montgomery's. He would rise at 6:30 a.m. and spend the mornings studying the latest news and holding meetings with senior staff officers, air commanders and allied representatives. He would leave his office at about three, read a novel for an hour, go for a walk in the cool of early evening with one of his staff, dine at 7:30 p.m., talk in the mess until 9:30 p.m., visit the operations room for a final look at the latest reports, and be in bed by 10:00 p.m.. Between then and 6:30 a.m. he would only permit being roused for a real crisis. His belief in the need for leisure to think and for unbroken sleep to regain energy was surely wise. Generals who are terribly busy all day and half the night, he remarked, 'wear out not only their subordinates but themselves'.[24] They then lack the reserves of mental and physical vigour to deal with a real emergency. It is evident that neither Slim nor Montgomery could have tolerated for long Churchill's propensity for keeping senior officers at his beck and call until the early hours. Alanbrooke somehow endured this routine but at the cost of tremendous strain.

Slim's staff organisation is also worthy of comment. He never adopted the 'Chief of Staff' system in which the senior staff officer serves as the mouthpiece of the commander to other staff officers and heads of support services. Slim preferred the older method of dealing directly with his principal staff officers because he felt it was essential to project his own personality. Interestingly Slim made his senior staff officer the major-general in charge of administration because he believed that in a theatre like Burma administrative considerations would loom larger than strategical and tactical issues.

It was Mountbatten who appointed Slim to the command of the newly-created Fourteenth Army soon after he arrived at SEAC headquarters and his continuing support was crucial throughout the campaign. Slim was glad to hear Mountbatten announce that there would be no more retreats and that, in event of a crisis, he would somehow find enough transport aircraft to maintain supplies. The two commanders also agreed that air transport would make it feasible to maintain operations through the monsoon, but this was only accepted reluctantly by some senior officers, including General Giffard. Giffard, for this and other reasons, lost the confidence of both Mountbatten and Slim. However relations between Mountbatten and Slim remained amicable despite the former's monstrous egotism and uninhibited showmanship. According to Lady Slim, when Mountbatten visited Slim on his deathbed the latter was heard to remark, 'We did it together, old boy.'[25]

An important attribute of a military leader is to select loyal and efficient subordinates and keep them together as a unified team. Slim did not believe in taking all his staff with him when he was promoted, but he 'inherited' several former Gurkha colleagues, such as Scott and Cowan, when he arrived in Burma and his selection both of staff officers and field commanders was admirable. Needless to say, a heroic defence leading on to an advance to victory breeds confidence and enhances a sense of team spirit, but it can hardly be doubted that in 1944–1945 Slim had gathered, and was supported by, a first class team including Stopford, Messervy (an import from Eighth Army), Rees, Cowan, Roberts, Evans and Christison. Among his outstanding staff officers were Snelling, Hasted, Steve Irwin and Lethbridge.

Slim had not selected Wingate and, like all the latter's nominal superiors, had difficulty in controlling him. In *Defeat Into Victory*, Slim leaves the impression that although he clashed with Wingate on some specific issues and had to overrule him, he broadly accepted Wingate's ideas and admired his imaginative schemes and dynamic leadership.

However, in his fine biography of Slim, Ronald Lewin revealed that the commander of Fourteenth Army had deliberately muted his animosity towards Wingate the man and his objections to his policies. Slim had remarked in a private letter that Wingate had been 'deliberately untruthful in some of his statements and most disloyal in passing such statements behind the backs of some commanders to others'.[26]

Wingate's numerous supporters continue to argue that Slim was unfair to their hero,[27] but the latter's standpoint as the Army commander is easily understood. Wingate's ambitions for expanding his Long Range Penetration forces were tantamount to giving them the main role in the reconquest of Burma with the remainder of Fourteenth Army in effect assigned to a supporting role. Slim could not tolerate this challenge to his authority, not only because he believed that the diversion of air transport and supplies would undermine his own plan, but also because he was opposed to 'special forces' in principle, being confident that ordinary divisions could be adapted, if necessary, for airborne operations behind enemy lines. Slim's post-war judgement was to deny that the contribution of the Chindits was either great in effect, or commensurate with the forces they absorbed.

In retrospect Fourteenth Army's victory in the attritional battle for the Imphal plain and its lifeline to India, followed by the brilliant offensive operations which carried it across the Irrawaddy, have an air of dramatic inevitability. But at the time the sequence of events and their timing were far from clear. Slim, in particular, was largely forced to wait upon others' decisions, whether they were Mountbatten's or Kawabe's. Slim, like most of the strategic planners, would have preferred the main allied offensive thrust to take the form of an amphibious landing somewhere on the coast of south-west Burma, with his Army and Stilwell's forces playing only the supporting roles in an overland north to south advance.[28] But at the end of 1943 it seemed extremely doubtful that the necessary shipping would be made available to Mountbatten. Consequently, Slim's strategic aim could only be the very general one of the total destruction of the Japanese forces in Burma.

In the first half of 1944 Slim's abilities as a defensive general were put to their severest test. In February a Japanese offensive in the Arakan took the British by surprise but this time there was no panic or hasty retreat The decisive action was fought around the 'administrative box' where rear-area troops dug in and waited for air supplies. Two fresh British divisions advanced from the north to inflict a crushing defeat on the Japanese who lost more than 5,000 men. This, however, was a secondary front to which Slim had committed four divisions to check what was essentially a Japanese diversion. Intelligence reports had suggested for several weeks that the main blow would fall on the Imphal front which was now thinly defended.

Slim's strategy was to draw the enemy into a battle of attrition on the Imphal plain where IV Corps would have an advantage in artillery and armour and where the Japanese lines of communications would be dangerously stretched. But Slim faced a critical command decision regarding the concentration of IV Corps' main component of two divisions each spread out and widely separated from the other in the mountains to the south. A premature withdrawal would suggest to the Japanese high command that their plans had been anticipated and might well prevent a decisive battle from taking place beyond the attackers' supply capacity. On the other hand if the order to withdraw was given too late the exposed British divisions might well be cut off and defeated piecemeal.

Slim was soon seen to have erred on the side of caution in giving orders to with-draw because the Japanese offensive began on 4 March rather than on 15 March as he expected. His cardinal error, as he admitted in *Defeat Into Victory*, was to leave this critical decision in the hands of IV Corps commander Scoones since he, Slim, was better placed to judge the whole situation. The outcome was nearly disas-trous.[29] Seventy miles south of Imphal 17th Indian Division was, indeed, cut off on the Tiddim road but managed to escape after fierce fighting and with help from the Imphal garrison. Fifty miles east of Imphal 20th Indian Division, though not cut off, also had to fight its way back along the Tamu road.

Slim also admits to what was potentially an even more serious error of judgement; namely that the attacker would not be able to supply more than a brigade group in a thrust towards Kohima and Dimapur, whereas it became clear that the whole Japanese 31st Division was committed in a daring long-range infiltration. Kohima was defended only by a small improvised garrison, Dimapur initially by none at all. Allied operations might just have survived the temporary loss of Kohima, but that of the base and railhead at Dimapur would have been disastrous. Its loss would have delayed the relief of Imphal, exposed British communications and airfields through the Brahmaputra valley, and cut off Stilwell's operations with the Chinese on the Ledo front.

Although Sir Geoffrey Evans, later to serve as one of Slim's divisional commanders in the reconquest of Burma, has argued that the latter was too self-critical about this episode in *Defeat Into Victory*,[30] the fact remains that the situation was only saved in the latter half of March by the remarkable airlift of 5th Indian Division with its infantry, guns, Jeeps and mules from the Arakan to the Imphal plain. While 2nd British Division moved in more slowly by rail, the airlift of 5th Indian Division was only made possible by Mountbatten's unilateral decision to divert American trans-port aircraft from the China front. As the crisis in the Imphal plain developed, Slim was also unintentionally aided by the Japanese 31st Division's commander, Sato, who persisted in attacking at Imphal rather than pressing on to capture the more valuable prize of Dimapur.[31]

During these critical weeks of March and April 1944 Slim's personal leadership qualities were most severely tested – and proven. The physical strain was enormous as he shuttled between his widespread commands in uncomfortable aircraft in order to keep abreast of events, not only at Imphal and Kohima, but also in the Arakan, on the Ledo front and regarding the Chindits, who were by now operating behind Japanese lines. The moral pressure was perhaps even greater in the need to appear calm and confident when things were going wrong. Slim succeeded in a military leader's greatest challenge: to take charge of a battle in which the enemy has siezed the initiative and by a wise disposition of existing forces and reserves turn the crisis decisively to his own side's advantage.[32]

As the battle of attrition ground on relentlessly through April and into May, Slim's initial strategic errors were more than offset by those of his opponents. Sato's relentless battering at Kohima gave Slim the chance to save Dimapur while, on a higher level of command, Mutaguchi's unwillingness to admit defeat condemned his 15th Army to a horrific retreat through the monsoon largely without food or medical supplies.

Although Imphal was not finally relieved and communications with Dimapur re-opened until 22 June, Slim was already confident of victory by mid-May when he realised that the enemy divisions could be effectively destroyed even before their retreat began. With characteristic generosity Slim stressed that his troops had really won the battle, but he insisted that his strategy had been basically sound. It had been 'to meet the Japanese on ground of our own choosing, with a better line of communications behind us than behind them, to concentrate against them superior forces drawn from Arakan and India, to wear them down, and, when they were exhausted, to turn and destroy them'.[33]

With Mountbatten's strong support, Slim's forces pressed on with their appalling slog towards the plains of central Burma through the monsoon.[34] Only two divisions of XXXIII Corps conducted this struggle against nature and the elements, 11th East African Division marching from Tamu eastwards to the Chindwin at Sittaung, while 5th Indian made for Kalewa along the equally difficult Tiddim road. Both divisions were obliged to depend largely on air supply and losses were high from sickness and disease. At an early stage it was realised that engineering resources made it impossible to convert more than a single route (down the Kabaw valley from Tamu to Kalewa) into an all-weather road. The Tiddim road was simply left to collapse as the Indian Division advanced. By mid-December 1944 bridgeheads over the Chindwin had been secured and an impressive Bailey bridge completed at Kalewa.

Logistics were therefore the critical factor as Slim and his staff began to plan for a decisive battle in central Burma. Staff studies suggested that the maximum force supportable beyond the Chindwin – some 400 miles from the railhead at Dimapur and 200 from the most advanced air-supply bases – was four complete divisions with two additional infantry and two tank brigades. Allowing for Japanese commitments in Arakan and on Stilwell's front, it seemed likely the enemy would deploy at least five divisions and numerous miscellaneous troops on the central front. Superior allied airpower would clearly be a great asset, but Fourteenth Army's skill in more open mobile warfare remained to be tested.

Slim had assumed that the newly-appointed Japanese commander, Kimura, would concentrate his forces for the decisive battle in the central plain north of the Irrawaddy. However Slim's two Corps, XXXIII (under Stopford) and IV (under Messervy) made such rapid progress that suspicions grew that he had made a huge strategic miscalculation. Air reconnaissance showed that Japanese movement was eastward across the Irrawaddy and not towards the advancing British forces. Other intelligence sources confirmed this suspicion: the enemy had no intention of making a stand within the Irrawaddy loop, but were going to defend Mandalay with the great river barrier in front of them. Slim had been on the verge of pouring his army into a vast cul-de-sac where he would have been faced with a frontal attack to cross a wide and fiercely-defended river before he could even begin the battle for Mandalay. Slim believed that this change in Japanese strategy was due to Kimura's generalship being more flexible and imaginative than his predecessor's (Kawabe's), but it later emerged that the high command in Tokyo had decided that southern Burma must be held at all costs; the territory within the Irrawaddy loop was consequently deemed to be expendable.[35]

Slim's drastic change of plan (from code name 'Capital' to 'Extended Capital') to deal with this unforeseen crisis was surely his most impressive achievement as a strategist.

The new plan, thoroughly discussed by Slim's staff but not cleared in advance with either ALFSEA or SEAC (i.e., Leese or Mountbatten) was described by Ronald Lewin as 'the most subtle, audacious and complex operation of his whole career'.[36] The essential feature of the plan was to convince the enemy that the main attack, by a whole Corps, would be made across the Irrawaddy with Mandalay as its objective. Meanwhile, under cover of this deception, the other Corps would approach the river further south using minor tracks to conceal its advance, cross at weakly held points and then drive all-out for Meiktila, the nerve centre of Japanese communications in central Burma. The second phase of this risky plan was to race for the sea to capture a port in southern Burma, Rangoon or perhaps Moulmein, before the advent of the monsoon in mid-May played havoc with Slim's already tenuous communications. Mountbatten would later describe Slim's master-stroke as 'a bold plan, relying for its fulfilment on secrecy, on speed and taking great administrative risks'.[37]

No matter how brilliant the plan, all would depend on the details of its implementation, which can only be summarised here. On 12 February 1945, 19th Division, supported by XXXIII Corps, began a series of fiercely contested crossings of the Irrawaddy which confirmed the Japanese assumption that this was the main attack directed against Mandalay. Meanwhile in January and early February IV Corps had moved some hundred miles to the west and marched south-east down little-known tracks to Pakokku nearly 50 miles south of the main Japanese defences. Its offensive, begun the day after XXXIII Corps' against Mandalay, did not go entirely smoothly or as planned,[38] but by 4 March its armoured spearhead had entered Meiktila. Kimura was taken by surprise, but once the threat to Meiktila became clear he rushed forces south to save this vital road and rail centre. The Japanese put up their usual fanatical defence of both cities but Mandalay was finally captured on 21 March and Meiktila a week later. After only a few days to rest and regroup, Slim's forces raced south in an attempt to reach Rangoon before the monsoon broke. Unfortunately for Slim, the monsoon arrived unusually early on 2 May while his leading units were still some 50 miles north of the city. But this hold-up, though an irritating anti-climax, soon proved unimportant because an amphibious landing by XV Corps launched from Arakan captured Rangoon virtually unopposed. The converging British forces linked up on 6 May so, to all intents and purposes, ending the campaign for the reconquest of Burma.

There was a scarcely credible episode in the days immediately following the victorious advance to Rangoon summarised above. General Sir Oliver Leese, Slim's immediate superior as Commander-in-Chief Land Forces South-East Asia (ALFSEA), informed Slim that he was relieving him of his command and giving him the humdrum role of 'mopping up' Japanese resistance in Burma while his successor planned the invasion of Malaya. Slim apparently took this astonishing blow calmly and did not openly protest nor, as far as is known, did he lobby privately either in the theatre or with the authorities at home. But he did remark to one of his officers, referring to Irwin's earlier attempt to have him dismissed in 1943: 'Don't worry my boy, this happened to me once before and I bloody well took the job of the chap who sacked me. I'll bloody well do it again.'[39] This proved prophetic. There was a general upsurge of opinion in Slim's favour throughout the Fourteenth Army and in India; Alanbrooke (the CIGS) intervened decisively; and Leese was indeed dismissed to be succeeded, after a brief interval, by Slim.

In conclusion, Bill Slim was a tough and successful Army commander who was also a charming and humane character. In this he was unlike most victorious generals, and in possessing so many admirable traits we may feel he was 'almost too good to be true'. Yet this unlikely combination of positive qualities, professional and private, has never been seriously questioned, let alone 'debunked'. He was a professionally well-educated and highly-trained soldier, a master of staff work and administration. He chose his subordinates wisely and gave them loyal support. He enjoyed good relations with most of his superior commanders (notably Mountbatten), and co-operated well with allies, including the notoriously prickly Stilwell. He was a good listener and adopted a relaxed, almost democratic, style in discussing plans with his staff, while leaving no uncertainty as to who bore the final responsibility for decisions. Slim was completely free from snobbery or self-importance; he excelled at winning the trust of all ranks and various nationalities – including even Chinese generals! One of his most important assets was his ability to speak to his troops in plain language which they could understand, explaining not only practical, soldierly matters but also dealing with more delicate issues of ideas and idealism. This gift for personal communication brought a rich reward in terms of loyalty and affection and goes far to account for his remarkable achievement in creating an *esprit de corps* at Army level.[40]

Slim's judgement as a strategist was sometimes faulty, but he never tried to gloss over his mistakes or put the blame on others. Nor, unlike Montgomery, did he later claim that his plans had all worked out perfectly in combat. He possessed the requisite physical robustness and the moral strength to overcome crises without showing the doubts and anxieties which privately assailed him.

In operational terms Slim demonstrated his leadership qualities in three very different circumstances. First, in sustaining morale and discipline through a devastating retreat which would have destroyed a lesser commander. Secondly, by maintaining his strategic aim through a long defensive battle of attrition where the outcome hung in the balance. Finally, in orchestrating a victorious advance through most difficult terrain against a formidable enemy; crowning the operation with a daring, improvised plan which succeeded brilliantly.

Slim may have to share with Montgomery the accolade of 'the finest (British) general the Second World War produced',[41] but as a sterling character on whom would-be military leaders might aim to model themselves, he was in a class of his own.

References

1. G. D. Sheffield (ed), *Leadership and Command. The Anglo–American Military Experience since 1861* (London: Brassey's, 1997), pp. 10–11, 126.
2. Sir John Smythe VC, *Leadership in War, 1939–1945* (Newton Abbot: David & Charles, 1974), p. 221.
3. John Keegan (ed), *Churchill's Generals* (London: Weidenfeld & Nicolson, 1991), pp. 298–322.
4. Basil Liddell Hart, *History of the Second World War* (London: Cassell, 1970).
5. Duncan Anderson in *Churchill's Generals*, op cit, pp. 298–300.
6. Ronald Lewin, *Slim: the Standardbearer* (London: Leo Cooper, 1976), p. 190.
7. Ibid, pp. 45, 50, 194.
8. Anderson, pp. 301–02.
9. Anderson, pp. 303–04. Lewin, pp. 53–54.
10. Lewin, pp. 64–67.
11. Anderson, pp. 304–05. Geoffrey Evans, *Slim as Military Commander* (London: Batsford, 1969), pp. 38–41.
12. Evans, pp. 51–52.
13. Anderson, pp. 307–10.
14. Field Marshal Sir William Slim, *Defeat into Victory* (London: Cassell, 1956), pp. 102–10.
15. Ibid, p. 86.
16. Lewin, p. 90.
17. Evans, pp. 82–84.
18. Slim, op cit, pp. 115–21.
19. Ibid, p. 146.
20. Ibid, pp. 182–87.
21. Anderson, pp. 312–14.
22. General Sir Rupert Smith, 'Should Generals be "Slim" Today?'. Lecture at the Imperial War Museum, 9 February 2002.
23. Slim, pp. 207–08.
24. Ibid, p. 213.
25. Lewin, pp. 128–29. Evans, p. 105
26. Slim, pp. 216–20. Lewin, pp. 142–44.
27. See, for example, David Rooney, 'Command and Leadership in the Chindit Campaigns' in Sheffield, op cit, pp. 141–57.
28. Anderson, p. 314.
29. Slim, pp. 294–308.
30. Evans, pp. 155–57.
31. Slim, p. 310. Sato may have been too doggedly fixated on Kohima but he also showed moral courage in refusing to divert units to Imphal and eventually forfeited his command by insisting that the remnants of his division must retreat. See Lewin, pp. 185–87.
32. Lewin, p. 176.
33. Slim, pp. 366–69. Lewin, p. 184. Evans, pp. 176–77.
34. Lewin, pp. 198–201.
35. Lewin, pp. 208–09. Evans, p. 184ff. Slim, pp. 390–93.
36. Lewin, pp. 210–13.
37. Evans, pp. 187–88, 214–15. Anderson, pp. 318–19.
38. Slim, pp. 428–29. The first attempt to cross the Irrawaddy failed completely but fortunately the Japanese had already abandoned the city of Pagan on the opposite bank. This was the longest river crossing in the Second World War.

39. Lewin, pp. 237–46. Rupert Smith, in the lecture mentioned earlier, suggests that although Slim was not a 'dabbler in politics' he was politically astute. It was a remarkable feat to be 'sacked' first as a Corps and then as an Army commander, and on both occasions to take the position of the general who had tried to dismiss him.
40. See Michael Howard's comments in Sheffield, op cit, pp. 120, 126–27.
41. Mountbatten had no doubt that Slim was the finest, see Evans, pp. 215–25.

Part IV
After 1945

13

Oh! What a Lovely War:
History and Popular Myths In Late Twentieth-Century Britain

This paper was prepared for Wm Roger Louis' celebrated seminar at the University of Texas in Austin and delivered in the Fall Semester, 2003. It was well-received by a large and enthusiastic audience but, not surprisingly, some of the references to the British role in the war were not fully appreciated. Subsequently, reading the paper to a branch of the Western Front Association I was surprised to find that some members of the audience had not seen the play or the film. For those who had seen either version I gained the impression that they had put entertainment far above historical accuracy and had not been bothered by the blatant historical bias or the polemics against the British commanders and staff officers. Perhaps one should accept that most people will believe what they want to believe, particularly if they have been emotionally stirred and entertained. Nevertheless, as I write at the end of the essay, I believe that historians, while paying due respect to these positive values, have a duty to point out the deceptions, evasions and inaccuracies which seriously mar what have become such influential contributors to First World War mythology.

In my book *The Unquiet Western Front: Britain's Role in Literature and History* (2002) I argued that the First World War had been rediscovered in the 1960s and presented to a new generation which had a very different cultural and political perspective from that of the 1930s. Furthermore I suggested that later twentieth century notions of Britain's role in the First World War had been decisively influenced by the books, plays, and films of the 1960s. I devoted only a few pages to discussion of the play and film *Oh! What a Lovely War* and the purpose of this lecture is to expand on that brief discussion.

Let me first provide the context in which a new generation was introduced to the history of the First World War. There was a pervasive fear of nuclear war which provided a grim undertone to the play under discussion. Only a year before the play's first showing in 1963 the Cuban missile crisis suggested that the world had teetered on the brink of annihilation. Far less dramatic, but of long-term social significance, National Service was ended in 1960, so the last conscripts left the armed services in 1963. Thus ended a tradition by which the majority of the male population had some familiarity with the realities of army life, and many conscripts actually experienced war itself.

The decade was also notable for the emergence of an independent youth culture and of much greater freedom in sexual matters. Homosexual relations between consenting adults in private ceased to be a crime; while the outcome of the 'Lady Chatterley' trial heralded a more liberal era for the publication and open discussion of formerly taboo topics. As Philip Larkin wistfully recalled in his poem Annus Mirabilis:

> Sexual intercourse began
> In nineteen sixty three
> (Which was rather late for me) –
> Between the end of the *Chatterley* ban
> And the Beatles' first L.P.[1]

The same year, 1963, was also that of the John Profumo scandal, in which the Secretary of State for War was disgraced for consorting with expensive call girls whose clientele included Stephen Ward, a society osteopath, and Captain Ivanov, a naval attaché at the Soviet embassy. This affair had all the ingredients to titillate the popular press: sleaze and hypocrisy in the Tory Party and high society with the possibility of espionage. Profumo's political career was ruined, Ward committed suicide, and the call girls became celebrities.

The increasingly dire plight of the American forces in Vietnam provided a focus for anti-American, anti-imperial, and anti-authority protest, especially in British universities. Only experts (at least in Britain) will now remember the rapid surge of the American military commitment in Vietnam and its even speedier contraction. In 1961 there were only some 3,000 American personnel in Vietnam but by 1966 there were 385,000. In 1968 the 'Tet' offensive against southern cities was defeated, but so unpopular was the war that President Johnson decided not to seek re-election and to begin peace negotiations. American forces in Vietnam reached a peak of 541,500 early in 1969 but the ebb tide was so rapid that the last personnel left in March 1973.[2]

Radical student protest and rebellion culminated in violent demonstrations and clashes with police in Paris and other European cities. In Britain, university lectures and administration were widely disrupted. Even at the conservative and largely apolitical King's College London, where I was then a young lecturer, we were worried (needlessly as it turned out) that departmental signs indicating 'War Studies' would provoke hostile demonstrations. At Field Marshal Earl Haig's former Oxford College his portrait in the hall was given a new caption 'Murderer of One Million Men,' while the College War Memorial was temporarily removed.

All this may seem beside the point since Britain was not involved in Vietnam, but as a teacher of military history I can assure you that the fallout was profound and enduring. For students who could not remember the Second World War, Britain's humiliation over the Suez crisis in 1956 and America's own involvement and eventual failure in Vietnam created a strong impression that even wars fought by democracies were unjust and futile.

It was in this generally anti-war setting that the entertainment *Oh! What a Lovely War* was put together and first performed in March 1963. Initially inspired by the soldiers' songs of the First World War, the play also drew heavily on anti-war historical writings of the inter-war decades, either directly or via their reappearance in derivative popular works of the early 1960s such as Alan Clark's *The Donkeys* (1961). I believe that the play (often revived)[3] and the film of *Oh! What a Lovely War* (1969) have had a significant role in shaping British beliefs and myths about the First World War from the 1960s to the present.

In my book I attributed the remarkable revival of interest in the First World War that occurred in the 1960s partly to the sense among publishers and television producers that the reading and viewing public needed a break from saturation coverage of the Second World War, followed by a sharp commercial perception that the imminent fiftieth anniversaries (1964–1968) would provide a splendid opportunity for re-visiting the First World War. But we need to explore further if we are to account for a new, more radical and even savage de-bunking approach to the First World War in the 1960s. Daniel Todman (who has generously allowed me to read part of his unpublished doctoral thesis), makes an interesting case for a demographic shift; his argument being that until the 1960s the generation of bereaved parents of soldiers killed in the First World War 'set boundaries on what was acceptable public discourse about the war'; i.e., criticism in books, plays, or films would be tacitly restrained by fear of causing further distress to this vulnerable group. This is a plausible argument but, as Dr Todman admits, it is difficult to document.[4]

I should like to offer a different kind of explanation based on the British public's perception of the nation's role in the two world wars. Paradoxically, Britain's role in the Second World War made it harder to understand, and appreciate, her role in the earlier conflict. The Kaiser's regime, though militaristic, was patently not such an evil force as Hitler's, and German atrocities in the First World War, seen after 1918 to have been exaggerated for propaganda purposes, were dwarfed by Nazi barbarism in the Second. Moreover, Nazi Germany had posed a more direct threat to Britain's survival with intensive aerial bombing and rocket attacks following the failure of the projected invasion in 1940. Thus, by the 1960s, Churchill's heroic leadership and the nation's 'finest hour' had acquired the status of myth, accompanied by the retrospective justification of a crusade to end the Holocaust. The radical historian A. J. P. Taylor concluded a popular history with the surprising verdict that, for all its suffering and destruction, the Second World War had been a 'good war.' By contrast, the First World War now seemed to many Britons to have been a very 'bad war' – in its origins, its conduct and its consequences.

The original program of the play *Oh! What a Lovely War* describes it as 'a musical entertainment based on an idea of Charles Chilton.' In 1958 Chilton had visited Arras military cemetery to take a photograph of his father's grave but was confronted with the bitter truth that his father had no grave: his name was included in the collective memorial to 35,942 officers and men with no known grave who had died in that area alone – and there were nearly twice as many names on the memorial at Thiepval for the Somme campaigns.[5] Reflection on this horrific statistic led to Chilton's celebrated 1961 radio program *The Long, Long Trail*, based on soldiers' songs of the period, and his passionate determination to portray the fate of the rank and file on the Western Front. Hence his collaboration with Joan Littlewood, a radical founder of Theatre Workshop, whose aim was to present politicized drama to working class audiences. It was her idea to stage the show in a music hall setting and performed by a troupe of pierrots. She insisted on a didactic, extreme left-wing perspective. For this reason, in Dr Todman's words, '[s]he rejected scripts which offered a realistic depiction of life in the trenches. The result is a black and white picture in which officers at all levels are stupid, callous cowards while their men are sardonic heroes.'[6]

The third, vital contributor to the stage production was Raymond Fletcher, military history buff and devotee of Liddell Hart, military commentator for the socialist journal *Tribune*, sometime Labour MP, and more recently revealed as a Soviet agent. Fletcher had no time for the generals or 'brass hats'; his sympathies were entirely with the ordinary soldiers. More ideologically committed than Charles Chilton, he fervently believed that the play should also convey a warning about the dangers of war in the nuclear age. Thus he described his three-hour harangue to the Theatre Workshop Group on the play's purpose as 'one part me, one part Liddell Hart, the rest Lenin!'[7]

The play was first performed at Stratford, in the East End of London, on March 19, 1963 and later transferred to the West End. As someone who saw an early performance, I can testify that the experience was not only highly entertaining, but also deeply moving. The puerile sneering at the generals and staff officers (mostly cribbed from Alan Clark) was partly offset by marvellous one-liners. For example:

> *The Master of Ceremonies (re the slide into war in August 1914):* 'Whenever there's a crisis, shoot some grouse, that's what I always say.'

Briton: 'I understand President Wilson is a very sick man?' *American:* 'Yes, he's an idealist!'

Haig reads a letter: 'Better conditions needed for officers. The other ranks don't seem to mind so much.'

Haig (at prayer): 'I ask thee for victory, Lord, before the Americans arrive.'[8]

But the overwhelming sense of sadness and nostalgia was mostly conveyed by the songs, thirty-one of which were listed in the program. These ranged from the music hall knockabout comedy of 'Belgium put the Kibosh on the Kaiser' and the bawdy 'I'll make a man of any one of you,' to the solemn 'Heilige Nacht,' the poignant 'Chanson de Craonne,' and 'They'll never believe us.' The majority, however, were irreverent and bitter tirades against the soldiers' predicament in the trenches including 'If you want the old battalion,' 'I don't want to be a soldier,' 'When this lousy war is over,' 'I want to go home,' and 'Forward Joe Soap's Army' sung to the hymn tune of 'Onward, Christian Soldiers.' The play's serious propaganda message was hinted at in various places in the text – such as the accidental nature of the war's outbreak, its unexpected duration and enormous casualty list – but it was spelt out in the author's notes, which read more like a political tract than the usual theater program.

Raymond Fletcher, like Joan Littlewood, was deeply concerned that the errors and miscalculations of 1914–1918 should not be repeated in the nuclear age. He was impressed by Herman Kahn's massive study *On Thermonuclear War* (1960), which was one of the many bizarre sources pressed on the Theatre Workshop players who were encouraged to contribute.[9] Before 1914, according to Fletcher, people had believed that the Balance of Power could preserve peace; today they believe in the Balance of Terror: 'But accident and miscalculations are still possible – and a third, nuclear world war could kill as many in four hours as were killed in the whole of World War One.' A series of notes drove home the lesson, the final one stating that '[o]ne atom bomb in 1945 caused as many casualties as the entire Battle of Arras. One Polaris missile is twenty-five times as destructive as the bomb that destroyed Hiroshima.' General Douglas MacArthur was quoted as saying in 1961: 'Global war has become a Frankenstein to destroy both sides. ... It [war] contains now only the germs of double suicide.' According to another note, '[i]n 1960 an American Research Team fed all the facts of World War I into the computers they use to plan World War III [sic]. They reached the conclusion that the 1914–1918 war was impossible and couldn't have happened. There could not have been so many blunders nor so many casualties.' Regarding the play's text it was stated (in italics): *Everything presented as fact is true.* This preposterous claim will be challenged later in this lecture, but for the moment we need only note Derek Paget's assertion that, from a Marxist viewpoint, Joan Littlewood's mode of representing war 'became dominant in historiography as well as in drama.' The play's historical sources provide a view 'now recuperated into the dominant cultural understanding of the great war.'[10]

The play's most original feature was its presentation of the war from what was assumed to be the common soldier's viewpoint: a revolutionary inversion of class authority in the 1960s though since then a much more common approach. A new generation in the 1960s was provided with the disturbing argument – later to be comically trivialized in the 1989 BBC television series *Blackadder Goes Forth* – that the Great War represented a betrayal of the ordinary people by the ruling class.[11] As will be suggested later, in discussion of the film version, these strident denunciations of the military leaders' incompetence have gradually achieved the status of popular myth, so much so that to many people it now seems perverse to contend that the majority of soldiers did not see themselves as hapless victims in a pointless war; that there were numerous brave and popular subalterns; and that most of the senior officers were neither callous nor incompetent.[12]

The anti-historical nature of the play is evident in its structure. There are only two Acts. The first dramatizes an innocent hope of victory in a spirit of optimism; the second presents recognition of defeat in a mood of despair and pessimism. The play draws heavily upon three popular texts: Barbara Tuchman's *August 1914* (for the accidental outbreak of war in that year), Alan Clark's *The Donkeys* for 1915 (and the battle of Loos), and Leon Wolff's *In Flanders Fields* for 1917 (and especially Passchendaele). Significantly, from a historian's viewpoint, it has almost nothing to say about 1918, thus avoiding having to explain how 'the donkeys' had secured victory. Indeed it was a crucial part of the play's message that there had been no winners. As early as page 61 of the text (cleverly transferred to the final scene in the film) a slide depicts a vast field with white wooden crosses stretching as far as the eye can see. This is what the war was 'about' and how it has ended – in desolation and mass slaughter.

The play, moreover, deliberately subverted traditional accounts of the war as related from the officers' standpoint, such as the hugely popular drama *Journey's End*, by giving a voice to a lower class (the rankers) who were supposed only to be able to express themselves through irony and humor. Irony is indeed the prevailing mode throughout, above all in the songs. The line taken was that the war as a whole was inflicted upon a compliant lower class by an upper class which assumed a superiority it had failed to justify. This is to take a breathtaking liberty with historical truth in the light of the disproportionate number of officer casualties, which included the Prime Minister's son, Raymond Asquith, killed on the Somme. These obtrusive political concerns, as Derek Paget damningly concludes, 'make the play a poorish source of knowledge about the Great War, (yet) such an excellent source of knowledge about the early 1960s.'[13]

The play was a considerable box-office success, both in Stratford East and later in the West End, followed by several international tours and frequent productions by repertory theatres. But did the play realise the political expectations of its progenitors? In the short term, say over the next decade, probably not. As Daniel Todman has rightly pointed out, the majority of the audience, even at the Theatre Royal, Stratford, were almost certainly middle class regular playgoers and not members of the working class which Joan Littlewood had hoped to attract. This was even more the case when the play moved to Wyndham's Theatre on the Aldwych. One of Joan Littlewood's colleagues even complained that the critics' enthusiasm had attracted the wrong kind of audience which was tantamount to a betrayal of the Theatre Workshop's socialist aspirations. The play ran for a year in the West End but closed after only fifteen weeks on Broadway with a loss of about £30,000 to the Theatre Workshop. Presumably many of the characters and references were lost on an American audience.[14] British theatergoers would be well aware that the Theatre Workshop's productions were experimental and left-wing and would therefore be prepared for a swingeing attack on the First World War generals, provided they were also entertained. Reviewers' reactions showed that the gap between Chilton's aim of paying tribute to the humor, stoicism, and comradeship of the ordinary soldier and the more radical intentions of Littlewood and Fletcher had not been entirely bridged. In other words, the most enjoyable and memorable aspect of the entertainment was the wonderful songs which evoked emotions of pathos, nostalgia, and even sentimentality, The songs received even more emphasis in the West End version when a cynical ending was replaced by a jolly reprise.[15] These are my own recollections of that memorable evening, and most contemporary critics concurred that sentimentality had taken the edge off the savage satire. Thus the *Sunday Times* reviewer, J. W. Lambert, commented that 'this immensely brisk charade gives nostalgia a top-dressing of belated anti-establishment respectability.' David Pryce-Jones remarked of the Aldwych version that 'showbiz has crept in to bespangle the poor relation from Stratford East' to the extent that audiences 'could imagine themselves back in the days of good old musical shows.'[16]

Few reviewers seem to have been worried by the play's blatant anti-military bias or its historical distortions, partly perhaps, as suggested earlier, because they gave priority to its entertainment value but also, I would argue, because the fundamental assumptions regarding the war's pointlessness, unspeakable conditions, unacceptable casualty figures, and incompetent generalship were already widely accepted. Liddell Hart, whose books were included in the source material, and who acted as a historical consultant, wrote to the *Observer* that there was 'more of the real war in the play than in recent "white-wash" history; it *did* faithfully reflect what his generation thought of the war.' Correlli Barnett, however, struck a dissenting note in savaging the production in a BBC Third Programme radio talk. He stressed the gulf between entertainment and history. As entertainment it succeeded brilliantly, but in terms of history '[i]t is a highly partisan, and often grossly unfair, presentation of the war from an extreme anti-Brass-hat point of view. Its intent is serious – it wants to make propaganda.'[17] Barnett made another telling criticism which applied to both the stage and film versions: while politicians were shown as responsible for the outbreak of war they were conspicuously absent during its conduct. There were 'butchers' aplenty (i.e., the Generals) but where was 'the Cur' (Lloyd George) asked Barnett rhetorically? If only officers were depicted, only officers could be charged – and their guilt was proven by the casualty figures.[18]

Richard Attenborough's film adaptation has largely eclipsed the original play in the public memory. It caused an immediate sensation when first shown in London in 1969, and on general release was acclaimed at international film festivals in the United States, Spain, and Japan. The film was one of the highest earners in Britain in 1969 but, interestingly, was outshone financially by *The Battle of Britain*.[19] Part of the appeal for regular cinema goers surely lay in the all-star cast. To mention just a few of the best-known actors: Jack Hawkins was a senile Emperor Franz Joseph; John Gielgud a cynical Count Berchtold; Michael Redgrave played Sir Henry Wilson; Laurence Olivier an outrageously blimpish Sir John French; Ralph Richardson an aloof Sir Edward Grey; Maggie Smith the seductive recruiting siren, and – starring throughout – John Mills was a cold and inflexible Sir Douglas Haig. Most of the play's songs and the dialogue were retained, but the setting was changed to Brighton Pier with the atmosphere and trappings of the 1914-era fairground and music hall. Attenborough also retained much of the stylized nature of the stage version, especially for Haig and his colleagues who remained on the pier, safely distant from the killing fields. The film made a strong impression by the frequent switches between the jolly scenes on the pier and the grim vignettes of front-line fighting, though from a critical historical standpoint the latter too were very unrealistic. A very successful innovation in the film was the introduction of a representative family, the Smiths, who provide continuity throughout from the five brothers' recruitment by the Maggie Smith character, through their experiences of battle, to their deaths in the trenches.

Attenborough's adaptation, though retaining the relentless critique of the officers and the upper classes in general (an elderly boss in his carriage cannot remember the name of his wounded employee, and wounded men on Waterloo Station are made to wait while wounded officers are at once whisked away), lacks Joan Littlewood's angry political drive. Feelings of nostalgia and sadness are evoked, even more powerfully than on the stage. In a brilliant piece of symbolism, which can easily be missed, poppies – normally the emblems of remembrance – are here handed to those about to die.[20] Also, as Todman notes perceptively, the audience's perspective has been changed. In contrast to the play, where the theater audience is made to feel involved in a tragedy without end, in the film the viewers are detached spectators of a 'war game' which ends with mass funerals and the same old statesmen (also located on the pier) re-drawing the map of Europe.

No one who has seen the film will forget the audacious final sequence. As hostilities draw to an end the remaining soldier of the Smith family (a ghost), is escorted from the battlefield and follows a tape which takes him back to England, past the peace-makers in session with the maps, and off the pier to emerge on the Sussex Downs. There he joins the reclining ghosts of his dead relatives and the female survivors who are enjoying a picnic on the hillside. When his small daughter asks the stock question 'granny, what did daddy do in the war?' the scene is transformed. As Jerome Kern's nostalgic melody 'They Wouldn't Believe Me' rises on the sound track, the dead soldiers dissolve into white crosses which are seen to stretch away into infinity, filling the whole screen. The effect is still powerful when viewed in solitude: in crowded cinemas the impression of sadness at the useless sacrifice of so many young men was reportedly overwhelming. Nevertheless it needs to be pointed out that this astonishing conclusion was not only deceitful as history but did a disservice to the memory of these young 'lions' who were made to seem to have thrown away their lives for nothing. This was the meaning Richard Attenborough intended to convey. He remarked recently that watching the closing scene always brings tears to his eyes.[21]

In its supplement pre-viewing the film the *Observer* had displayed Field Marshal Haig (John Mills) on the cover amid this sea of white crosses with the comment: 'the hated objects in this film turn out to be a parcel of imbecile aristocrats and politicians, and the British High Command – French and Haig especially.' Its review noted that the film is on the side of the workers who do all the dirty jobs. Ironies are to be found everywhere. For example, the superficially glamorous lady who recruits Harry Smith and his pals with a broad hint of sexual favours to follow ('I'll make a man of every one of you'), is glimpsed off stage as 'a raddled bag as hard as nails,' suggesting that from the very outset the innocent recruits have been deceived by their social superiors. The *Sunday Telegraph*'s review described the film as 'the most pacifist statement since *All Quiet on the Western Front*.' Derek Malcolm in the *Guardian* and Kenneth Allsop in the *Observer* both felt that the film was inferior to the play because its glossy production tended to elicit comfortable feelings of nostalgia. Malcolm also felt that the film-makers had been enamored as well as repelled by the terrible images of trench warfare. 'In a way difficult to explain, it unwittingly indulges itself. ... Its basic nostalgia is too comfortingly fond. ... It seems almost ridiculous to admire it so much, but to be moved by it so little.' Allsop admitted that: 'The raw, caustic savagery which burned through the Theatre Workshop evening still haunts me. I esteem what Mr. Attenborough has done, but he hasn't disturbed my nights.'[22] Between them the film and the play had managed to transform a terrible and devastating European tragedy into an entertaining 'War Game.'

Dr. Todman has thoughtfully analyzed the dilemma between the requirements for commercial success and the risks of brutal realism in comparing the film versions of *Oh! What a Lovely War* and *King and Country*, directed by Joseph Losey in 1964. The latter tells the story of the execution of a shell-shocked young British soldier called Hamp, and is 'unremitting in its depiction of the horror of the Western front,' culminating in the (improbable) scene of the defending officer, Captain Hargreaves, having to blow Hamp's head off with his revolver after the firing squad had botched its task. That film was a disaster at the box office whereas the phrase 'Oh! What a Lovely War' has passed into popular language and both the play's and the film's contents and message are widely remembered. As Todman sums up: 'For all that they might talk about the mud, blood and official stupidity, audiences would not accept such a bitter interpretation of the war (as Losey's) without a sugaring of sentimentality.'[23]

In view of what was said earlier about the polemical intent and political bias of both the play and the film of *Oh! What a Lovely War*, it may seem otiose to make some detailed criticisms. I do so here because I believe that the media has had an insidious influence in shaping public opinion towards a view of the war that is largely false. I will concentrate on the film, partly because it has reached a wider audience, but also because I have been able to study it more carefully on video cassette.

The First World War can easily be portrayed as pointless if the Great Power rivalries before 1914 are completely ignored or the outbreak of war attributed to the mishandling of a petty incident at Sarajevo. Richard Attenborough has recently confirmed that he does indeed believe the war had no cause, that it resulted only from the pride of statesmen and diplomatic maneuvering.[24] While it would be unrealistic to expect a faithful adherence to chronology and an accurate depiction of the main events, the film's structure (following the play) creates enormous distortions. For example, so much time is devoted to scene setting and recruiting (on Brighton Pier) that nearly half the total time (one hour) is taken up with events in 1914, culminating in the Christmas Truce. This episode is given prominence to show that the ordinary soldiers on either side are reluctant to fight each other: the German spokesman, Fritz, actually says so. Indeed the Scots soldiers' real hostility is directed more towards 'the bastard English' who end the truce with gunfire! After 1914 the rest of the war is drastically condensed. There is only brief coverage of Loos (September 1915), the first day of the Somme offensive (July 1, 1916) and the Third Ypres campaign in 1917.

Again, while it would be ridiculous to expect a fair and balanced portrayal of Sir Douglas Haig, still a controversial figure among historians, here he is crudely caricatured as completely unimaginative, stubborn, and inhuman in his calm acceptance of huge losses – a War Office official notice records, 'British casualties on the Somme 600,000: ground gained nil.' On a specific point, Haig is shown as complacent and overly optimistic about his troops' readiness before the Somme offensive, whereas we know that in fact he was very anxious about the inexperienced Kitchener divisions' inadequate training and tried in vain to persuade the French commander Joffre to postpone the start of the offensive.

The irony and pathos implicit in most of the soldiers' songs is fully exploited to engage the sympathy of the viewers, but the impression is created that pessimistic and anti-war lyrics should be taken literally, thus ignoring the traditional humor, grumbling, and stoicism of Tommy Atkins. It is ridiculous, for example, to place a disenchanted song as early as the battle of Mons in August 1914 where all the soldiers were regulars or pre-war reservists.

Although Richard Attenborough apparently felt that the stage production had been too harsh on the officers, his own depiction of officer-men relations was nevertheless an unhistorical caricature. No officers were shown leading their men in the trenches or in the attack; look for example at the officer-less group of Ulstermen stranded in an advanced position near Thiepval on July 1, 1916. The staff officer shown in the trenches at Loos is a pompous ass, ending his embarrassing harangue with the comforting words, 'You're white men all,' which indeed they were.

The British front-line soldiers are shown as passive, impotent cannon fodder who mostly die impersonally from shell fire and machine gun bullets. Their own role as attackers and killers is overlooked. Above all, they are portrayed as victims of their own incompetent staff officers and callous commanders, epitomized by the wooden characterization of Haig who believes that he is carrying out God's will.

The final criticism concerns the outcome of the war, on which both the play and the film were evasive. To be sure, the Allied victory was bought at a terrible price in lives, destruction, and the disruption of European society, and its political benefits soon came to seem disappointing. There was still a large gulf between victory and defeat, however, and this was generally appreciated by the generation that had fought, or endured, the war. In the film the only clue that the war on the Western Front has ended in an allied victory is a Tommy's remark that they are back at Mons where he and his brother fought in August 1914. There is an inference that the Americans' arrival in 1917 will lead to victory, hence of course Haig's prayer that God will allow *him* to win the war before the Americans become the dominant partner. The brief glimpse of the elderly statesmen redrawing the map of Europe after the Armistice suggests that they are again trying to establish a balance of power, having learned nothing since their failure in 1914. Finally the surreal closing scene on the Sussex Downs creates the impression that all the soldiers have been killed and have died in vain – an utterly negative conclusion which Attenborough still believes to be true.

In my book, *The Unquiet Western Front*, I may have exaggerated the extent to which the unsubtle polemical views of the play and film of *Oh! What a Lovely War* gained public acceptance in Britain in the 1960s and early 1970s. But the new, more insistent emphasis on the futility of the war and the vain sacrifice of a generation of brave ordinary young men by uncaring and incompetent upper-class officers put down deep roots which have since been continuously nourished in books, journals and, above all, television, until by the 1990s the farcical but enormously popular series *Blackadder Goes Forth* could be widely accepted as purveying the essential truths about the most unlovely war. In Derek Paget's perceptive analysis, 'The myth of the Great Men of Empire with their tales of derring-do dissolved first into the Lions led by Donkeys, then into General Melchett and Captain Darling (the epitome of the incompetent commander and staff officer in *Blackadder*). ... Crucial changes have taken place not only in representation, but also in national self-perception since 1963.'[25] Furthermore, as Daniel Todman neatly puts it, 'By the 1990s, the texts which had first arrived in the 1960s were themselves the subject of myths.'[26] In August 2003 a reviewer could write, before addressing a book which robustly challenges these myths: 'For many people, perhaps most people, "futility" seems to be the word that best sums up Britain's martial endeavors on the Western Front. Few believe throwing away the flower of the nation's manhood for the gain of a few square miles of Flanders mud was worth it. ... New Age pacifists, hip satirists and reactionary Edwardian summer sentimentalists all agree: the Great War came at too high a price.'[27]

How is the military historian to react to what the majority of his professional colleagues regard as pernicious myths, misunderstandings, and misrepresentations which are blatantly out of touch with modern scholarship? He can shrug his shoulders and take the line that most people are not deeply interested in history and can be left to embrace any old myths that suit them. He can counterattack with righteous indignation as the likes of John Terraine and Correlli Barnett did in the late twentieth century and Gordon Corrigan is doing now. Or, as I tried to do in my recent book, and as Daniel Todman has explored in his doctoral thesis from a slightly different angle, they can trace the origin and development of myths as historical phenomena which acquire a life of their own. However in the case of such a huge and controversial subject as the First World War most military historians will feel that they have a professional duty to present 'the truth' as they see it, based on the best documentary evidence and with as much objectivity as they can muster. As regards *Oh! What a Lovely War* and its pervasive influence, their task may be comparable to that of Sisyphus, forever fated to push an enormous boulder uphill. But, unlike him, they may eventually succeed when the First World War takes its place as just another great conflict in history and one in which Britain's very impressive contribution will be recognized.

References

I am indebted to Stephen Badsey, John Lee, and Daniel Todman for their help in preparing this lecture.

1.   Philip Larkin, *High Windows* (London, 1979 pbk edn), p. 34.
2.   Arthur Marwick, *The Sixties: Cultural Revolution in Britain, France, Italy and the United States 1958-1974* (New York, 1998), pp. 533-63 and 632-42. Some early American viewers of the film of *Oh! What a Lovely War* thought it 'speaks as much for the young protesting generation of today as for their grandparents who survived the Great War.' *Sunday Telegraph*, Apr. 6, 1969, Liddell Hart Papers, Liddell Hart Centre for Military Archives, King's College, London: hereafter LH. LH 13/61.
3.   The play was performed in London's Regent's Park Open Air Theatre as recently as July 2002.
4.   Daniel Todman, 'Representations of the First World War in British Popular Culture, 1918-1998' (Ph.D. Thesis, University of Cambridge, 2003), Ch. 2, 'Drama and the First World War, 1960-1998,' pp. 41-45 and 80-84. See the revised version of the thesis entitled *The Great War: Myth and Memory* published by Hambledon in 2005.
5.   I have retained a copy of the original program. See also Alex Danchev's essay in Brian Bond, ed., *The First World War and British Military History* (Oxford, 1991), p. 281.
6.   Todman, 'Representations,' p. 91.
7.   Bond, *First World War*, p. 282. I owe the point about Fletcher's links with the Soviet Union to Dr. Gary Sheffield.
8.   *Oh! What a Lovely War* (1965) pp. 46, 48, 49, 80, and 83. More than the film, the play stresses the evil influence of arms manufacturers and war profiteers. In the play, for example, an American profiteer remarks 'Do you realise that there have been two peace scares in the past year? Our shares dropped 40 percent.'
9.   Derek Paget, 'Remembrance Play: *Oh! What a Lovely War* and History,' in Tony Howard and John Stokes, eds., *Acts of War* (1996), p. 83. For an example of the current interest in the 'myths' rather than the 'history' of the First World War, see Graham S. Galer, 'Myths of the Western Front' (Ph.D. Thesis, University of Kent, 2002); Bond, *First World War*, p. 283. For a list of the historical sources consulted see Paget, 'Remembrance Play,' p. 91
10.   Paget, 'Remembrance Play,' p. 83.
11.   Ibid., p. 89.
12.   John Bourne, 'British Generals in the First World War' in Gary Sheffield, ed., *Leadership and Command* (London, 1997).
13.   Paget, 'Remembrance Play,' p. 89.
14.   *Sunday Telegraph*, Jan. 31, 1965, in LH 13/61.
15.   Ibid.

16. I quoted some of these reviews from the Liddell Hart Papers (file LH 13/61) in my book, but I am grateful to Dr. Todman for his references to additional material in this file which I have subsequently checked.
17. Liddell Hart letter to the *Observer*, June 20, 1963 and typescript of Correlli Barnett's talk on July 10, 1963, both in LH 13/61.
18. Bond, *First World War*, p. 285.
19. Ibid., p. 283.
20. I owe this important insight to Dr. Todman. Richard Attenborough also mentioned this deliberate use of symbolism in a BBC 2 Arena program celebrating his career on Aug. 24, 2003.
21. Attenborough, *Arena* program.
22. Kenneth Allsop, 'War Game Comparisons,' *Observer*, Apr. 13, 1969; Derek Malcolm 'Fun and Games,' *Guardian*, Apr. 9. 1969. Copies of all the reviews mentioned are to be found in the Liddell Hart Papers LH 13/61. In re-reading this bulky file of press cuttings I was deeply depressed by the abysmal lack of historical understanding of the First World War, with the late John Terraine and Correlli Barnett honourable exceptions.
23. Todman, 'Representations,' p. 108.
24. Attenborough, *Arena* program.
25. Paget, 'Remembrance Play,' p. 86.
26. Todman, 'Representations,' p. 86.
27. Graham Stewart reviewing Gordon Corrigan's *Mud, Blood and Poppycock, Spectator*. Aug. 9, 2003.

A Farewell to Arms

I gave my last lecture as a member of staff at King's College on 13 June 2001 and called it 'A Farewell to Arms'. I had good reason to believe that I would be invited to continue to teach part-time for a few years, or be given an honorary position which would enable me to maintain a working relationship with the Department where I had spent 35 years. When my farewell lecture turned out to be precisely that, not *au revoir* but a definite goodbye, I was, to say the least, disappointed. I felt I had sufficient energy, enthusiasm and expertise to make a useful contribution, especially in supervising PhD candidates and teaching MA special subjects. After I reached 70, however, I came to accept that I had had a good innings and could appreciate the advantages of being back in the pavilion: no more stressful commuting, attending tedious committees or marking sheaves of essays based on the same limited sources.

I have already, in the introductory essay for this volume, given some idea of the early days of the Department of War Studies and my role there. In retrospect the 1970s and early 1980s were a relatively tranquil period. Laurence Martin succeeded Michael Howard as head of Department and Michael Dockrill and Barrie Paskins joined us as lecturers in military history/foreign policy and ethics/war literature respectively. We took on more and more MA and PhD candidates but otherwise the rate of change remained steady. In a more financially stringent and competitive era, however, the Department's small size (and lack of an undergraduate intake of its own) made it vulnerable. More dynamic leadership and a broader concept of the future of War Studies was urgently needed and these attributes were supplied in abundance by Lawrence Freedman, who became head of the Department in 1982. After a few years of playing himself in Lawrie introduced changes which transformed the nature of the Department and greatly extended its responsibilities in its relationship with the armed services. Lawrie's international reputation and prodigious output of volumes on contemporary conflicts attracted a rapid increase in graduates interested in this field of modern strategic studies, and the members of the academic staff expanded accordingly. In the early 1990s the critical decision was taken to accept undergraduates for a new three year course for a BA in War Studies. The idea was to build up this course gradually to allow for the inevitable problems of time-tables, lecture rooms and library facilities, but from the outset the BA course was enormously popular so that, even with high entry standards and rigorous interviewing, the annual intake soon exceeded the target of 30 originally deemed to be manageable. The extra stress on staff was considerable; including the search for ever-changing teaching rooms in obscure parts of the College; and classes continuing through the lunch period and extending well into the evening. Although I was not greatly affected by this upheaval, it was undoubtedly a period of turmoil which drastically altered the atmosphere in the Department.

The remit of the Department was also expanding in other ways. A Centre of Defence Studies was set up nearby in the Strand under the excellent direction of Michael Clarke. Even more remarkable, after tortuous negotiations with the Ministry of Defence, the Department took over responsibility for the academic side of education at the three Services' Staff Colleges at Bracknell, Greenwich and Camberley. When, a few years later, the three separate Services institutions were merged and moved to a new location at Watchfield near Shrivenham, the resulting Joint Services Command and Staff College became an outpost of King's College. This creation of an academic empire was largely the work of Lawrie (now Sir Lawrence) Freedman. Although I had been short-listed for headship of the Department in 1982 when he was appointed I freely admit that I would not have had the drive, energy or vision to carry through these momentous developments.

My own career had made steady but not spectacular progress, which was only to be expected in a Department of only five members where there was already a professor and a reader (Wolf Mendl who had been recruited a year before me in 1965). But I was elected a Reader in 1977 and awarded a personal chair (in Military History) in 1986. In my last few years at King's my modest personal ambitions were nearly all realised. I was honoured with a Fellowship of the College (FKC) in 1996; made the first of five demanding but rewarding lecture tours to Japan; elected in 2000 to a Visiting Fellowship at All Souls College, Oxford; and later that year delivered the Lees Knowles Lectures at Cambridge.

I should not wish to leave the impression that after the abrupt ending of my career at King's College I found nothing to do but cultivate my garden. I remained President of the British Commission for Military History (BCMH) until 2006 but then felt I should step down, after 20 years in the post, rather than stay on until members began asking about my future plans. Finding a successor who would continue the developments introduced during my tenure – an expanded membership, annual battlefield tours, regular conferences and early ventures in publishing – was not easy because of the time involved, but the Committee eventually discovered someone who seemed ideal. Professor Richard Holmes was not only an eminent military historian with a number of excellent books to his credit, but also an outstanding presenter of battles and campaigns on television. Alas, though he soldiered on bravely and stoically for several years, Richard was already seriously ill on taking over as President and died suddenly in April 2011.

In retirement I continued to attend conferences in, for example, Breda and the Hague and gave frequent lectures in Britain, mainly for the Historical Association and the Western Front Association. Thanks to the determined support of Michael Dockrill I was able to deliver the Saki Dockrill Memorial Lecture at King's College, London in November 2011. Meanwhile, in 2008, I had published *Survivors of a Kind: Memoirs of the Western Front*, many of whose subjects including Robert Graves, Siegfried Sassoon, Edmund Blunden and Frederic Manning had been discussed in my lively and most enjoyable MA Seminar. I had found it a pleasure to write this book, not least because of its fascinating personnel and their evocative accounts of front-line experience. Who could write a dull book about the above characters and others such as Charles Carrington, Guy Chapman, Frank Crozier, Anthony Eden and Harold MacMillan? I hoped that the book would draw attention to war memoirs as a comparatively neglected source for the study of war literature and their value as history, at schools as well as universities, but it received little publicity and seems to have made no impact at all. Shaking off this disappointment I recently published a bold, concise account of *Britain's Two World Wars against Germany* (2014), contending that the received public wisdom caricaturing the First World War as unnecessary, criminally mismanaged and futile whereas the Second was a necessary crusade, well-conducted, economical in lives and a triumph for good over evil, was in need of considerable revision. So far this too has received little publicity but since the centenary commemorations of the First World War still have three years to run I must hope that these wider comparative issues, and particularly the gulf between historical scholarship and popular myths, will be discussed.

In my youth and early manhood I was a keen cricketer so the earlier reference to having had 'a good innings' was appropriate. Inevitably one now spends more time in retirement as a spectator, but I hope to remain active in the study and writing of history.

In 2001 I concluded my farewell lecture by quoting Henry V's melancholy musing on the eve of the battle of Agincourt:

> We are but warriors for the working day: Our gayness and our gilt are all besmirched with rainy marching in the painful field.

But I have never accepted the later line 'and time hath worn us into slovenry'. So long as health and mental faculties permit we have to soldier on and look for fresh challenges and opportunities.

Index

INDEX OF PEOPLE

INDEX OF PLACES

INDEX OF MILITARY FORMATIONS & UNITS

INDEX OF MISCELLANEOUS TERMS